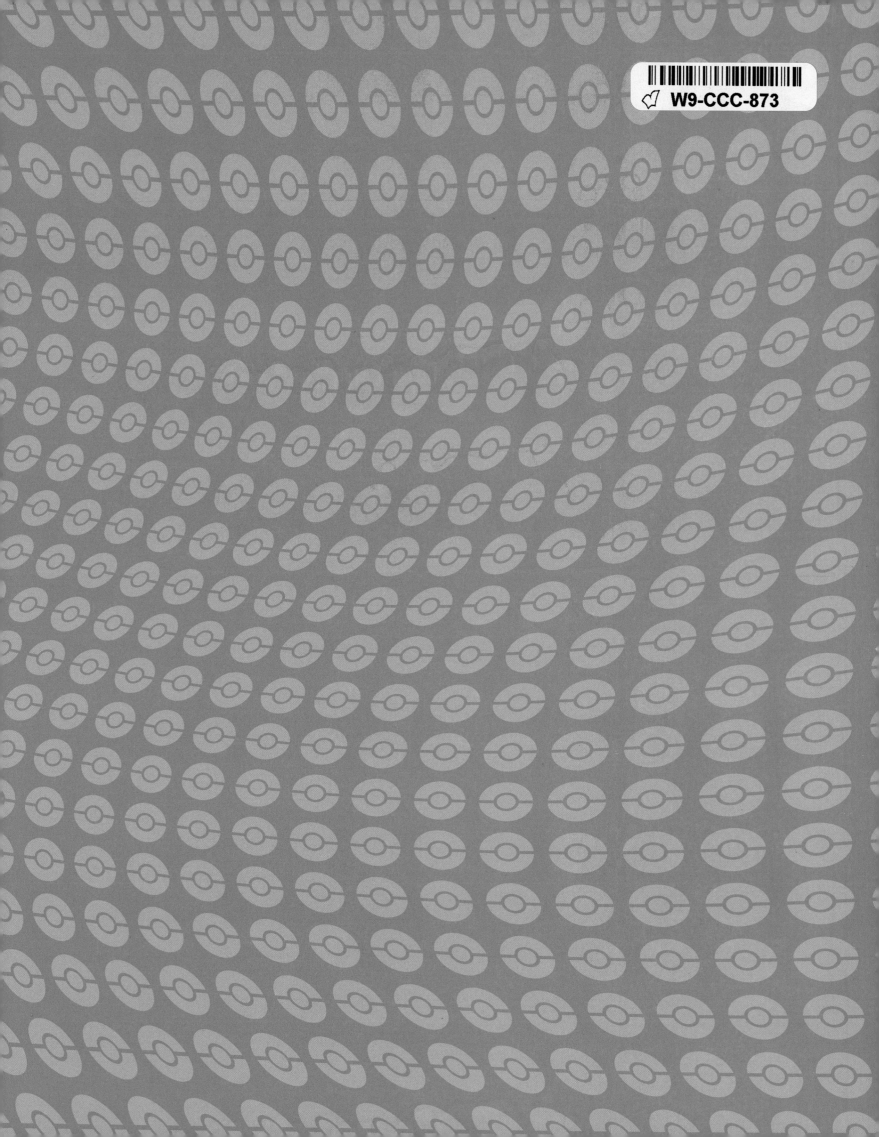

Pokémon

VISUAL GUIDE

CRIS SILVESTRI & KATHERINE FANG

THE WORLD OF POKÉMON

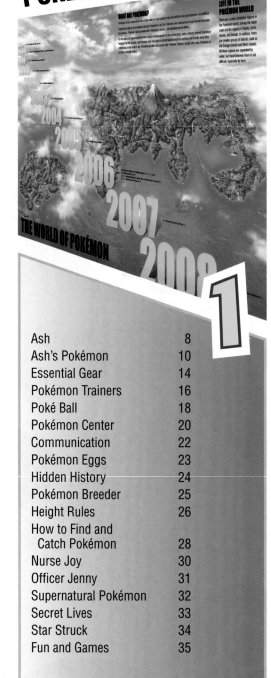

KANTO

ORANGE ISLANDS

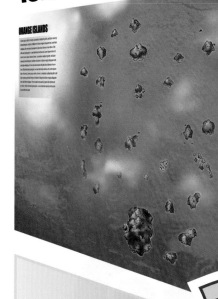

JOHTO

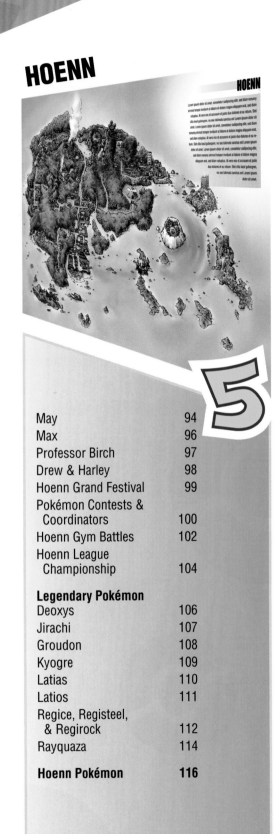

HOENN

SINNOH

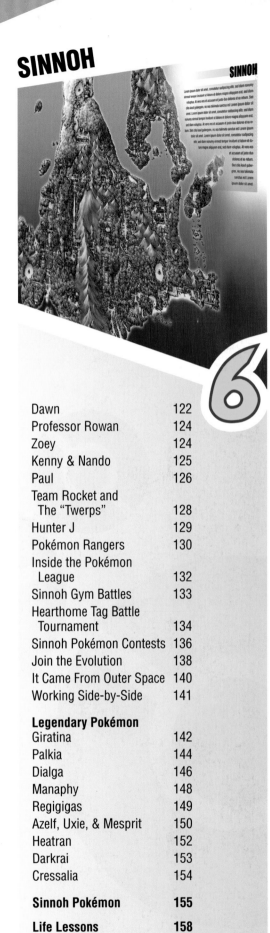

WELCOME POKÉMON FANS!

Welcome to the wide world of Pokémon—a world filled with mystery and adorable creatures known as Pokémon.

What is a Pokémon? Read through this book and you'll discover everything you need to know about Pokémon.

But Pokémon do not live alone. They live in harmony with humans, and the world around them. This book will introduce you to some of the bravest, sneakiest, and important people in the Pokémon world. You will see what it takes to become a Pokémon Trainer, a human that makes Pokémon and human partnership his or her priority, a Contest Coordinator, and a Pokémon Breeder.

Are you ready? Are you gonna catch 'em all? If that's your path, you'd better start reading now!

Dates apply to U.S. only.

1998 | September: *Pokémon (The Indigo League)*

1999 | September: *Pokémon (The Indigo League) / Pokémon (Orange Island Adventures)*

2000 | September: *Pokémon: Johto League Journeys*

2001 | September: *Pokémon: Johto League Champions*

2002 | September: *Pokémon: Master Quest*

2003 | September: *Pokémon Advanced*

2004 | September: *Pokémon: Advanced Challenge*

2005 | September: *Pokémon: Advanced Battle*

2006

THE WORLD OF POKÉMON

WHAT ARE POKÉMON?

Pokémon: unique creatures of every shape and size, each species endowed with its own special powers and abilities.

Pokémon are able to communicate amongst themselves, but few Pokémon have been known to use human language. Nevertheless, Pokémon clearly demonstrate intelligence, feelings, and individual personalities.

For the most part, people and Pokémon coexist in relative peace. In the ancient past, some cultures revered Legendary Pokémon for their powers, and Pokémon have lived and worked alongside people as partners and friends since time immemorial. In the modern day, Pokémon are often seen paired with Pokémon Trainers, people who raise Pokémon to compete in friendly battles.

LIFE IN THE POKÉMON WORLD

There are various inhabited regions in the Pokémon world; among the major areas are the regions of Kanto, Johto, Hoenn, and Sinnoh. In addition, there are smaller groups of islands, such as the Orange Islands and Whirl Islands. All these regions are separated by water, but travel between them is not difficult, especially by ferry.

April: *Pokémon: Mastermind of Mirage Pokémon*
June: *Pokémon Chronicles*
September: *Pokémon Mystery Dungeon: Team Go-Getters Out of the Gate!*
September: *Pokémon: Battle Frontier*

June: *Pokémon: Diamond and Pearl*

2007

2008

April: *Pokémon Diamond and Pearl: Battle Dimension*
September: *Explorers of Time and Darkness*

ASH

He is a Pokémon dreamer who wants to one day have it all—including becoming a Pokémon Master. Ash battles impossible odds while maintaining personal relationships with all his friends and Pokémon.

Almost every season brings on new surprises and new conflicts—and also new outfits. Ash has an outfit redesign with every new region he visits, but he does maintain some basics: rolled-up blue jeans, a baseball cap, fingerless gloves, and a vest.

BRASH ASH

Ash, like any ten-year-old boy, finds it hard to see the world in anything but black and white. His arrogance usually ends up hurting him somehow, but he usually ends up learning from his mistakes. Don't let the boy-ego fool you, he is exceedingly compassionate and often sacrifices himself for his friends and Pokémon.

WHAT'S A MOTHER TO DO?

Ash's mother is Delia Ketchum. She resides in Ash's hometown of Pallet Town with her own Pokémon, Mr. Mime. Often calling Ash to praise him after a victory or worry about him in a particularly dangerous adventure, like all mothers, she supports him in everything he does.

READY TO BATTLE
Ash's Sinnoh threads reflect a more mature approach to his Pokémon Master quest. A larger, looser black vest with a horizontal yellow stripe, more relaxed flared pants, and a new backpack highlights the new outfit.

SLEEPING LATE

Pikachu was not Ash's first choice (he wanted Squirtle). After sleeping in and missing his chance to choose, he was given Pikachu. Pikachu was not very pleased with being paired with Ash and didn't listen very well, and thus one of the funniest partnerships ever was created. After many shocking developments the two, who once seemed destined for disaster, bonded in the face of mutual danger and the legend of Ash and Pikachu was born.

Ash's first outfit was very straightforward. Very sporty and to the point, it survives remarkably well in both form and function. The original hat was a special Pokémon Expo hat that Ash got by mailing in cereal box tops.

The most notable change in the second coming of Ash is the baseball cap, which does away with the swoop logo, and moved to a pattern that resembles half of a Poké Ball. This symbol can also be seen on Ash's shirt.

Badge Master

From Kanto, through the Orange Islands, to Johto and Hoenn, Ash has won his share of badges during his travels. He's also won 7 Frontier symbols from The Battle Frontier, making him a Battle Frontier Champion. He is currently working on his Sinnoh badges.

ASH'S POKÉMON

Ash and Pikachu are certainly well paired, but there's no way that Ash is going to make it through all of his Pokémon championships and badges without a little more help...without a *lot* of help, actually. Ash has a number of Pokémon at his side helping with the hundreds of battles he's experienced. All are very important to Ash. Everyone has had an opportunity to shine, and because of Ash's training and tenacity they have all succeeded.

PIKACHU

Although Ash's first Pokémon and long time companion is Pikachu, they didn't get along at all in the beginning.

CATERPIE

Caterpie is the first Pokémon that Ash ever catches, but he catches it in a fashion that is not standard with Pokémon Trainers—he doesn't weaken it first!

BUTTERFREE

METAPOD

PIDGEY

Ash mistakenly catches a Pidgey, which stayed with him until it evolved.

PIDGEOTTO

PIDGEOT

TOTODILE

Ash had to fight Misty for this one. They each threw a Poké Ball at it, but because they didn't know whose Ball caught it, they battled for it. Ash won the battle.

CHARMANDER

After rescuing Charmander from a rainstorm, Ash nurses the fiery Pokémon back to health. It evolves two more times.

CHARIZARD

CHARMELEON

CHIKORITA

Ash severely injured Chikorita in a battle, but after nursing it back to health, Chikorita becomes enamored with Ash. It even gets jealous when Pikachu is around! Chikorita evolved into a Bayleef to protect Ash from Team Rocket.

BAYLEEF

SQUIRTLE

After forming a bond with Ash, Squirtle becomes a vital member of his team, but decides to go back to its roots after the Squirtle Squad starts to fall apart.

CYNDAQUIL

Caught almost by accident, Cyndaquil has proven a formidable partner, after overcoming early bouts of shyness. Ash leaves it with Oak before setting out for Hoenn.

BULBASAUR

Bulbasaur is a reluctant addition to Ash's arsenal. It agrees to go if Ash beats it in a battle, which he does.

TREECKO

Ash catches a Treecko after defending the Giant Tree. Treecko evolved into a Grovyle during its battle with a fellow Trainer's Loudred. It later evolved into a Sceptile to protect a Meganium it loved, although it lost forgot how to use its abilities after Meganium didn't return its affection.

GROVYLE

SCEPTILE

SNORUNT

Snorunt steals Ash's Badge Case and hat (Pokémon love Ash's hats). Snorunt joins Ash. It evolves into a Glalie after some intensive training to help it use Ice Beam better.

GLALIE

TAILLOW

Taillow makes off with chocolate from Ash and his crew, and as Ash hunts down Taillow for this misdeed, it becomes the leader of a larger flock of Taillow and attacks him. A battle ensues, and Ash eventually captures it. During the final round of a flying tournament, it evolved into a Swellow to achieve victory.

SWELLOW

AIPOM

Aipom befriends Ash, but only after it steals his hat (the hat has got to be some kind of Pokémon-catching charm!). Ash captures Aipom in battle, but eventually trades it to Dawn for her Buizel.

TURTWIG

Turtwig is a mediator, helping other Pokémon with their squabbles, and facing down those that don't want to let things go. It befriends Ash, who later captures it in battle.

GLIGAR

The Gligar that Ash comes across is a slow one—slower than the rest of its flock. After Ash's rival, Paul, captures Gliscor, the leader of the flock, Gligar decides to go with Ash.

GLISCOR

STARLY

Ash's Aipom injures a wild Starly, which in turn attacks. Ash captures the Starly, evolving it into a Staravia during a battle with Team Rocket. A powerful Pokémon, Staravia has mastered Brave Bird.

STARAVIA

SNORLAX

Ash captured Snorlax in the Orange Islands after he found out that it was consuming nearly all the island's plant life. Snorlax doesn't travel with Ash much, because he can't keep it fed.

PHANPY

Ash's prize for winning a Pokémon Riding Contest is a Pokémon Egg that hatches into Phanpy. Phanpy evolved into a Donphan while attempting to take down a Team Rocket mecha. Don't let it fool you, Donphan packs quite a powerful punch in its trunk.

DONPHAN

HERACROSS

Heracross is the first Pokémon that Ash catches in Johto, and although this sweet-loving herbivore seems harmless, it is one of the more powerful Pokémon that Ash has known.

CORPHISH

After doing a number on Dewford Town and its citizens, the jealous Corphish was captured and calmed down quite a bit. Although it joined Ash's team, it still flared with envy when another teammate evolved or received praise.

TORKOAL

Torkoal befriended Ash after he defended it. Although Torkoal fled, it followed Ash and eventually joined up with his team. Ash used Torkoal quite a bit, but decided to leave him with Professor Oak for a while.

CHIMCHAR

Ash never lets a Pokémon in need suffer. Chimchar was abandoned by its original Trainer, Ash's rival, Paul. Ash offers Chimchar a spot on his team.

KRABBY

In an effort to prove his capturing prowess to Misty, Ash caught Krabby. It immediately was sent to Professor Oak's as Ash already had six Pokémon with him. Krabby evolved into a Kingler when Ash battled Mandi in the first round of the Pokémon League.

KINGLER

BUIZEL

Acquired in a trade with Dawn, Buizel wanted to battle instead of competing in Contests.

NOCTOWL

Noctowl is a rare shiny Pokémon that glitters when released from its Poké Ball. Noctowl is highly intelligent, and even fooled Ash, who eventually captured it. He leaves it at Professor Oak's lab.

ESSENTIAL GEAR

Pokémon Trainers do not take their mission lightly. In order to maintain the high standards of training, raising, and caring for Pokémon, there is an essential list of items that each Trainer should carry at all times.

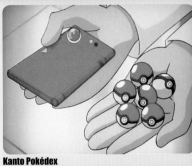

Kanto Pokédex

Sinnoh Pokédex

SCREEN

Although the Sinnoh Pokédex has a dual-screen, earlier versions only had one screen. The screen shows the Pokémon being observed, and various stats about it.

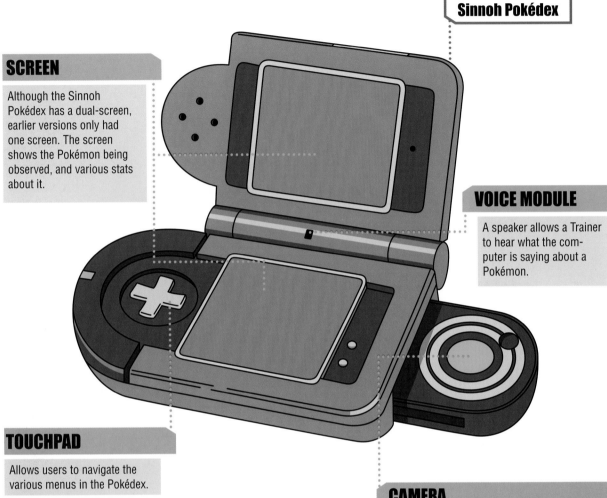

VOICE MODULE

A speaker allows a Trainer to hear what the computer is saying about a Pokémon.

TOUCHPAD

Allows users to navigate the various menus in the Pokédex.

POKÉDEX

Everyone needs information, but for Pokémon Trainers that information is a vital part of their training. The Pokédex acts as a miniature electronic encyclopedia of Pokémon facts and figures.

CAMERA

This allows the Pokédex to scan an image of wild Pokémon for later reference. The Pokédex has pre-loaded information—you don't have to physically see every Pokémon to hear its breakdown.

Voices Carry

The Kanto and Johto Pokédex have male voices, and are nicknamed "Dexter" by Ash. While the Hoenn and Sinnoh versions have a female voice and Ash nicknamed it "Dextette."

POKÉ BALLS

If you're gonna catch 'em all, you're going to need something to catch them with. The Poké Ball is the most common capture system. It is thrown at a weakened Pokémon to ensnare it. Poké Balls come in many varieties.

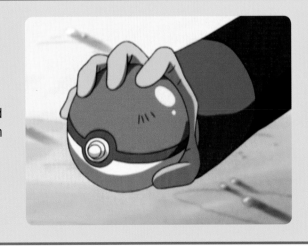

FOOD

Food is used by Trainers to sustain themselves during long journeys. Brock is especially food-conscious, and one of the few humans who carries cooking supplies with him wherever he goes.

Sitrus Berry

Oran Berry

Tamato Berry

Pecha Berry

Pokémon also enjoy food in the form of berries and Pokéblocks. Expert breeders such as Brock make extremely delicious and helpful Pokéblocks perfect for any occasion.

Boulder

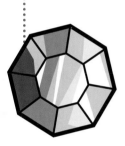

Rainbow

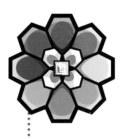

Hive

Knuckle

Forest

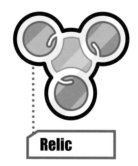

Relic

BADGE CASE

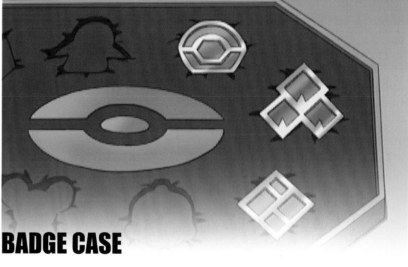

Most Trainers don't wear their badges on their clothing, so you've got to put them somewhere. Ash has had his Badge Case stolen on more than one occasion, which must have been greatly upsetting considering how hard he had to work to fill it with badges. Badges are symbols of a Pokémon Trainer's prowess. They are given by Gym Leaders for victory and are necessary to enter League Championships.

POKÉTCH

The newest gizmo for Trainers is the Pokétch. It is a kind of pocket watch that has all sorts of amazing abilities. Dawn receives hers after being fooled by an imitation.

POKÉMON TRAINERS

A Pokémon Trainer can be considered anyone who owns a Pokémon and works with it for a specific purpose—Pokémon breeders and Coordinators are also Trainers, in a sense. But for the most part, a Pokémon Trainer is thought of as someone who trains their Pokémon to battle, forging a bond that makes both partners stronger.

KANTO

SQUIRTLE

BULBASAUR

CHARMANDER

JOHTO

CHIKORITA

CYNDAQUIL

TOTODILE

TO EVOLVE OR NOT TO EVOLVE?

Sooner or later, most Trainers will have to figure out what to do about their Pokémon's Evolution. Evolving a Pokémon makes it stronger, which seems like a no-brainer decision for someone interested in battles. But raw power alone doesn't determine whether Evolution is the best choice for a Trainer; since Pokémon can excel in different things for each stage of Evolution, it might not make sense to evolve a Pokémon right away. To make it more complicated, some Pokémon are simply happy the way they are and have no interest in evolving.

Ash and Pikachu now know Pikachu is happy to stay a Pikachu, but Ash was excited when he thought his Bulbasaur would evolve. As it turned out, Bulbasaur

didn't want to evolve at all—so Ash not only apologized to Bulbasaur for being inconsiderate, he made a speech about how a Pokémon should be able to freely choose when it wants to evolve.

TRUST YOUR POKÉMON

Trainers need to trust their Pokémon, but Pokémon are also intelligent enough to pick up on a Trainer's uncertainty. It's a two-way street; if a Trainer hesitates when giving orders or doesn't feel comfortable with a Pokémon, the Pokémon reacts accordingly.

Honesty is the best policy: Pokémon dislike being the butt of a joke as much as anyone else, so when Ash tries to spook his Corphish to teach it a lesson, Corphish is none too happy to discover it's been tricked. It doesn't take much for Corphish to turn on Ash when it thinks it's been played for a fool a second time, either!

KNOW YOUR POKÉMON

Good Trainers also need to be in synch with their Pokémon. Ideally, Trainer and Pokémon should work together as if each knows what the other is thinking. That doesn't mean teaching a Pokémon to blindly obey commands; instead, a Trainer needs to be aware of a Pokémon's own rhythms and preferences in order to work as an effective team in battle.

THE JOURNEY BEGINS

Each Trainer's journey can start as early as age 10, when a kid can become a Trainer and select one of three first Pokémon to be their first partner. The selection varies by region, but Trainers can always choose from a Fire-type, Grass-type, or Water-type Pokémon.

A starting Trainer also receives Poké Balls so they can start catching Pokémon. There's no limit to how many Pokémon a Trainer can catch, but they can only bring up to six Pokémon with them at any time. If they want to use another Pokémon after they've reached their limit, they'll need to send at least one of their Pokémon back to a Professor or other person for holding.

I will journey to gain the wisdom of Pokémon training.

~Ash Ketchum

HOENN

MUDKIP

TREECKO

TORCHIC

SINNOH

PIPLUP

TURTWIG

CHIMCHAR

WHAT ARE THE QUALITIES OF A GOOD TRAINER?

There's no "right" way to train a Pokémon; every Pokémon's personality is unique, just as every Trainer's personality is unique. Ash may be an excellent Trainer, but not all good Trainers have to interact with their Pokémon just like he does. The one thing that all good Trainers do have in common, however, is a bond of trust and understanding with their Pokémon.

WHEN POKÉMON JUST WON'T OBEY

It takes more than a badge to make a Trainer an expert, and even good Trainers may find themselves outmatched by a Pokémon. That in itself is no great shame, but a Trainer shouldn't use a Pokémon if they're not sure they can control it. A good example is Ash's Charizard; perfectly obedient as a Charmander, it became more and more unruly as it quickly evolved into Charmeleon and then Charizard. As Charizard, it was simply too powerful and willful for a novice Trainer like Ash to control.

Time, experience, and a few hard lessons helped Ash regain control over Charizard, but he simply wasn't ready to handle a Pokémon like that back in his Indigo League days.

Dawn and her Buizel had trouble battling at first, since Dawn was out of synch with Buizel's timing. After a helpful lesson from Lucian of the Elite Four, Dawn learned how to work with Buizel—although it remained more interested in battles than Contests.

Why Become a Pokémon Trainer?

No one can deny it looks fun to travel the world with a best friend who rides on your shoulder and unleashes high voltage blasts on your opponents. But beyond making powerful new Pokémon friends, what's the real point of becoming a Pokémon Trainer?

Just as caring for a pet can teach children responsibility, training Pokémon is a growth experience. A Trainer has to work hard to help a Pokémon achieve its full potential—beyond simply putting in the time for training workouts, a Trainer also learns to understand another living creature's needs and desires.

A Pokémon journey itself is also a catalyst for growth. Most young Trainers still have a lot of hard lessons to learn about winning, losing, and how they relate to their Pokémon. The experience of leaving home and facing new situations helps both people and Pokémon develop maturity and confidence.

POKÉ BALL

You can travel the lands of Pokémon far and wide—and see hundreds of Pokémon—but you can't capture them if you don't have the right tool. The Poké Ball is the Trainer's capture system of choice, and the many varieties of Poké Balls ensure that you can match the Poké Ball to the situation, increasing your odds of a capture. These are only some of the Poké Balls available.

THE MECHANICS

How a Poké Ball works remains a mystery, even to the most dedicated Trainers and fans. Poké Balls seem to not only be a capture system, but an information storage system as well, since Pokémon captured in Poké Balls automatically have their information transferred to the Pokédex. Ash's Pokémon have been transferred from Professor Oak's lab to a nearby Pokémon Center for Ash to pick up.

Inside, the Poké Ball features many of what appear to be mirror panels. When the Trainer needs a Pokémon, they have only to throw the ball and call the Pokémon to action. When retrieving their Pokémon, a Trainer will simply point the Poké Ball at the Pokémon in question and press the button on the front of the ball. The Poké Ball itself can be miniaturized to the size of a golf ball for easy storage and mobility while out in the field.

LUXURY BALL

This special Poké Ball helps the Pokémon captured in it bond with you more quickly. The Luxury Ball was shown in *Pokémon: Jirachi Wishmaker.*

PREMIER BALL

The same as the basic Poké Ball.

MASTER BALL

The ultimate Poké Ball. It enables you to capture any Pokémon. The elusive Master Ball has been seen by Ash only once. These are often used to capture Legendary or one-of-a-kind Pokémon. Unique in every sense of the word, these balls have a letter "M" emblazoned upon the upper hemisphere of the Poké Ball.

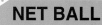

NET BALL

A special Poké Ball, the Net Ball excels in the capture of Bug-type and Water-type Pokémon.

TIMER BALL

The longer the battle lasts, the better this Poké Ball works.

GREAT BALL

The intermediate Poké Ball, it is slightly more effective than the basic Poké Ball.

REPEAT BALL

Awesome against Pokémon the Trainer has already captured. The Repeat Ball was shown in *Pokémon: Jirachi Wishmaker.*

ULTRA BALL

The advanced Poké Ball, it is slightly more effective than the Great Ball.

NEST BALL

This is the Poké Ball of choice when capturing weaker Pokémon.

DIVE BALL

The Dive Ball is highly effective against Pokémon encountered in or under the water.

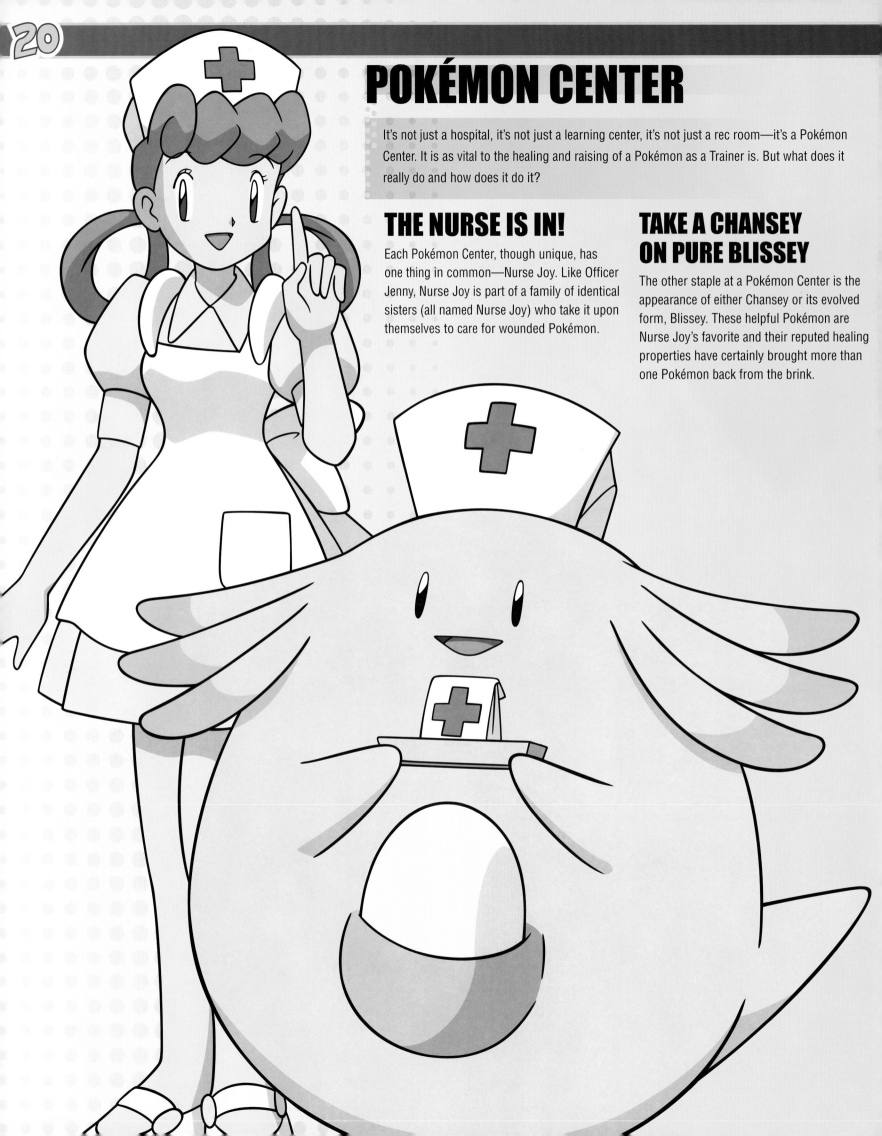

POKÉMON CENTER

It's not just a hospital, it's not just a learning center, it's not just a rec room—it's a Pokémon Center. It is as vital to the healing and raising of a Pokémon as a Trainer is. But what does it really do and how does it do it?

THE NURSE IS IN!

Each Pokémon Center, though unique, has one thing in common—Nurse Joy. Like Officer Jenny, Nurse Joy is part of a family of identical sisters (all named Nurse Joy) who take it upon themselves to care for wounded Pokémon.

TAKE A CHANSEY ON PURE BLISSEY

The other staple at a Pokémon Center is the appearance of either Chansey or its evolved form, Blissey. These helpful Pokémon are Nurse Joy's favorite and their reputed healing properties have certainly brought more than one Pokémon back from the brink.

ONE-STOP SHOP

Pokémon Centers are central gathering areas for Trainers, Contest Coordinators, Tournament participants, and generally anyone who needs a break from the rigors of Pokémon competition.

Video phones and the ability to retrieve Pokémon left with Professors, the Pokémon Center is a must stop for thriving Pokémon Masters.

A CENTER OF ATTENTION

Pokémon Centers all vary in appearance, except for one distinguishable landmark—they all have a giant "P" on or near their building. Their architectural differences are due to the varying habitats and cultures.

NOT JUST FOR POKÉMON

The Pokémon Center is a healing place not only for Pokémon, but for Trainers as well. Many a weary Trainer has come through the doors, and Nurse Joy has always been there to greet them.

The Pokémon Center can be a very supportive place—even more supportive than home for most Trainers! They can eat at a Pokémon Center without charge, and can even extend their stay until their Pokémon recover.

COMMUNICATION

Many Pokémon communicate using a variation of their name or the entire name spoken with inflection and emotion. Still others make sounds that aren't discernable, but they are still clearly communicating. But there are some that speak our language.

Very few Pokémon have language skills that can be interpreted by humans. Even Ash mostly guesses what his Pokémon are feeling, and never speaks directly to them. However, there are a few Pokémon that have bridged the communication gap and actually speak to humans.

They fall into two categories: telepathy and real language skills.

UNTIL SPOKEN TO

Most of the other Pokémon that communicate with humans are Legendary Pokémon, and they mostly communicate through telepathy.

Lugia and Mewtwo have both used telepathy to communicate diretly with Ash. Entei and Darkrai both streamed their thoughts to thos nearby. Lucario, through its Aura power, is able to speak with Ash through telepathy.

SPEAK UP!

The most talkative of all Pokémon is Meowth, the third wheel in the Team Rocket trio. To his credit, Meowth has been used by Ash and others to interpret for a hurt or scared Pokémon, and often shows compassion and a willingness to help other Pokémon in need. Meowth's ability to communicate is unprecedented among Pokémon.

POKÉMON EGGS

Pokémon Eggs are usually the same size and shape, regardless of species—it's the patterns on the Eggs that hint at the species of the Pokémon within. Eggs are surprisingly hardy, capable of surviving some bounces and jolts. Gentle loving care is always preferable. An Egg is ready to hatch once it starts to glow.

Where do Pokémon come from? The true origins of Pokémon have yet to be revealed, but all Trainers know that Pokémon normally hatch from Eggs.

WHAT DOES A POKÉMON EGG FEEL?

If a Pokémon Egg can survive a couple of misadventures and still hatch okay, then it's no harm done, right? To the contrary, Ash's experience with a troubled baby Larvitar shows that trauma to a Pokémon Egg can affect the baby Pokémon even after it hatches. Once the Larvitar hatched, it remained unresponsive and sick due to its experiences while still in the Egg.

POKÉMON EGG RAISERS

Similar to the Pokémon Nesters, Pokémon Egg Raisers take care of both their own Pokémon Eggs and the Eggs they've received for safekeeping. In Hoenn, May and Ash visit an Egg Nursery that's as big as a veritable farm, housing five large barns filled with Pokémon Eggs.

Before Larvitar hatched, its Egg would glow but then fade. Once it hatched, the baby Larvitar was cold and unmoving, a sign that something was dreadfully wrong; it had to be kept warm so it could recover.

Even after it physically recovered, Larvitar refused to respond to stimuli. Ash figured out the problem after he fell asleep with the baby Larvitar in his lap and had a bad dream: he saw the Egg being stolen, knocked into a stream, kicked around, and almost run over. It might all have been part of Larvitar's own nightmares, but it suggests that Larvitar had some awareness of the outside world even while inside the Egg.

DAY CARE

There are facilities known as Day Cares that are devoted to the care of Pokémon Eggs and baby Pokémon. One place where Day Cares proliferate is the rural town of Eggseter, located in a lush area of Johto with ideal weather. The area has long been home to Nesters, the people who care for baby Pokémon and Pokémon Eggs, and visitors will see a variety of Day Care facilities as they travel through the area.

In addition to a high-tech room for monitoring Eggs that are about to hatch, there's no substitute for old-fashioned hands-on care. That includes gently polishing each Pokémon Egg with a cloth.

HIDDEN HISTORY

From long-forgotten civilizations to temples dedicated to Dialga and Palkia, there's abundant evidence that Pokémon had a tremendous influence on the history of their world.

POKÉMOPOLIS

Stories speak of an ancient city where people believed Pokémon symbolized nature's power and even built temples to them. Although the city was supposedly destroyed in a storm and never seen since, its relics have since been uncovered not far from Pallet Town.

Contained within some of the artifacts of Pokémopolis are giant Pokémon, including a giant Alakazam and Gengar who immediately begin to battle each other when released. Fortunately, among the artifacts is a large bell that's awakened by the song of Jigglypuff. Contained within the bell is a giant Jigglypuff, which is the only thing that can put Alakazam and Gengar back to sleep and into their respective artifacts.

BALTOY CIVILIZATION

Not all ancient civilizations involve dangerous giant Pokémon and sinister spirits. Long ago, there was said to be a Baltoy civilization where Baltoy lived together with humans. Today, the remains of this civilization can be found within Kirikiri Mountain in Hoenn, and the legends say that the relics of this civilization include the most precious thing in the universe—time.

POKÉLANTIS

There are always people who unwisely wish to control the power of Legendary Pokémon, and the fate of ancient Pokélantis is an example to others. Under the rule of an arrogant king, this once-great empire attempted to use Ho-Oh's power to conquer the world. Pokélantis was completely destroyed, but the king escaped and supposedly got his revenge on Ho-Oh by sealing it in underground in a stone orb.

Within the ruins lies the King's Chambers, where a stone orb was found on a throne at the base of the king's statue. But instead of Ho-Oh, the orb contained the King's malevolent spirit, eager to possess a body and use it to revive his plans of world domination.

RUINS

Archaeologists and researchers continue to come across undiscovered relics and secrets of long-forgotten civilizations, from the prehistoric Pokémon fossils in the ruins of Alph to the Solaceon Ruins in Sinnoh, where Dialga and Palkia were once revered.

In Johto, the ruins of Alph and its abundant fossils have made it an ideal place to set up a domed research center. But fossils aren't the only finds here: the Alph ruins have also yielded many ancient artifacts.

The Solaceon Ruins are just one of several places in Sinnoh where statues of Dialga and Palkia can be found. These Pokémon play a key role in the region's legends and origin stories.

POKÉMON BREEDERS

Every Pokémon Trainer should know how to raise their Pokémon to be healthy and strong, but Pokémon breeders take special pains to bring out the best qualities in their Pokémon. Despite the name, they're not necessarily concerned with breeding more Pokémon, just raising healthy Pokémon.

Pokémon breeders sometimes use their Pokémon for battle, and they even endorse battling as a good way for Trainers and Pokémon to bond with each other. However, breeders focus on a Pokémon's overall health and appearance, not just its battling strength. As such, breeders like Brock may not have many battle trophies to boast of, but they're often the best source of advice on how to keep a Pokémon in peak physical shape.

Two Types of Breeders: Suzie and Zane

Even among Pokémon breeders, opinions differ on what's most important for a Pokémon. Suzie, the breeder who lent Brock her Vulpix, believes that a Pokémon's inner beauty is what counts. She may have run a noted Pokémon salon, but she doesn't believe that Pokémon need to be cut and styled to look their best. Suzie's old friend and rival, Zane, believes it's outward beauty that matters the most, and he's a successful breeder too. There's no right answer to the question of whether outer looks or inner beauty counts the most—instead, both breeders pool their different talents and outlooks to open a Pokémon salon together.

STRUTTING THEIR STUFF

If Coordinators have Contests and Trainers have tournaments, what do breeders have? There's a World Pokémon breeders' Contest, but no formal competitive system exists for Pokémon breeders as it does for Trainers and Coordinators. Nevertheless, breeders do compete in special events to see whose Pokémon shines the brightest.

Breeders turn out in droves for Bonitaville's Pokémon beauty contest, where Pokémon accessories aren't required but definitely help. A similar trend exists in Sinnoh, where fans of the fashion magazine PokéChic dress up themselves and their Pokémon.

Outside of competitions, some breeders congregate around certain neighborhoods. Celadon City's Scissor Street, also known as "Breeder's Lane," is where Pokémon beauty parlors abound. Not all Pokémon breeders believe in decking out Pokémon with accessories and fancy cuts, but this is where their latest fashions are on display.

Nutrition

Although anyone can keep a Pokémon well fed with just basic Pokémon chow, any breeders worth their salt develop their own recipes for Pokémon food formulas to suit an individual Pokémon's needs. This includes food designed for a particular Pokémon type or specially formulated for a picky eater.

Grooming

Grooming is another must for Pokémon breeders, even though their Pokémon are already in good physical condition. During grooming sessions, a breeder can closely examine a Pokémon's health of the Pokémon. It also gives breeders an opportunity to bond with their Pokémon.

Exercise

Just because a Pokémon can remain in a Poké Ball indefinitely, that doesn't make it a good idea to keep it there. Pokémon benefit from regular outings, even if it's just to play. A Pokémon's type should also be considered: Water-type Pokémon will benefit from getting regular opportunities to swim in a large body of water.

Health Care

For most Trainers, all a Pokémon needs after a battle is some healing at a Pokémon Center and plenty of rest. A Pokémon can thrive with that alone, but it's not enough for serious breeders! They're more likely to recommend additional post-battle treatment such as therapeutic massages.

My Pokémon Won't Listen to Me!

Problem: Autumn's new Miltank Ilta doesn't listen to a thing she says, and she's so frustrated she's ready to give it away. Once again, Brock comes to the rescue with a hands-on demonstration of how to repair the rift between Autumn and Ilta.

Solution: Giving up on a Pokémon is the wrong answer—instead, it's key to develop a friendship with a Pokémon through various activities. Stay calm, give lots of encouragement, interact with it as a friend and not just a boss, and groom regularly—all these things may not come automatically, but they'll provide the foundation for a solid relationship.

It takes a few false starts, but before long, Autumn and Ilta are battling and acting just like a team should.

HEIGHT RULES

While Pokémon has always been about the size of Ash's and his Pokémon's hearts, height and weight cannot be ignored. From the titanic Wailord to the tiny Wurmple, Pokémon come in all shapes and sizes. Have you ever wanted to see the majestic Lugia beside the rotund Snorlax? Here is your chance.

BLAZIKEN
Height: 6'03" (1.9 m)

LUGIA
Height: 17'01" (5.2 m)

SHEDINJA
Height: 2'07" (0.8 m)

BEAUTIFLY
Height: 3'03" (1.0 m)

MILOTIC
Height: 20'04" (6.2 m)

SNORLAX
Height: 6'11" (2.1 m)

DUSKNOIR
Height: 7'03" (2.2 m)

SANDSHREW
Height: 2'00" (0.6 m)

ALTARIA
Height: 3'07" (1.1 m)

COMBEE
Height: 1'00" (0.3 m)

FLYGON
Height: 6'07" (2.0 m)

YANMEGA
Height: 6'03" (1.9 m)

SALAMENCE
Height: 4'11" (1.5 m)

HO-OH
Height: 12'06" (3.8 m)

WAILORD
Height: 47'07" (14.5 m)

GROUDON
Height: 11'06" (3.5 m)

TORTERRA
Height: 7'03" (2.2 m)

HITMONTOP
Height: 4'07" (1.4 m)

WURMPLE
Height: 1'00" (0.3 m)

HOW TO FIND AND CATCH POKÉMON

Every new Trainer can visit a Pokémon Professor to receive a first Pokémon, but catching more Pokémon isn't as easy. Wild Pokémon are easy to find, at least if a Trainer isn't choosy; it's learning the art of capture that takes time.

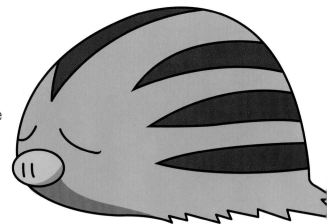

In addition to a first Pokémon, each Trainer normally receives several Poké Balls. There's more to catching Pokémon than just throwing a Poké Ball—unless injured, weak, or willing to be caught, a wild Pokémon is normally too strong to be caught without battling it first to tire it out.

A Trainer must remember to first click the button on the front of the Poké Ball to expand it to normal size. The Poké Ball is then thrown at the target Pokémon, but even if the Pokémon is absorbed inside the Poké Ball, it doesn't mean the capture is complete. The Poké Ball rocks back and forth and its button will glow red while the capture is in progress.

Once the Poké Ball chimes and the button returns to its normal white color, the capture is complete. If the capture fails, the Poké Ball reopens and the Pokémon is once again released. Odds are it won't be keen on sticking around to facilitate another capture attempt.

When a Pokémon Just Doesn't Want to Be Caught

Some Pokémon will swat away any Poké Ball thrown in their direction, while others will avoid any attempt to battle and catch them. It can take true persistence to convince a reluctant Pokémon to stick around—when Pietra wants to battle a swimming Rhydon that she needs to finish constructing a tunnel, she has to chase it multiple times and gets it to battle her only after clinging to it so stubbornly that she nearly drowns!

FISHING

Not all Pokémon can be found on land. Large numbers of Pokémon prefer aquatic habitats, so a different approach is required: fishing! With a fishing rod and a lure, all that's needed is to find the nearest promising body of water, throw out a line, and wait for a bite.

Of course, as with any other capture, once you hook a Pokémon, you still have to subdue and catch it. Otherwise, like this Octillery, it'll simply scurry around and then leap back into the water.

WHERE TO FIND POKÉMON

Pokémon can be found just about anywhere, but most Trainers head to the wilderness to look for them. Some Pokémon are more common than others and thus easier to catch—they can be found hanging from trees, standing in the grass, or even just nosing across a forest path.

Pokémon aren't always so obliging as to hang around in the open waiting to be caught, so special lures or strategies are sometimes called for. A Trainer's Pokémon may know moves that can help, but putting out bait and waiting can work too.

Owned Pokémon

From time to time, a Trainer accidentally tries to catch a Pokémon that's already owned by another Trainer. If a Pokémon has already been captured, it can't be caught by using another Poké Ball on it.

FRIENDSHIP

Sometimes, wild Pokémon take an interest in people and are actually interested in accompanying a Trainer. Ash and his friends have caught plenty of Pokémon this way, but even if a Pokémon wants to accompany a Trainer, it typically wants to battle that Trainer first.

Ash's Turtwig wanted to tag along with him, and Ash observed proper Trainer protocol by first having a friendly battle with it.

TRADING

Pokémon Trainers often trade Pokémon with each other, whether it's because they see a Pokémon they like or think a Pokémon will do better with someone else. Trade machines are found at special events and Pokémon Centers, and they all accomplish the same thing: swapping Pokémon between two different Poké Balls. Trainers insert the Poké Balls holding the Pokémon they want to trade in the machine, and it does the rest.

In the Johto town of Palmpona, the annual festival is a great opportunity for people to show off and trade Pokémon.

When They Were Young

Even the best Trainers sometimes have a rocky start—it's not uncommon for a few mistakes to be made in the beginning.

Ash's First Catch

Caterpie was the first Ash ever caught, and he did it just by using a Poké Ball. But before that, he tried to catch a Pidgey, a Pokémon that's normally easy for beginners to get, without having Pikachu battle it. After using a Poké Ball, then a shirt, and finally a rock, he learned his lesson when he brained a wild Spearow by mistake and incurred its wrath.

May's First Catch

Hoping to someday have a gorgeous Beautifly, May chases down a Wurmple and tries to catch it with Torchic's help. But one hit from Torchic isn't enough—Wurmple escapes from the Poké Ball and attacks Torchic. Fearing a repeat performance of her first attempt to catch an Azurill, in which she failed miserably, she has Torchic attack again with Ember. This time Wurmple is tired enough that May makes a successful catch on her second try.

Dawn's First Catch

Ash tried to coach Dawn through her first catch, but they got on each other's nerves and the Pokémon easily escaped. The next time around, Dawn tried to get a Buneary, but it easily overpowered her Piplup. On her second try, she was prepared for Buneary's attacks and managed to subdue it with Piplup so she could make the catch.

NURSE JOY

Every Pokémon Center needs a nurse, and every one has the same nurse—Nurse Joy! These nurses are actually identical members of the same family. Brock's goggle-eyed love of Nurse Joy doesn't stop them from their initial duties—to help care for and protect Pokémon!

JOY TO THE WORLD

Nurse Joys have been known to act as assistants to the Professors from time to time, handing out Pokémon to able Trainers when there is no Professor available to do so. The Nurse Joy in Slateport City has handed out Treecko, Mudkip, and Torchic Pokémon to Trainers.

There is one group of Joys that is different from the others. These would be the Nurse Joys who reside in the Orange Islands. The Orange Island Nurse Joys are a little leaner, and a little more tanned (Island living does that). They aren't above traveling; there is a traveling clinic, going from small island to small island in the Orange Archipelago when resources are tight.

NOT YOUR TYPICAL NURSE

Nurse Joy can be a lot of things besides nurses. Ash has been rescued by an undercover Official Pokémon League Inspector, who also happened to be a Nurse Joy!

Ash and friends go on a rescue mission for a Nurse Joy that is actually kidnapped by a menacing Shiftry. After battling against gangs of Seedot, Nuzleaf, and Oddish, they face down the Shiftry and find that it is merely trying to help an injured Nuzleaf. Nurse Joy attends to the Pokémon, wiping down the chlorophyll from one of its appendages.

Ash, Misty, and Brock come across a deep-sea diving Nurse Joy in charge of the Lake Lucid Pokémon Center. She also happens to be a star among Trainers who love Water-type Pokémon. However, she turns out to be the least compassionate Nurse Joy you'll ever meet. She can't bear to be around Water Pokémon unless she's wearing her deep-sea suit.

Judge Not, Lest You Be Joy

Pokémon Contests are contests where Pokémon are judged by how strong or how beautiful they are. One of the judges in these contests is usually a Nurse Joy.

Active Duty

Nurse Joy even has a memorable turn as a protector of Pokémon legend. She leads an expeditionary team to research the healing properties of Kabuto shells. When it is later learned that the Kabuto will rise and return to the sea, she does everything she can to protect them and get Ash to safety. That's some nurse!

OFFICER JENNY

Another loyal civil servant is Officer Jenny. Officer Jenny, like Nurse Joy, is not one entity but many who share the name. She shares other traits with Nurse Joy as well: they are all female, they exist to serve and protect Pokémon, and the only one who can tell them apart is the love-stricken Brock!

JENNY TO THE RESCUE

Growlithe isn't the only Pokémon Officer Jenny uses. Depending upon the situation and the area she is from, she could have many types of Pokémon helpers.

While in Cattalia City, Ash and crew meet up with an Officer Jenny whose ancestor caught a thief using a loyal Spinarak. Since then, all Officer Jennys in Cattalia City use Spinarak as their main Pokémon. Likewise, in Wobbuffet Village on their way to Ecruteak City, the Officer Jenny has a Wobbuffet as her sidekick.

Sometimes Pokémon are used in very specific circumstances; Gastly's psychic powers are used by Officer Jenny to hunt down the person or persons responsible for turning Pokémon against their Trainers. Elsewhere, we are introduced to an Officer Jenny who enlists the aid of a Pidgeot to track down Team Rocket and Ash's Pikachu. Most recently, Officer Jenny in Eterna City in the Sinnoh region used a Stunky as her partner Pokémon to disable Team Rocket with Poison Gas.

PARTNER PERFECT

Like Chansey and Blissey for Nurse Joy, every Officer Jenny needs a helpful Pokémon sidekick. Loyal, fierce, and dedicated that Pokémon helper is Growlithe.

Although Officer Jenny tries to uphold the law, she is hampered by understaffing. If she had more Jennys on her side, couldn't she easily stop Team Galactic, Team Aqua, Team Magma, and Team Rocket?

SQUIRTLE SQUAD

When the Squirtle Squad was first formed, it was nothing but a source of trouble, and Officer Jenny soon became involved. The Squirtle Squad then became a very effective fire-fighting crew under her tutelage.

Officer Jenny's cap, much like Nurse Joy's, is one way to tell them apart. Different regions have different symbols.

SUPERNATURAL POKÉMON

Pokémon are behind many unexplained happenings and hauntings in the Pokémon world. But it's a world where anything can and often does happen; even people have been known to possess spooky psychic powers.

THE GASTLY GHOST OF MAIDEN'S PEAK

Over 2000 years ago, a maiden fell in love with a young man who sailed off to war. She promised to await his return, but waited in vain until she finally turned into the stone known as Maiden's Rock. At least, so goes the legend in one of Kanto's seaside towns. Her portrait now hangs in a shrine near Maiden's Rock, and a local Gastly disguises itself as both a local crone and the Maiden's ghost to keep the stories alive to honor the real Maiden's spirit.

Brock and James are bewitched by an illusion of the Maiden, and soon they can think of nothing else but her. In its guise as an old woman, Gastly then sells Ash and his friends paper charms that are supposed to keep the Maiden's ghost at bay.

When Jessie decides to confront the Maiden's ghost, Gastly uses its powers to unleash a swarm of frightening apparitions. Fortunately, this Gastly is weak against sunlight, so the break of dawn drives it away…but only until next year's summer festival!

A HAUNTED NINETALES

Lost in a deep mist, Ash and his friends meet a girl named Lokoko and her faithful Ninetales. Lokoko invites them all to stay at her home, a palatial mansion otherwise devoid of residents. The mansion's owner left home long ago, and all the staff except for Lokoko have quit and gone away.

Brock is instantly at home, thanks to Ninetales' affection and Lokoko's lavish hospitality. When Lokoko asks him to stay for good, he's ready to accept! On the other hand, Ash and Misty are spooked by Lokoko's lack of a reflection—or even a corporeal body—and Brock's obliviousness to how his clothes have suddenly changed. The key to the mystery lies in an old-fashioned Poké Ball and a photo of a man who looks just like Brock, except *that* man was the mansion's owner from over 200 years ago.

The truth is revealed: for over a century and a half, Ninetales has waited for its master, during which time it gained the power to create the illusion of Lokoko. Although deeply lonely, it could never bear to leave and instead tried to bewitch Brock into staying. It's not until Brock breaks Ninetales' antique Poké Ball that it's finally free to leave the mansion.

XATU FORETELLS THE FUTURE

It's said that Xatu can look backward and forward in time and their insight is vitally important to Calista, one in a long line of people who interpret Xatu prophecies. Even though Calista has access to a high-tech weather center, Calista's people rely on the Xatu to forecast the weather; the Xatu use their wings to speak in a form of semaphore, and Calista translates their gestures into predictions.

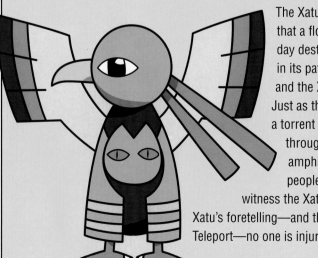

The Xatu long ago predicted that a flood would one day destroy everything in its path, ending Calista and the Xatu's duties. Just as they prophesied, a torrent of water sweeps through the canyon and amphitheater where people once gathered to witness the Xatu. But thanks to the Xatu's foretelling—and their ability to use Teleport—no one is injured by the disaster.

SECRET LIVES

Pokémon Professors have only scratched the surface of the mysteries of Pokémon. Evolutions, migration patterns, communication, social structure—these are just some aspects of Pokémon life that still pose intriguing questions.

THE BLUE MOON RITUAL OF THE QUAGSIRE

Johto's Cherrygrove City prohibits the battling and capturing of Quagsire, since the presence of Quagsire indicates to humans where the cleanest water can be found. Once a year, during the full moon, masses of Quagsire swim down the river that runs from Blue Moon Falls into the city; they grab any round object they can find and return upstream. The locals tolerate this because all the missing items float back downstream the next day, and it's good luck if your item is returned. Whoever owns the last thing to float back downstream is considered the luckiest of all.

No one in Cherrygrove knows what the Quagsire want with all those round things, but Ash, May, and Brock have seen the Quagsire's secret with their own eyes. The Quagsire take the items back upstream, where they gather in large numbers and watch the moon until just the right moment. Acting on some unknown cue, the Quagsire then toss the round objects in the air and blow water jets to shoot the objects toward the moon. They seem to celebrate when a Quagsire shoots its item higher than the rest.

THE SECRET GARDEN OF THE BULBASAUR

Conventional Trainer wisdom says that Pokémon usually level up by battling. But for Pokémon, and especially wild Pokémon, Evolution is sometimes part of a natural cycle.

At a certain time of the year, Bulbasaur from all over the world gather in a secluded part of Kanto known as the Mysterious Garden. These Bulbasaur are all ready to evolve. During this time, the presence of the Bulbasaur causes plants in the area to bloom unnaturally quickly.

The Mysterious Garden seems to be nothing more than a field with a barren tree at its center, but soon the Pokémon cause the entire area to burst into fresh blossoms. Inside the tree lives a Venusaur who leads the Evolution ceremony.

The Venusaur who lives in the Garden leads the Evolution, beginning with a form of call and response between Venusaur and the gathered Bulbasaur. When the moment is right, the Bulbasaur all evolve—unless, like Ash's Bulbasaur, they defy the crowd and refuse to become Ivysaur.

STARSTRUCK

After Meowth saw a screening of *That Darn Meowth*, it was so entranced that it headed west in search of the wonderful food it saw in the film. But Meowth isn't the only one in the Pokémon world who's been affected by the media—there are plenty of stars and celebrities who have crossed paths with Ash and his friends.

DJ MARY

DJ Mary is Poké Radio's famous radio host, broadcasting live from Goldenrod City. She's a real pro who's good at easing her guests' stage fright. She also works together with Professor Oak on his own Poké Radio show. The two of them have done several live broadcasts from towns in the area.

Pokétalk Radio's enthusiastic producer doesn't just stay in the studio, he'll even go out himself to grab interviewees. Everyone who wins a Plain Badge is interviewed on the show, so he goes to find Ash in person and ask him to come to the station.

Fiorello Cappucino

Fiorello's not just the movie star cohost of the Queen of the Princess Festival Contest, he's also the prize: in addition to a set of rare dolls, the winner receives a photo together with Fiorello. He's a perfect pick for the Princess Festival, since all the ladies just love him!

KLIEBAN SPIELBUNK

Winner of the Golden Growlithe for Best Director, Spielbunk is an artiste who's prone to melodrama. He takes a break from directing people to direct *Pokémon in Love*, a tragic Pokémon romance starring a prima donna Wigglytuff and Misty's Psyduck.

Spielbunk also directed *I Saw What You Ate Last Tuesday*, which was a big hit with Brock but a big flop at the box-office.

BRAD VAN DARN

Cooler than Articuno and hotter than Moltres: that's how the previews describe Brad van Darn, star of action films like *Ultra Maximum*. Behind the tough guy image is a man who dotes on his Smoochum, which upsets his manager. What would happen to Brad's image if his frenzied female fans saw him toting around a tiny Kiss Pokémon?

Ultimately, Brad decides he can't give up his precious "Smoochie-kins." Smoochum always supported him during his early days when he was washing dishes to earn meals and struggling through dance lessons. After Brad demonstrates some real-life heroics to save his Smoochum from Team Rocket during a live stage show, the fans go wild with delight. Now Brad and Smoochum act in films together and they're more popular than ever.

FUN AND GAMES

Sports and athletics are always popular in the Pokémon world, even when the athletics involve Pokémon instead of people! Most of the time Pokémon shouldn't be playing, but there are some exceptions.

BASEBALL

Baseball is a big sport with passionate fans, none more passionate than Ash's friend Casey. She's a die-hard fan of the Electabuzz, but the team was known for its losing ways during Ash's Johto journeys—perhaps because they lost their starting pitcher, Corey Demario, to a shoulder injury. Corey's absence helped turn the Electabuzz from first in the league to a team on a 10-game losing streak, but Casey would later help Corey regain the confidence to get back on the mound.

Other baseball teams include the Starmie, who play out of Cerulean City, and the questionably named Magikarp.

POKÉMON SUMO

What's Pokémon sumo? Like the actual sport of sumo, it's a 1-on-1 grappling match between Pokémon, using nothing more than sheer physical power. Pokémon sumo is the favored sport of a small village in Johto—the art was developed by local Trainers who were big fans of human sumo wrestling. Trainers in the village breed Pokémon just for sumo wrestling; Pokémon must weigh at least 80 kilograms in order to compete.

The town even has its own Pokémon Sumo Society and an annual Pokémon Sumo Conference, which has been held for over 35 years. The winner receives a King's Rock and a year's supply of Pokémon food.

SURFING

Islands like Kanto's Seafoam Island and Hoenn's Dewford Island are home to big waves and the surfers that love them. People do most of the surfing but Pokémon can get in on the fun, too: Brawly, the Dewford Gym Leader, has trained his Makuhita to surf, and Pooka the blue-eyed Pikachu rides a surfboard together with its human friend, Victor.

Seafoam Island and Humungadunga

The tsunami-sized wave called Humungadunga strikes Seafoam Island once every 20 years, an event that fills surfers' hearts with excitement. There's a tall rock spire just offshore, and surfers love to ride past it and see how high on the rock they can plant their flags.

EXTREME POKÉMON

Extreme Pokémon races are the most popular sport in Eggseter, a small Johto town. This type of racing involves a person riding a skateboard pulled by a harnessed Pokémon.

Eggseter holds an annual Extreme Pokémon race, with the golden Poké Ball trophy as the prize. The course leads out of town and out to the Shellby Ranch, where competitors pick up a dummy Pokémon Egg and then bring it back to the starting line using any route they wish.

KANTO

Kanto is Ash's home. Hailing from the small village of Pallet Town, which also happens to be the home of Professor Oak, Ash traveled across this region exploring everything from Mt. Moon in the north to the Indigo Plateau in the east.

From the island resort of Cinnabar Island in the south to Pewter City and Cerulean City in the north, Kanto offers many different walks of life. Kanto's Saffron City is the largest metropolis in the region, located in the center of Kanto, between Celadon City and Lavender Town.

Perhaps the most unique man-made feature is the oceanic bridge. Spanning the entire gulf area of Vermilion City, travelers can ride, walk, or bike across the great expanse.

PROFESSOR OAK

Professor Oak is an important figure in the Pokémon universe, and to Ash. He often serves as his mentor and friend. He is always there for Ash with timely advice or a piece of his world famous Pokémon poetry.

PROPS FOR THE PROF

Professor Oak is the first in a line of arborous professors we meet throughout the Pokémon universe. Professors are usually named after some type of tree or plant: Professor Birch, Professor Elm, Professor Ivy, and even Professor Rowan.

First and foremost, Professor Oak is a Pokémon researcher—a man who studies the behavior of Pokémon and their interaction with the human community. He's credited with a ton of material that's related to Pokémon, and all that data helped him to build his greatest invention ever—the Pokédex.

While he always shows a keen intellect and sage wisdom, Professor Oak actually knows a bit about battling as well. His Pokémon of choice is an extremely powerful Dragonite.

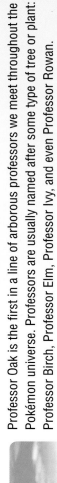

POETRY

Professor Oak is a poetry master, making up thoughtful *haiku* about Pokémon that not only describe a Pokémon, but answer some of life's questions as well.

Wobbuffet

When life is a mystery, it is your answer.

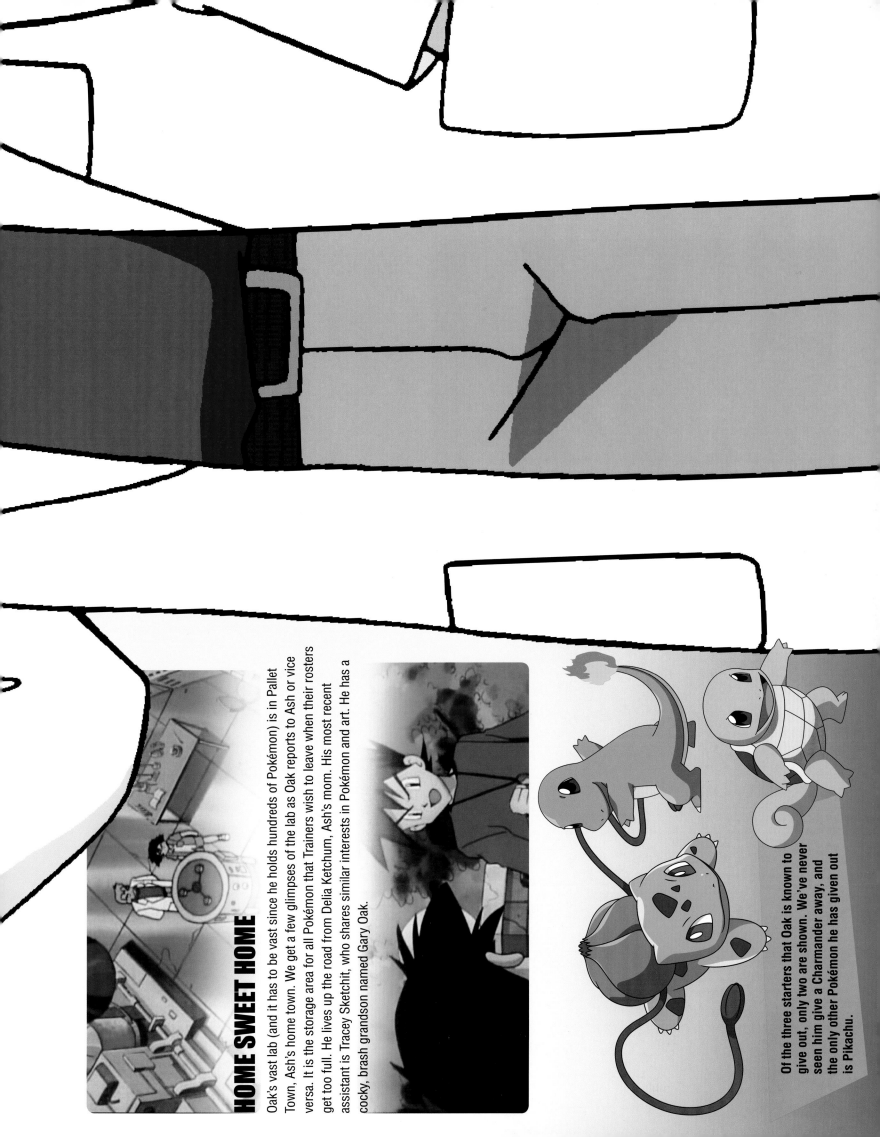

HOME SWEET HOME

Oak's vast lab (and it has to be vast since he holds hundreds of Pokémon) is in Pallet Town, Ash's home town. We get a few glimpses of the lab as Oak reports to Ash or vice versa. It is the storage area for all Pokémon that Trainers wish to leave when their rosters get too full. He lives up the road from Delia Ketchum, Ash's mom. His most recent assistant is Tracey Sketchit, who shares similar interests in Pokémon and art. He has a cocky, brash grandson named Gary Oak.

Of the three starters that Oak is known to give out, only two are shown. We've never seen him give a Charmander away, and the only other Pokémon he has given out is Pikachu.

MISTY

She's a hothead, cranky, and very emotional. She also has a tender side that comes out when caring for Togepi. But what Misty has that few others possess is a determination to be the best fueled by sibling rivalry.

WATER, WATER, EVERYWHERE

Misty loves Water-type Pokémon, and she'd better—her sisters run the Cerulean Gym in Cerulean City. But her chance encounter with Ash sets off a series of events that turn her life upside down. But the biggest mystery surrounding Misty is how (or when) she and Ash will finally come to realize that they're made for each other.

Misty and her three older sisters, Daisy, Violet, and Lily, run the Cerulean City Gym. In order to make a name for herself, Misty sets off on her own to become the greatest Water-type Pokémon Trainer ever. She eventually returns to the Gym out of a sense of duty, and makes a name for herself as a much better Gym Leader than her sisters.

THAT'S MY BIKE!

So how did Misty and Ash meet? Pikachu was fleeing a flock of Spearow, and Ash was in hot pursuit. After snagging Ash and Pikachu on her fishing pole, they beat a hasty retreat on Misty's "borrowed" bike.

Later, when Pikachu bravely faces down the flock, its ThunderShock fries everything to a crisp, including Misty's bike. Misty's bike was repaired and returned to her by the Viridian City Nurse Joy.

TRAUMA DRAMA

Misty fears a number of Pokémon, most notably Bug-type Pokémon. She won't even befriend Bug-types caught by Ash—she lists them as one of the three most disgusting things in the world: carrots, peppers, and Bug-types. She once had a fear of Gyarados—one tried to eat her when she was a baby. She got over it after calming and gaining the trust of an angry Gyarados at the Cerulean City Gym.

Misty's Pokémon

HORSEA

After befriending this Horsea, it was later transferred back to the Cerulean City Gym for further strengthening.

PSYDUCK

Misty got Psyduck by accident. Misty trips, falls, loses a Poké Ball, and Psyduck hops in.

STARYU

Another original for Misty, this unassuming Pokémon has counted for quite a few victories.

STARMIE

This Pokémon was also one of Misty's original Pokémon, but was seldom seen in the show. She did use it against Ash in her Gym Battle for the Cascade Badge.

CORSOLA

Corsola was caught after Misty found it terrorizing other Corsola in the Whirl Islands. She used it in many battles, where it proved to be an admirable fighter.

TOGEPI

Togepi began as an Egg that became the center of a battle between everyone involved. Ash found the Egg. Brock took care of it. Meowth raised the Egg. But when it hatched, Togepi connected with Misty.

GOLDEEN

One of the Pokémon that Misty originally started out with. It is can only be used in the water.

POLIWAG

Misty befriends Poliwag in the Orange Islands after a Vile Plume uses its Stun Spore attack on Ash and Tracey. Although seldom used, it evolves into a powerful Poliwhirl later.

LOMBRE

CASERIN

Caserin is a Luvdisc that Misty acquired in Kanto. After trying unsuccessfully to foster a romantic relationship with another Luvdisc, it battles its way out of trouble and wins the affection of its target.

AZURILL

Ash is reunited with old friends, including Misty, who now has an Azurill she hatched from an Egg.

SENSATIONAL SIBLINGS

Misty's sisters perform a synchronized swimming act under the stage name The Three Sensational Sisters. Apparently, they don't count Misty as being that sensational, and refer to her as a "runt." But it was Misty, not her sisters, who battled Ash for the Cascade Badge when he fought at the Cerulean Gym.

BROCK

Steady as the Rock-type Pokémon he once favored, Brock is a wise, talented Pokémon breeder with one big weakness: pretty girls. Most of the time, Brock takes care of his friends, dispensing sage advice and making sure everyone is fed. But when Brock goes ga-ga over a girl, it's his friends who have to rein him in.

Brock is a born caretaker, an ace hand at caring for his nine younger siblings as well as all types of Pokémon. His specialty is cooking delicious food for people and Pokémon, but he has a knack for just about anything domestic, from sewing to sweeping floors. What's more, he genuinely enjoys domestic work, but his household duties kept him chained to the Gym until his absent father Flint returned to take over the Gym.

Brock thought he'd found paradise in the Orange Islands helping out Professor Ivy, but he returned a broken man. For a time, he recuperated at Ash's house and fought with Mr. Mime for the privilege of doing chores and errands.

Brock has a book for everything—whenever he finds himself in a new situation, he takes diligent notes in his notebook. He also has a book to keep track of pretty girls and the instructions for all his chores are recorded in a notebook as well. It's not all cooking and laundry; polishing his Rock-type Pokémon with sand and a scrub brush is another one of Brock's regular chores. After Brock joined Ash and Misty, he eased up on the stern Gym Leader act. Not only did he start to show his goofy girl-crazy side, he's the gang's go-to man when it comes to region information, Battle strategy, and Pokémon - Trainer relationships.

Brock's Pokémon

GEODUDE

Like Brock's original Onix, Geodude was a mainstay of his Gym battling team at the Pewter Gym. Now it's back at the Gym under Forrest's care.

ONIX

Back when Steelix was an Onix, it was already so imposing that Pikachu tried to sneak out of their Gym battle. Brock left Onix with his brother Forrest, who raised it into a Steelix.

ZUBAT

Zubat took a very long time to evolve into a Golbat. Finally evolving in a battle with Team Rocket. It reached its final stage, a sleek Crobat, in attempting to chase down Team Rocket in of all things a rocket.

STEELIX

CROBAT

GOLBAT

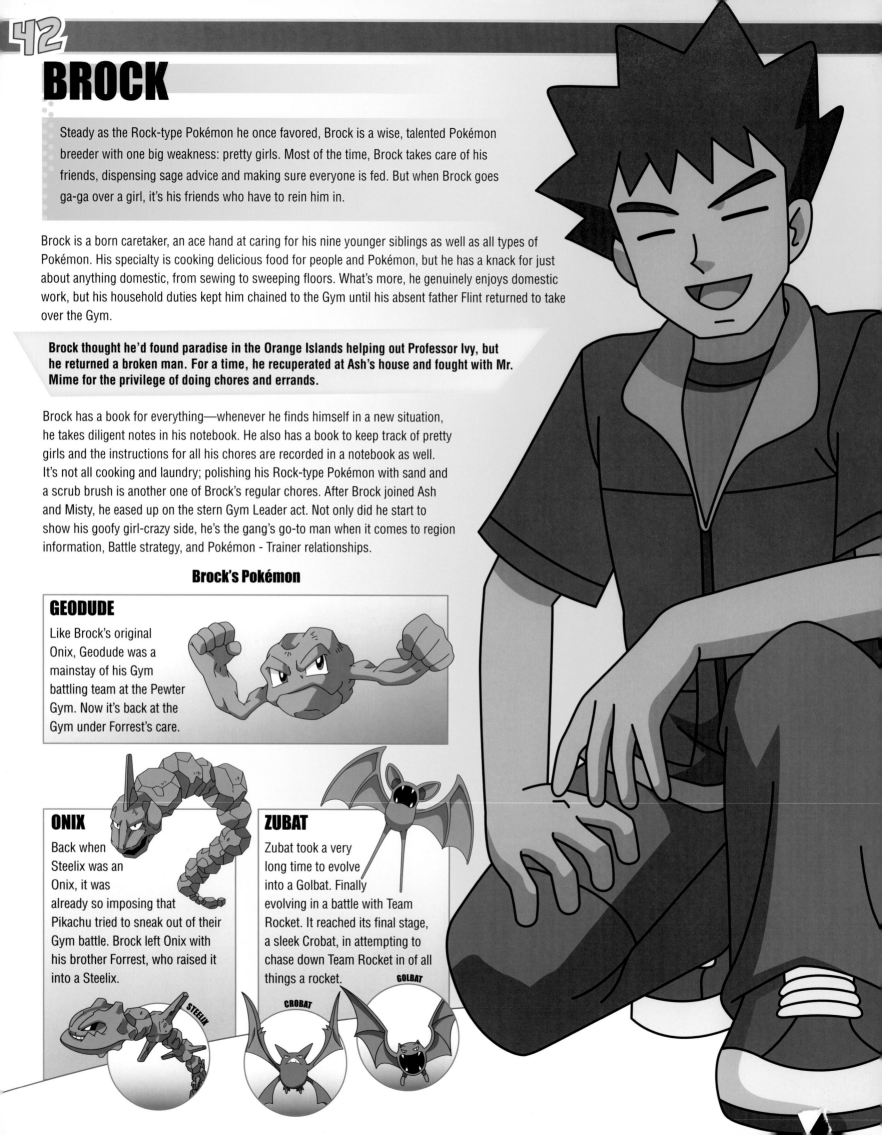

ALL IN THE FAMILY

To understand Brock, it's essential to understand his family. Brock's parents, Flint and Lola, met in a Pokémon battle. They've kept the romance alive to this day, but Flint has difficulties adjusting to life as a family man: when things get tough, he runs off to the Pewter City outskirts and sits there in disguise. The first time, it was because he never became the Pokémon Trainer he wanted to be and couldn't face his family. The second time, he simply couldn't bear to stand up to his dear wife Lola.

Brock's mother Lola is loving but flighty, always busy with new hobbies. She likes to paint and decorate the house—and the Pewter Gym, unless she's stopped by Brock. Flint is hard in name only, and he had no choice but to let Lola turn the Pewter Gym into a Water-type Gym.

As for Brock's siblings, all nine of them (Forrest, Salvador, Yolanda, Tommy, Cindy, Suzy, Timmy, and the twins Tilly and Billy) look to him to keep the household functional.

Brock the Gym Leader

Before Ash and Brock were pals, Ash was another challenger at the Pewter Gym. Brock was unimpressed with Ash's ability to raise his Pokémon and let him know as much; even then, he cared more about being a Pokémon breeder than battling.

The Many Loves of Brock

Brock professes his love to just about every pretty girl he sees, but fate has it that it never works out even when there's a girl who's attracted to him.

From time to time, Brock's unerring attraction for pretty girls does have its uses. For one thing, he's always able to tell Nurse Joys and Officer Jennys apart, based on their scent, or sometimes just a vibe. And even when the eyes may be fooled, Brock's heart isn't—just as a Pokédex correctly identifies Meowth even when it's in disguise, Brock feels nothing for Jessie disguised as Nurse Joy or Phantom Thief Brodie disguised as a lovely female researcher.

Temacu

She loves him, she loves him not… For once, Brock isn't interested when a girl falls in love with him, but he soon realizes he feels for Temacu after all. By then, it's already too late: fickle Temacu is completely over Brock and head over heels for the local doctor instead.

Pike Queen Lucy

The daring Pike Queen of the Battle Frontier is quiet, almost shy in person, but she blushes when Brock tries to charm her and seems to take a real interest in him.

MUDKIP

Marshtomp evolved from a responsible Mudkip that shared its caretaker instincts with Brock. It left its other Mudkip charges to join Brock's team and eventually evolved into a Marshtomp, but suffers from the same unluckiness in love as its Trainer.

MARSHTOMP

LOTAD

Brock's shy and earnest Lotad evolved into a Lombre after falling into a dry well. Lombre had a poor romantic track record, it lost the heart of another Trainer's Mawile when it evolved into a boisterous, outgoing Ludicolo after coming into contact with a Water Stone.

LOMBRE

LUDICOLO

PINECO

While in Johto looking for apricorns, Brock saved a Pineco from Team Rocket. Pineco had a habit of self-destructing at the most inconvenient moments, but once it evolved into Forretress, it became a dependable member of Brock's team.

FORRETRESS

BONSLY

Brock lovingly cared for a baby Bonsly that he found haunting a ninja school. From that Bonsly, too young to even eat solid food, Brock eventually raised a loyal Sudowoodo that mimics anyone it's around.

SUDOWOODO

HAPPINY

Hatched from an Egg, Happiny was won when Brock entered Croagunk into a Pokémon dress-up contest. After rescuing Happiny from Team Rocket, Brock was able to bond with it.

CROAGUNK

Brock and Croagunk share a bond that can only be described as "special." Croagunk acts taciturn yet always looks out for Brock in its own way, usually by hitting him with Poison Jab whenever he tries to woo a beautiful lady.

TODD SNAP

Team Rocket once hired Todd Snap to capture Pikachu. What they didn't realize is that Todd only knows how to capture Pokémon one way, and that's with a camera—he doesn't call himself a number one photomaster for nothing!

Todd lives and breathes Pokémon photography—he has no Pokémon of his own, but he's captured countless on film and claims to have the world's best collection of candid Grass-type Pokémon photos. He first met Ash in Kanto and the two of them didn't hit it off immediately, even though they share a unique connection: Todd took a famous photo of the Aerodactyl that was carrying Ash away.

His obsession with photographing an Articuno finally paid off, and a print of his photo now hangs in the Snow Top Peak Pokémon Center in Johto. He decided to stay there for a while and continue photographing Pokémon that live in the mountains.

Todd and Ash soon bonded over their shared love of Pokémon, and he's even done some traveling with the gang in Kanto and Johto. Todd has smoothed out his early flashes of ego, but he's still obsessed with photography and will risk life and limb just to get the perfect shot.

RICHIE

Picture Ash, only mature for his age and adept at everything from solving problems to jump-starting a defunct elevator. That's Richie: he even has a Pikachu that likes to ride on his shoulder!

Richie and Ash first met at the Indigo League, where they teamed up to stop a Team Rocket Pokémon heist. Richie was taken aback by Ash's reckless antics, but they became great friends once they discovered just how similar they are. To their shock, they faced each other in the fifth round of the Indigo League; even though Ash was almost a no-show thanks to Team Rocket, Richie believed in his new friend and refused to let the referee call the match until Ash arrived.

Richie can go a little crazy over Pokémon, just like Ash, but he's usually the more level-headed of the two. Even when he loses in the Indigo League, he doesn't indulge in self-pity. He simply decides he'll do better next time, a maturity that makes an impression on Ash.

Richie's Pokémon

"ROSE" (TAILLOW)

"HAPPY" (BUTTERFREE)

"CRUZ" (PUPITAR)

"ZIPPO" (CHARMELEON)

"SPARKY" (PIKACHU)

EEVEE

PALLET TOWN

Throughout all of Ash's journeys, Pallet Town remains stable, the center of his adventures. There may not be much excitement in this little town, but there's everything a Trainer needs to welcome him home: a warm bed, a home-cooked meal, and the friendly faces of family and friends.

Pallet Town is a quiet town surrounded by rolling hills and fields, not far from a river, mountains, and even a rocky valley.

Much of Pallet Town is rural, and even the center of town is small and sleepy. But there's usually some activity at the local shop, run by an elderly lady who's always happy to chat with Professor Oak about the latest issue of *Pokémon Monthly*. She's always happy to chat, period—she's the biggest gossip in Pallet Town.

Inside her shop is a booth where she has her own one-woman DJ gig. From there, she can make announcements over the town's loudspeaker system and play music—her "station's" callsign is WPOK.

Delia Ketchum loves her garden, and she's taken Ash on many visits to nearby Xanadu Nursery for supplies. Filled with plants from top to bottom, Xanadu looks more like a botanical garden than a nursery. As lovely as it is, visitors must be careful since some of the plants have toxic defenses.

ASH'S HOUSE

Located on an unpaved road in a quiet neighborhood, Ash's house is as peaceful as can be. In the absence of her son, Ash's mother Delia keeps busy with her garden and social visits to Professor Oak; her Mr. Mime helps her out with the chores.

The upper level of the house has a workspace where Delia sews Ash's clothes.

PROFESSOR OAK'S LABORATORY

Professor Oak and his assistant Tracey live and work in a complex on top of a hill, just across a small river. Behind his home and laboratory is a sprawling ranch that has ample room for lots of Pokémon to run free.

Trainers come to Professor Oak to receive their first Pokémon or consult his expertise, while researchers contact him with their own scientific issues.

In addition to computers and scientific equipment, the lab has a storage area full of Poké Balls being held for traveling Trainers.

GARY OAK

Every hero has a rival—someone who brings out the best in him. Rivals from day one, Gary and Ash seemed destined to get on each other's nerves. But their passion to always do better drives each to excel.

Their epic rivalry started very early. While fishing one day, Ash and Gary snag the same Pokémon. After some heated words, they both yank from opposite sides of a river at their prize. It turns out to be a Poké Ball. When the Poké Ball snaps in half, each youngster claims it as their own. To this day each keeps his half as symbol of their competition.

Cheerleaders

Gary is so overconfident that he has his own team of cheerleaders. Unfortunately, the cheerleaders have a bad effect on Brock, who becomes so infatuated with them in the finals that he can't seem to stay focused on his friend Ash's battles.

A REPUTATION TO UPHOLD

Gary Oak needs to be Gary Oak—that is, he needs to uphold the Oak family name. His grandfather is, after all, the famous and world-renowned Professor Samuel Oak, and those are some mighty big shoes to fill. Unfortunately, he doesn't get a lot of favoritism shown to him, and his brash and arrogant manner could be part of the problem. His overconfidence and attitude begin to change as he experiences more of the world.

In a furious 6-on-6 battle for the Silver Conference Finals, Ash beats Gary. Cocky at the beginning, Gary finally admits to Ash that they would have been better friends than rivals. Soon after he decides he wants to become a Pokémon researcher—just like his grandfather.

Gary's Pokémon

BLASTOISE

This was Gary's first choice and it also would have been Ash's first choice as well. Only revealed, as a fully evolved Blastoise, this was Gary's first Pokémon.

NIDOKING

In an early epic battle with Giovanni, Gary Oak goes for the Earth Badge at the Viridian City Gym. Giovanni plays the battle hard and fast…

NIDOQUEEN

When Oak's lab comes under attack by Team Rocket, a mysterious stranger, who turns out to be Gary, saves the day with his Nidoqueen.

SCIZOR

After some back and forth between Ash and Gary in the Johto League Silver Conference, the battle comes down to Snorlax and Scizor. Scizor defeats Snorlax.

"At least you get the chance to meet me…
Mr. Gary to you. Show some respect."

ARCANINE

…bringing a Mewtwo in that wipes out almost everything thrown at it, including two of Gary's Pokémon, Nidoking and Arcanine.

DODUO

Although making only a brief cameo as Gary returns to Professor Oak's lab, this Pokémon does end up evolving into Dodrio and playing a more major role later on.

DODRIO

EEVEE

Eevee is one of those rare Pokémon that can evolve a number of different ways: the time of day, the opponent, and it's feeling for the Trainer all are factors. So it's no wonder that Gary's Eevee evolved into Umbreon, but not before defeating Ash and Pikachu.

UMBREON

MAGMAR

Magmar is Gary's second Pokémon used against Ash in the finals. Magmar is sent packing by Ash's Heracross.

GOLEM

Golem comes in to battle Charizard, which seems like it would be a bad match-up for Charizard, but of course, Ash thinks outside the box and comes up with a unique way to defeat it!

ELECTIVIRE

Larger than Pikachu, Electivire has won the only time it has faced off with Pikachu.

Listen, is that a voice I hear?
It's speaking to me loud and clear.
On the wind.
Past the stars.
In your ear!
Bringing chaos at a breakneck pace.
Dashing hope, bringing fear in its place.
A rose by any other name is just as sweet.
When everything's worse, our work is complete.
Jessie!
James!
And Meowth, now dat's a name!
Putting the do-gooders in their place...
...we're Team Rocket...
...in your face!
Wobbuffet!

JESSIE

How could a trio of ineffective criminals possibly make it through dozens of lands, hundreds of adventures, and thousands of misfires into the annals of Pokémon lore? You'd have to be so spectacularly bad at your job that people would notice. And on that note, we introduce you to Team Rocket.

HUMBLE BEGINNINGS

Both Jessie and James have very intricate backstories that actually have you feeling sorry for them. Jessie had a troubled childhood. She was incredibly poor, having to eat snow to survive. Jessie tried nursing school for a while, but flunked out and eventually met James.

DUSTOX

Completely convinced that her Wurmple, which had evolved into a Cascoon, was going to evolve into a Beautifly, she is disappointed at first when it finally evolves after a battle with May. She quickly comes to adore Dustox and only releases it so it can mate.

CASCOON

WURMPLE

ARBOK

Ekans was an obedient Pokémon that Jessie used often. It evolved into Arbok and became her go-to Pokémon. She eventually released it so that it could help a group of Ekans being threatened by poachers.

EKANS

WOBBUFFET

Wobbuffet was obtained mistakenly when Jessie accidentally dropped her Ball a real Tracing Machine. She was unaware that her Lickitung had been traded until later in a battle with "the Twerps."

SEVIPER

A sturdy battler on Jessie's team, Seviper has a long running feud with Zangoose. It obeys Jessie, but will never back down from a fight with Zangoose. This has been Jessie's Pokémon of choice for some time.

YANMEGA

Caught as a Yanma, Jessie's Yanmega evolved very quickly.

JAMES

James was born to a wealthy family, and has always enjoyed his status and wealth. So why would he give it all up for a life of crime? After attending Pokémon Tech (a school for Pokémon education), James grew bored of his lifestyle and ran away leaving Growlie at home. After a short stint in the Bridge Bike Gang, James set his sights somewhat higher and decided to join the Team Rocket syndicate.

GROWLITHE

Growlithe, or "Growlie" as James calls him, was one of his first Pokémon. His pet was beloved, but when James ran away from home, he left Growlie behind. When James does meet up with him again, he leaves Growlie as guardian over his scheming parents.

VICTREEBEL

Although Weepinbell was one of James's first Pokémon, he leaves it at a daycare center to evolve into Victreebel. He loses Victreebel in a Pokémon swap.

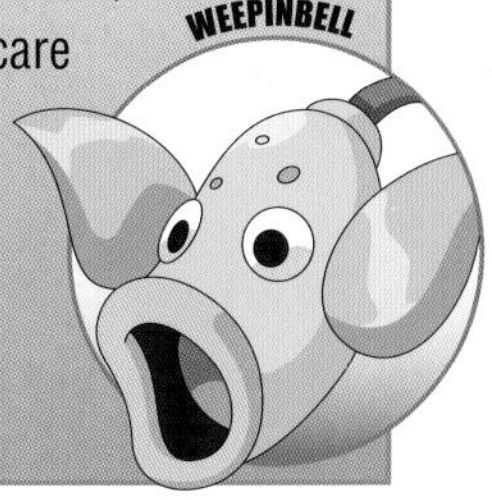

WEEPINBELL

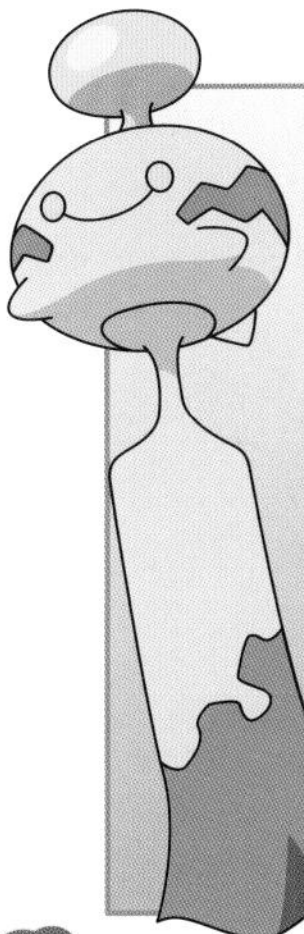

CHIMECHO

James calls Chimecho his first love. But after almost being duped into buying a Hoppip, a real Chimecho agrees to become one of his Pokémon. After it comes down with a fever, James leaves it with his Nanny and Pop-Pop, but vows to return for it after it heals.

MIME JR.

James' Nanny and Pop-Pop are helping to heal his sick Chimecho. Mime Jr. jumps into an empty Poké Ball that falls to the ground, voluntarily becoming his newest Pokémon.

KOFFING

Koffing is seen when we first meet Team Rocket, and has proven itself to be a formidable battler. It eventually evolves into a Weezing along with Jessie's Ekans. It was released along with Jessie's Arbok.

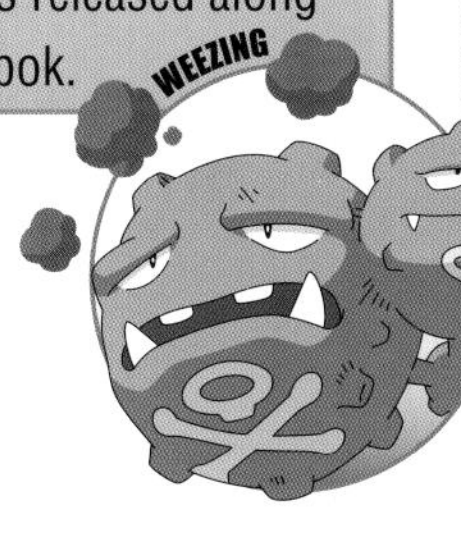

WEEZING

CARNIVINE

Early in Sinnoh, Team Rocket is trudging along after another defeat. They come across the old mansion where James spent his summers, and inside the playroom, James finds a beloved, albeit forgotten, childhood Pokémon of his—Carnivine.

MEOWTH

Meowth's story is heartbreaking, but its desire remains constant. It wants to supplant Giovanni's favorite pet Pokémon, Persian. All of Meowth's schemes almost work, but he always ends up paying for the bungling antics of Jessie and James.

CERULEAN CITY

Kanto's Cerulean City is Misty's hometown, a modern city located on the ocean. In keeping with its location, one of its featured attractions is the Water-type Cerulean Gym, but the city is home to other attractions with an oceanic theme. Cerulean City's own lighthouse is a scenic rendezvous spot in an area surrounded by trees.

CERULEAN CITY GYM

One look at the Cerulean Gym and it's clear what type of Gym it is. But it's more than just a Gym; Misty's sisters love to stage water ballet shows with the Gym's central tank as their stage.

For battles, the tank is usually recessed into the ground, just like a normal pool…but the tank can be elevated aboveground for special events and shows.

Although Misty's sister Daisy can't wait to get Misty and Tracey into some water ballet outfits and into the pool, Misty is happy to hand over the spotlight to Lily and Violet, the scriptwriting sister. Misty was already drafted to play a mermaid in one underwater show, and she's not keen on a repeat performance. Her Pokémon, including Goldeen, Starmie, Corsola, Horsea, and Staryu, continue to appear in water shows, while Kasurin and Loverin, two Luvdisc recently acquired by the Gym, can also help provide special effects.

The ceiling above the pool features lots of windows to let in light, and those windows can also swing open or shut. In the Gym's basement is an aquarium room filled with additional tanks for the Gym's Water-type Pokémon.

Making the Cascade Badge

The Cerulean Gym's Cascade Badges aren't just for show, they're handcrafted works of art. When supplies run out, Misty, Sakura, and Tracey pay a visit to the artist, Mr. Kinzo, who lives in Rafore Village. There they learn

through hands-on experience that making a badge is a grueling process that involves smithing, filing, welding, and a light hand with a brush!

Earning the Cascade Badge

But for all that work, Misty's sisters tend to be lax about the requirements for earning a Cascade Badge whenever Misty isn't around—it's not unusual for them to practically give the badges away. One Trainer, Jimmy, "earned" his Cascade Badge for helping Daisy clean the pool—although Tracey has also done the same thing and has yet to receive a badge for his troubles.

INDIGO CONFERENCE

The Kanto region's Indigo Conference is Ash's first big tournament and the culmination of everything he's worked for so far—not the least of which is the fact that his rival Gary will be there. Eight Kanto Gym Badges earn entry into the tournament, after which it's down to a series of elimination rounds.

The Indigo Conference takes place on the Indigo Plateau. Located near a sparkling lake, Indigo Stadium is where the tournament's main events take place, but the first four rounds are held in other outlying stadiums.

Competitors can look forward to comfortable accommodations in the Pokémon League Village and free meals at area restaurants; parades and other special events add to the festive atmosphere for Trainers and spectators alike.

President Goodshow, a Pokémon League Torch Committee official, presides over the opening ceremonies. There's a ceremonial release of a flock of Pidgey and a parade of all the competing Trainers, followed by the lighting of the stadium's central torch.

TOURNAMENT STRUCTURE

The first four rounds are 3-on-3 battles in separate stadiums, each with one of four different battlefields: Rock, Grass, Water, and Ice. Each competitor must win matches on all four types, and competitors are assigned to fields at random.

Once a competitor advances past the first four rounds and into the top 16, they battle on a standard field in Indigo Stadium. Starting at the quarterfinal stage, battles are 6-on-6 instead of 3-on-3. For the top 16, brackets are determined by having each Trainer fish for a numbered Magikarp. Ash must battle Richie.

RICHIE DEFEATS ASH

Several of Ash's Pokémon are exhausted after a running struggle to escape Team Rocket and get to the stadium on time, so Ash's options are limited. Charizard is his last Pokémon, but when it refuses to battle, Ash loses the round and his final 16 match by default.

ASSUNTA DEFEATS RICHIE

Richie's own run ends here. His match comes down to a battle between Sparky and Assunta's Ivysaur. Despite the type advantage, Sparky is knocked out.

CLOSING CEREMONIES

Everyone wins *something* in the Indigo League, so to speak. At the closing ceremonies, the winner receives a trophy, the rest of the competitors parade into Indigo Stadium and receive a commemorative badge, then bask in the light of a spectacular fireworks display.

KANTO GYM BATTLES!

On his way to becoming a Pokémon Master, Ash must first find and defeat the Gym Leaders for each area. He starts in Kanto, where the Gyms are spaced pretty far apart, leaving open the possibilities of endless adventures!

VERMILLION CITY GYM

GYM LEADER: LT. SURGE

Lt. Surge, a fierce Gym Leader, uses Pikachu's evolved form, Raichu. Raichu is more powerful and knows more moves than Pikachu, so their first meeting is disastrous. While recuperating at the Pokémon Center, Nurse Joy offers Ash a Thunderstone, which would evolve Pikachu into Raichu, but Pikachu refuses, instead opting to face Surge and his Pokémon on its own terms.

The first outing ended fairly quickly, as Lt. Surge predicted. Pikachu tried to use ThunderShock, but Raichu easily absorbed it, using a ThunderShock that was much more powerful. By the time Raichu got around to using Mega Punch, the match was over.

Pikachu was emboldened by its promise to protect its honor and not level up using the Thunderstone. Raichu was ready with Body Slam, but Pikachu's Agility outmaneuvered it.

PEWTER CITY GYM

GYM LEADER: BROCK

Gust works like a charm—a really, really bad charm. Flying attacks are weak against Rock-type Pokémon.

Geodude is no match for the strengthened Pikachu. Brock recalls Geodude.

Pikachu fares better against Onix, but in the end, Brock stops the fight when it appears that it may hurt Pikachu. Luck is on their side, though, when a damaging sprinkler malfunction weakens Brock's Rock-type Pokémon.

Ash meets his first Gym Leader, Brock, while in Pewter City. Brock runs the Pewter City Gym, but also acts as a father to his abandoned siblings. Ash is reluctant to defeat Brock in front of his brothers and sisters, but his chivalry is rewarded when Brock joins his team, and grants him the Boulder Badge.

SAFFRON CITY GYM

GYM LEADER: SABRINA

Pikachu is confused by Abra's indifference—which actually is a form of telekinesis. Abra evolves into the much stronger Kadabra, then proceeds to wipe the floor with Pikachu using Psychic attack and Confusion.

Using Psybeam, Kadabra expects to win easily, but then Haunter shows up and makes Sabrina laugh. This immobilizes her Kadabra and wins Ash the Marsh Badge.

CERULEAN CITY GYM

GYM LEADER: THE SENSATIONAL SISTERS

Ash is a little overconfident going against Misty, and the battle volleys until Butterfree's Stun Spore does a number on Staryu. Staryu delivers a hard blow, and Ash recalls it.

Realizing Staryu probably couldn't take much more, Misty recalls it and sends out Starmie. Wing Attack and Gust give Pidgeotto the edge, but before anyone can finish the match, Team Rocket arrives and rains on the parade.

The Sensational Sisters (Misty's sisters) are about to give the badge to Ash when Misty intervenes. She wants to battle Ash for the badge, and does an admirable job. Unfortunately for Ash, Pikachu doesn't want to battle his new friend, Misty. When Team Rocket stops the pitched battle, Pikachu comes forward and blasts them off. The Sensational Sisters award the badge to Ash for saving the Gym.

CELADON CITY GYM
GYM LEADER: ERIKA

On their arrival in the sweet-scented Celadon City, Misty and Brock are taken by the town's perfume shop – but Ash is rude and dismissive, which angers the shop's owner and the town's Gym Leader, Erika. Ash now must find some other way into the Gym, and he enlists the help of Team Rocket to sneak in "Ashley". Pikachu uncovers his drag act, and Erika angrily takes him on in a battle for the Rainbow Badge.

Bulbasaur tries Vine Whip to attack Tangela from a distance, but Tangela counters with Constrict. After using Stun Spore effectively on Bulbasaur, Ash withdraws it.

Weepinbell uses Razor Leaf, but Charmander's Flamethrower easily burns the Grass-type Weepinbell. Ash finishes with Skull Bash, and Erika removes Weepinbell from battle.

Erika calls out Gloom against Charmander, and because she has such a tight bond with her Pokémon, it lays the smack down on Charmander pretty easily.

Team Rocket shows up during the fracas to steal the secret formula for the Gym's world-renowned perfume, and sets the Gym on fire. Ash puts aside his battle to save the Pokémon, and in particular, Erika's Gloom, for which she rewards him with the Rainbow Badge.

CINNABAR ISLAND GYM
GYM LEADER: BLAINE

Squirtle seemed like an obvious choice for a lava gym, but Ninetales uses Fire Spin, the most powerful attack in its repertoire, and Squirtle is knocked out.

Pikachu has to pick up for Charizard, and its use of Rhydon's horn as a lightning rod leads to an easy victory for Ash.

Charizard actually sleeps throughout the whole match, and forfeits the battle. It embarrasses Ash and disobediently leaves the arena.

No match. Pikachu is so outmatched that Ash forfeits the battle to save Pikachu.

The volcanic conclusion to the battle with Blaine is epic. A battle of Flamethrower attacks is useless, so Magmar uses Fire Blast, the most powerful move it knows. Charizard deflects it, and finally wins the match with its Seismic Toss.

FUCHSIA CITY GYM
GYM LEADER: KOGA

Bulbasaur and Venonat parry with limited results, until Bulbasaur's Leech Seed takes Venonat down.

Charmander takes over for the fainted Pidgeotto, and gains the advantage with Flamethrower. Their battle, however, is interrupted by Team Rocket.

Venonat evolves almost immediately into Venomoth, which uses Stun Spore and Sleep Powder with devastating results.

Continuing their earlier battle, Charmander faces Golbat, and uses Ember attack to great effect. Golbat counters with Screech, but Charmander's Fire Spin does it in.

VIRIDIAN CITY GYM
GYM LEADER: GIOVANNI

Giovanni, the Gym Leader of Viridian City, is also the head of Team Rocket. He has a super-powerful Pokémon at his side, a Pokémon that wiped out all of Gary's Pokémon—Mewtwo. Giovanni is absent when Ash arrives, and he has to battle Jessie and James.

Machamp treats Squirtle like the squirt it is, and ends up hurting Ash in the process.

A combination of Quick Attack and Double-Edge attack puts things right for Ash.

Bulbasaur's Vine Whip has no effect when Kingler uses its Harden. When it hits Bulbasaur with Bubble attack, it seems as if Ash is destined to lose.

Pikachu evens everything out with a powerful Thunderbolt that wipes out the competition.

Team Rocket has rigged the battlefield so that Trainers feel the pain of their Pokémon. In true Team Rocket fashion, they rigged both sides of the field. When Ash uses Pikachu's Thunderbolt, and Team Rocket blasts off, he wins the eighth and final badge—the Earth Badge.

BELIEVE IT OR NOT!

STRANGE MEOWTH BALLOON FLOATING ABOVE SINNOH.

Story on Page 74

SINISTER HUNTER J WANTED ON MULTIPLE COUNTS OF THEFT.

Story on Page 129

A planet full of Pokémon is a fantastic place to begin, but the Pokémon world is full of other unusual sights. Magic? Mystical kingdoms? Giant Pokémon? Ash and his friends have encounter all this and more…

Giant Claydol Spotted On Izabe Island!

According to legend, a maiden crafted it from the mud of Lake Izabe, and the Claydol searched for her after it was released. That's how Ash and Team Rocket lure the Claydol toward the stone Poké Ball on the cliff—Wobbuffet bears a certain resemblance to the original maiden.

IS THE GIANT CLAYDOL EVEN A REAL POKÉMON?

Lombre the Water Lord?

The locals have a shrine to Lombre

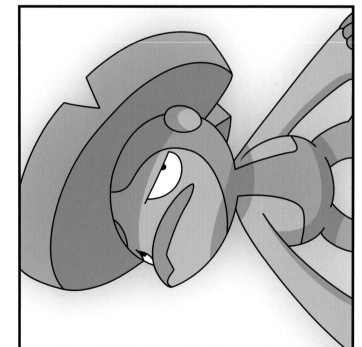

Mighty Pokémon such as Dialga and Palkia have long been revered for their power, but Lombre? There is indeed a town in Hoenn where the locals have a shrine to Lombre, their Water Lord, who is said to live in a spring upstream from their village. The Water Lord is honored with music and dancing in the hopes that it keep the village supplied with water. But after a fateful encounter with Ash, Brock's Lombre, and a Solrock, the villagers now venerate Solrock instead.

Red Gyarados Scares Locals!

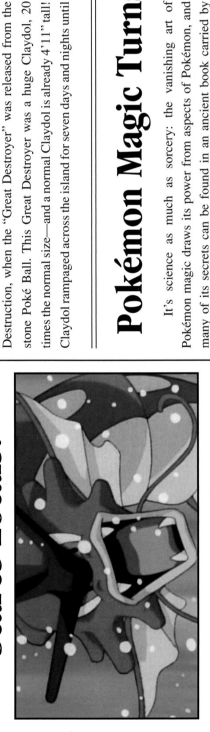

Especially viscious, the Red Gyarados is rumored to be much more aggressive and territorial than the average Gyarados. Often found in secluded underwater caves or in hidden underground lakes, the Red Gyarados is slightly larger but otherwise identical.

Although clearly believed to be a myth by many, Team Rocket has seen, and been blasted off by a Red Gyarados.

Togepi From Another World!

Hoenn residents aren't likely to find the Mirage Kingdom listed in any guidebook. To reach it, visitors must use an airship to cross a desert and the ring of rocky peaks that hides the Kingdom from outside eyes.

That alone is remarkable, but what makes the Mirage Kingdom truly unusual is a centuries-old connection with Togepi, its guardian of peace and freedom.

The palace and nearby temple both incorporate design elements reminiscent of Togepi, as do the fashions of the royal family.

Because Togepi are sensitive to the goodness—or lack thereof—that dwells in human hearts, conditions in the Togepi Paradise are closely linked to conditions in the Mirage Kingdom. That's why Princess Sarah, who (after a little help from Misty and her friends) now rules the Mirage Kingdom, has sworn to protect the Togepi Paradise. Misty's Togepi, now evolved into Togetic, is a stalwart guardian of the Paradise as well.

Pokémon Magic Turns a Boy Into a Pikachu!

It's science as much as sorcery: the vanishing art of Pokémon magic draws its power from aspects of Pokémon, and many of its secrets can be found in an ancient book carried by Lily the Pokémon Magician. Passed down across generations of her family, the book is written in an obscure script and describes how to work Pokémon magic—but bear in mind that this "magic" doesn't always work the way one would expect. A spell to make a girl's skin smooth and soft might involve summoning Spinarak to show up and cocoon the spell's target in silk. And a spell that lets a person read the thoughts of Pokémon—well, the full text of the spell is smudged, so it temporarily turns Ash into a talking Pikachu. Caster beware!

The pages of Lily's book describe the components for the Pokémon communication spell: Shuckle's secret cure, powdered Stantler horns, yogurt made from Miltank milk, a flower petal marked with a Jynx's kiss. That's not all—it calls for Aipom's tears and Parasect's Stun Spore, too.

There's one more ingredient to go before it's time to use Pikachu's Thunderbolt to activate the spell. Dirt from a Meowth's claw is another ingredient, and Lily the Pokémon Magician isn't shy about marching right up to Team Rocket to get it.

(Claydol)

On Hoenn's Izabe Island lies the Valley of Destruction, where a giant stone Poké Ball was once perched high on a cliff. The valley acquired its ominous name in the Time of the Destruction, when the "Great Destroyer" was released from the stone Poké Ball. This Great Destroyer was a huge Claydol, 20 times the normal size—and a normal Claydol is already 4'11" tall! Claydol rampaged across the island for seven days and nights until a White Sage conjured up a giant Poké Ball and used it to seal Claydol in Lake Izabe.

The Claydol remained in the lake for a thousand years until Team Rocket let it out, and the stone Poké Ball in the lake was lost in the process.

Fortunately, Claydol's original Poké Ball was still perched on the valley cliff. After Claydol was sealed in the Poké Ball, the Poké Ball rolled into the lake, restoring the balance.

Downtown Rocked by a Battle of Giant Pokémon!

Professor Jacuzzi is a Gulpin expert who has a plan to save a town from its annual Gulpin infestation. One of his inventions is the Mach 3 Particle Cannon, which absorbs Gulpin using a subatomic particle beam and then uses power from the Gulpin's own attacks to launch them out of the city at Mach 3. But when the Particle Cannon is damaged, it causes a Gulpin and Ash's Treecko to grow to humongous size!

As the two battle in the middle the town, the exertion causes Treecko to return to normal size—but Gulpin remains a giant. Professor Jacuzzi captures Gulpin with a Heavy Ball and he's determined to return it to normal size, sooner or later…

Giant Flying Pokémon!

Could a little candy make a Pokémon huge? Dr. Gordon's Mystery Candy Complete was invented by accident, but it's no dud. Just one of these blue candies makes Caterpie grow to the height of a ceiling and then beyond. Soon it's big enough to knock over the top of a metal tower, and when it evolves into Metapod and then Butterfree, it can easily carry people on its back.

Team Rocket uses some stolen candy to make their own giant Pokémon out of Cacnea and Dustox, setting up a giant aerial clash with Butterfree. Fortunately, the effects of the Candy are only temporary.

ARTICUNO • (ART-tick-COO-no)

Height: 5'07" (1.7 m)   **Weight: 122.1 lbs (55.4 kg)**

A brilliant blue and white Pokémon, the beat of Articuno's wings chill the air, causing snow to fall wherever it flies. One of the Titan Trio, Articuno represents the element of ice.

Extremely agile, Articuno's most unique feature is its long flowing tail. Like a dancer's ribbon, the tail rolls and whips behind Articuno as it flies, accentuating the majestic birds path through the air.

ZAPDOS • (ZAP-dos)

Height: 5'03" (1.6 m)   **Weight: 116.0 lbs (52.6 kg)**

The electric crash of yellow and black announces Zapdos like a bolt of Thunder across the sky. Zapdos is the second of the Titan Trio and represents the element of electricity.

Zapdos gains power when struck by lighting. Enormously strong, Zapdos is a formidable and intimidating opponent whose Electric-type attacks inspire and awe with their destructive power.

MOLTRES • (MOLE-trace

Height: 6'07" (2.0 m)   **Weight: 132.3 lbs (60.0 kg)**

Frightening and beautiful, Moltres' fiery wings send it effortlessly through the air rousing both fear and wonder. Moltres represents the last of the Titan Trio.

Completely at home in fire, if injured, Moltres dips its body in molten magma to burn and heal itself. The heat radiating off of Moltres' wings makes it difficult to see the great Pokémon if it is stationary.

MEW • (myu)

Height: 1'04" (0.4 m)   **Weight: 8.8 lbs (4.0 kg)**

Fun loving and innocent, Mew seems to inspire the best in people and Pokémon. Able to transform into any Pokémon at will, Mew is said to possess the genetic composition of all Pokémon.

Mew seems to be connected to the world of Pokémon unlike any other Pokémon. Severely affected when the environment is unbalanced, Mew's life has been in jeopardy on more than one occasion.

KANTO POKÉMON

This is the region that started it all—the home of Ash (Pallet Town), and the beginning of great adventures!
You'll meet all sorts of Pokémon in Kanto, including everyone's favorite, Pikachu! It's also the home of the
Titan Trio: Articuno, Zapdos, and Moltres!

ABRA

Height: 2'11" (0.9 m)
Weight: 43.0 lbs. (19.5 kg)

PSYCHIC

AERODACTYL

Height: 5'11" (1.8 m)
Weight: 130.1 lbs. (59.0 kg)

ROCK	FLYING

ALAKAZAM

Height: 4'11" (1.5 m)
Weight: 105.8 lbs. (48.0 kg)

PSYCHIC

ARBOK
Height: 11'06" (3.5 m)
Weight: 143.3 lbs. (65.0 kg)

POISON

ARCANINE

Height: 6'03" (1.9 m)
Weight: 341.7 lbs. (155.0 kg)

FIRE

ARTICUNO
Height: 5'07" (1.7 m)
Weight: 122.1 lbs. (55.4 kg)

ICE	FLYING

BEEDRILL

Height: 3'03" (1.0 m)
Weight: 65.0 lbs. (29.5 kg)

BUG	POISON

BELLSPROUT

Height: 2'04" (0.7 m)
Weight: 8.8 lbs. (4.0 kg)

GRASS	POISON

BLASTOISE

Height: 5'03" (1.6 m)
Weight: 188.5 lbs. (85.5 kg)

WATER

BULBASAUR

Height: 2'04" (0.7 m)
Weight: 15.2 lbs. (6.9 kg)

GRASS	POISON

BUTTERFREE

Height: 3'07" (1.1 m)
Weight: 70.5 lbs. (32.0 kg)

BUG	FLYING

CATERPIE

Height: 1'00" (0.3 m)
Weight: 6.4 lbs. (2.9 kg)

BUG

CHANSEY

Height: 3'07" (1.1 m)
Weight: 76.3 lbs. (34.6 kg)

NORMAL

CHARIZARD

Height: 5'07" (1.7 m)
Weight: 199.5 lbs. (90.5 kg)

FIRE	FLYING

CHARMANDER

Height: 2'00" (0.6 m)
Weight: 18.7 lbs. (8.5 kg)

FIRE

CHARMELEON

Height: 3'07" (1.1 m)
Weight: 41.9 lbs. (19.0 kg)

FIRE

CLEFABLE

Height: 4'03" (1.3 m)
Weight: 88.2 lbs. (40.0 kg)

NORMAL

CLEFAIRY

Height: 2'00" (0.6 m)
Weight: 16.5 lbs. (7.5 kg)

NORMAL

CLOYSTER

Height: 4'11" (1.5 m)
Weight: 292.1 lbs. (132.5 kg)

WATER	ICE

CUBONE

Height: 1'04" (0.4 m)
Weight: 14.3 lbs. (6.5 kg)

GROUND

DEWGONG

Height: 5'07" (1.7 m)
Weight: 264.6 lbs. (120.0 kg)

WATER	ICE

DIGLETT

Height: 0'08" (0.2 m)
Weight: 1.8 lbs. (0.8 kg)

GROUND

DITTO

Height: 1'00" (0.3 m)
Weight: 8.8 lbs. (4.0 kg)

NORMAL

DODRIO

Height: 5'11" (1.8 m)
Weight: 187.8 lbs. (85.2 kg)

NORMAL	FLYING

DODUO

Height: 4'07" (1.4 m)
Weight: 86.4 lbs. (39.2 kg)

NORMAL	FLYING

DRAGONAIR

Height: 13'01" (4.0 m)
Weight: 36.4 lbs. (16.5 kg)

DRAGON

DRAGONITE

Height: 7'03" (2.2 m)
Weight: 463.0 lbs. (210.0 kg)

DRAGON	FLYING

DRATINI

Height: 5'11" (1.8 m)
Weight: 7.3 lbs. (3.3 kg)

DRAGON

DROWZEE

Height: 3'03" (1.0 m)
Weight: 71.4 lbs. (32.4 kg)

PSYCHIC

DUGTRIO

Height: 2'04" (0.7 m)
Weight: 73.4 lbs. (33.3 kg)

GROUND

EEVEE

Height: 1'00" (0.3 m)
Weight: 14.3 lbs. (6.5 kg)

NORMAL

EKANS

Height: 6'07" (2.0 m)
Weight: 15.2 lbs. (6.9 kg)

POISON

ELECTABUZZ

Height: 3'07" (1.1 m)
Weight: 66.1 lbs. (30.0 kg)

ELECTRIC

ELECTRODE
Height: 3'11" (1.2 m)
Weight: 146.8 lbs. (66.6 kg)

ELECTRIC

EXEGGCUTE

Height: 1'04" (0.4 m)
Weight: 5.5 lbs. (2.5 kg)

GRASS | PSYCHIC

EXEGGUTOR

Height: 6'07" (2.0 m)
Weight: 264.6 lbs. (120.0 kg)

GRASS | PSYCHIC

FARFETCH'D

Height: 2'07" (0.8 m)
Weight: 33.1 lbs. (15.0 kg)

NORMAL | FLYING

FEAROW

Height: 3'11" (1.2 m)
Weight: 83.8 lbs. (38.0 kg)

NORMAL | FLYING

FLAREON

Height: 2'11" (0.9 m)
Weight: 55.1 lbs. (25.0 kg)

FIRE

GASTLY

Height: 4'03" (1.3 m)
Weight: 0.2 lbs. (0.1 kg)

GHOST | POISON

GENGAR
Height: 4'11" (1.5 m)
Weight: 89.3 lbs. (40.5 kg)

GHOST | POISON

GEODUDE

Height: 1'04" (0.4 m)
Weight: 44.1 lbs. (20.0 kg)

ROCK | GROUND

GLOOM

Height: 2'07" (0.8 m)
Weight: 19.0 lbs. (8.6 kg)

GRASS | POISON

GOLBAT

Height: 5'03" (1.6 m)
Weight: 121.3 lbs. (55.0 kg)

POISON | FLYING

GOLDEEN

Height: 2'00" (0.6 m)
Weight: 33.1 lbs. (15.0 kg)

WATER

GOLDUCK

Height: 5'07" (1.7 m)
Weight: 168.9 lbs. (76.6 kg)

WATER

GOLEM

Height: 4'07" (1.4 m)
Weight: 661.4 lbs. (300.0 kg)

ROCK | GROUND

GRAVELER

Height: 3'03" (1.0 m)
Weight: 231.5 lbs. (105.0 kg)

ROCK | GROUND

GRIMER

Height: 2'11" (0.9 m)
Weight: 66.1 lbs. (30.0 kg)

POISON

GROWLITHE

Height: 2'04" (0.7 m)
Weight: 41.9 lbs. (19.0 kg)

FIRE

GYARADOS

Height: 21'04" (6.5 m)
Weight: 518.1 lbs. (235.0 kg)

WATER | FLYING

HAUNTER

Height: 5'03" (1.6 m)
Weight: 0.2 lbs. (0.1 kg)

GHOST | POISON

HITMONCHAN

Height: 4'07" (1.4 m)
Weight: 110.7 lbs. (50.2 kg)

FIGHTING

HITMONLEE

Height: 4'11" (1.5 m)
Weight: 109.8 lbs. (49.8 kg)

FIGHTING

HORSEA

Height: 1'04" (0.4 m)
Weight: 17.6 lbs. (8.0 kg)

WATER

HYPNO

Height: 5'03" (1.6 m)
Weight: 166.7 lbs. (75.6 kg)

PSYCHIC

IVYSAUR

Height: 3'03" (1.0 m)
Weight: 28.7 lbs. (13.0 kg)

GRASS | POISON

JIGGLYPUFF

Height: 1'08" (0.5 m)
Weight: 12.1 lbs. (5.5 kg)

NORMAL

JOLTEON

Height: 2'07" (0.8 m)
Weight: 54.0 lbs. (24.5 kg)

ELECTRIC

JYNX

Height: 4'07" (1.4 m)
Weight: 89.5 lbs. (40.6 kg)

ICE | PSYCHIC

KABUTO

Height: 1'08" (0.5 m)
Weight: 25.4 lbs. (11.5 kg)

ROCK | WATER

KABUTOPS

Height: 4'03" (1.3 m)
Weight: 89.3 lbs. (40.5 kg)

ROCK | WATER

KADABRA

Height: 4'03" (1.3 m)
Weight: 124.6 lbs. (56.5 kg)

PSYCHIC

KAKUNA

Height: 2'00" (0.6 m)
Weight: 22.0 lbs. (10.0 kg)

BUG | POISON

KANGASKHAN

Height: 7'03" (2.2 m)
Weight: 176.4 lbs. (80.0 kg)

NORMAL

KINGLER

Height: 4'03" (1.3 m)
Weight: 132.3 lbs. (60.0 kg)

WATER

KOFFING

Height: 2'00" (0.6 m)
Weight: 2.2 lbs. (1.0 kg)

POISON

KRABBY

Height: 1'04" (0.4 m)
Weight: 14.3 lbs. (6.5 kg)

WATER

LAPRAS

Height: 8'02" (2.5 m)
Weight: 485.0 lbs. (220.0 kg)

WATER | ICE

LICKITUNG

Height: 3'11" (1.2 m)
Weight: 144.4 lbs. (65.5 kg)

NORMAL

MACHAMP

Height: 5'03" (1.6 m)
Weight: 286.6 lbs. (130.0 kg)

FIGHTING

MACHOKE

Height: 4'11" (1.5 m)
Weight: 155.4 lbs. (70.5 kg)

FIGHTING

MACHOP

Height: 2'07" (0.8 m)
Weight: 43.0 lbs. (19.5 kg)

FIGHTING

MAGIKARP

Height: 2'11" (0.9 m)
Weight: 22.0 lbs. (10.0 kg)

WATER

MAGMAR

Height: 4'03" (1.3 m)
Weight: 98.1 lbs. (44.5 kg)

FIRE

MAGNEMITE

Height: 1'00" (0.3 m)
Weight: 13.2 lbs. (6.0 kg)

ELECTRIC | STEEL

MAGNETON

Height: 3'03" (1.0 m)
Weight: 132.3 lbs. (60.0 kg)

ELECTRIC | STEEL

MANKEY

Height: 1'08" (0.5 m)
Weight: 61.7 lbs. (28.0 kg)

FIGHTING

MAROWAK

Height: 3'03" (1.0 m)
Weight: 99.2 lbs. (45.0 kg)

GROUND

MEOWTH

Height: 1'04" (0.4 m)
Weight: 9.3 lbs. (4.2 kg)

NORMAL

METAPOD

Height: 2'04" (0.7 m)
Weight: 21.8 lbs. (9.9 kg)

BUG

MEW

Height: 1'04" (0.4 m)
Weight: 8.8 lbs. (4.0 kg)

PSYCHIC

MEWTWO

Height: 6'07" (2.0 m)
Weight: 269.0 lbs. (122.0 kg)

PSYCHIC

MOLTRES

Height: 6'07" (2.0 m)
Weight: 132.3 lbs. (60.0 kg)

FIRE | FLYING

MR. MIME

Height: 4'03" (1.3 m)
Weight: 120.1 lbs. (54.5 kg)

PSYCHIC

MUK

Height: 3'11" (1.2 m)
Weight: 66.1 lbs. (30.0 kg)

POISON

NIDOKING

Height: 4'07" (1.4 m)
Weight: 136.7 lbs. (62.0 kg)

POISON | GROUND

NIDOQUEEN

Height: 4'03" (1.3 m)
Weight: 132.3 lbs. (60.0 kg)

POISON | GROUND

NIDORAN ♀

Height: 1'04" (0.4 m)
Weight: 15.4 lbs. (7.0 kg)

POISON

NIDORAN ♂
Height: 1'08" (0.5 m)
Weight: 19.8 lbs. (9.0 kg)

POISON

NIDORINA

Height: 2'07" (0.8 m)
Weight: 44.1 lbs. (20.0 kg)

POISON

NIDORINO

Height: 2'11" (0.9 m)
Weight: 43.0 lbs. (19.5 kg)

POISON

NINETALES

Height: 3'07" (1.1 m)
Weight: 43.9 lbs. (19.9 kg)

FIRE

ODDISH

Height: 1'08" (0.5 m)
Weight: 11.9 lbs. (5.4 kg)

GRASS | POISON

OMANYTE

Height: 1'04" (0.4 m)
Weight: 16.5 lbs. (7.5 kg)

ROCK | WATER

OMASTAR

Height: 3'03" (1.0 m)
Weight: 77.2 lbs. (35.0 kg)

ROCK | WATER

ONIX

Height: 28'10" (8.8 m)
Weight: 463.0 lbs. (210.0 kg)

ROCK | GROUND

PARAS

Height: 1'00" (0.3 m)
Weight: 11.9 lbs. (5.4 kg)

BUG | GRASS

PARASECT

Height: 3'03" (1.0 m)
Weight: 65.0 lbs. (29.5 kg)

BUG | GRASS

PERSIAN

Height: 3'03" (1.0 m)
Weight: 70.5 lbs. (32.0 kg)

NORMAL

PIDGEOT

Height: 4'11" (1.5 m)
Weight: 87.1 lbs. (39.5 kg)

NORMAL | FLYING

PIDGEOTTO

Height: 3'07" (1.1 m)
Weight: 66.1 lbs. (30.0 kg)

NORMAL | FLYING

PIDGEY

Height: 1'00" (0.3 m)
Weight: 4.0 lbs. (1.8 kg)

NORMAL | FLYING

PIKACHU

Height: 1'04" (0.4 m)
Weight: 13.2 lbs. (6.0 kg)

ELECTRIC

PINSIR

Height: 4'11" (1.5 m)
Weight: 121.3 lbs. (55.0 kg)

BUG

POLIWAG

Height: 2'00" (0.6 m)
Weight: 27.3 lbs. (12.4 kg)

WATER

POLIWHIRL

Height: 3'03" (1.0 m)
Weight: 44.1 lbs. (20.0 kg)

WATER

POLIWRATH

Height: 4'03" (1.3 m)
Weight: 119.0 lbs. (54.0 kg)

WATER | FIGHTING

PONYTA

Height: 3'03" (1.0 m)
Weight: 66.1 lbs. (30.0 kg)

FIRE

PORYGON
Height: 2'07" (0.8 m)
Weight: 80.5 lbs. (36.5 kg)

NORMAL

PRIMEAPE

Height: 3'03" (1.0 m)
Weight: 70.5 lbs. (32.0 kg)

FIGHTING

PSYDUCK

Height: 2'07" (0.8 m)
Weight: 43.2 lbs. (19.6 kg)

WATER

RAICHU

Height: 2'07" (0.8 m)
Weight: 66.1 lbs. (30.0 kg)

ELECTRIC

RAPIDASH

Height: 5'07" (1.7 m)
Weight: 209.4 lbs. (95.0 kg)

FIRE

RATICATE

Height: 2'04" (0.7 m)
Weight: 40.8 lbs. (18.5 kg)

NORMAL

RATTATA

Height: 1'00" (0.3 m)
Weight: 7.7 lbs. (3.5 kg)

NORMAL

RHYDON

Height: 6'03" (1.9 m)
Weight: 264.6 lbs. (120.0 kg)

GROUND | ROCK

RHYHORN

Height: 3'03" (1.0 m)
Weight: 253.5 lbs. (115.0 kg)

GROUND | ROCK

SANDSHREW

Height: 2'00" (0.6 m)
Weight: 26.5 lbs. (12.0 kg)

GROUND

SANDSLASH

Height: 3'03" (1.0 m)
Weight: 65.0 lbs. (29.5 kg)

GROUND

SCYTHER

Height: 4'11" (1.5 m)
Weight: 123.5 lbs. (56.0 kg)

BUG | FLYING

SEADRA

Height: 3'11" (1.2 m)
Weight: 55.1 lbs. (25.0 kg)

WATER

SEAKING

Height: 4'03" (1.3 m)
Weight: 86.0 lbs. (39.0 kg)

WATER

SEEL

Height: 3'07" (1.1 m)
Weight: 198.4 lbs. (90.0 kg)

WATER

SHELLDER

Height: 1'00" (0.3 m)
Weight: 8.8 lbs. (4.0 kg)

WATER

SLOWBRO

Height: 5'03" (1.6 m)
Weight: 173.1 lbs. (78.5 kg)

WATER | PSYCHIC

SLOWPOKE

Height: 3'11" (1.2 m)
Weight: 79.4 lbs. (36.0 kg)

WATER | PSYCHIC

SNORLAX

Height: 6'11" (2.1 m)
Weight: 1014.1 lbs. (460.0 kg)

NORMAL

SPEAROW

Height: 1'00" (0.3 m)
Weight: 4.4 lbs. (2.0 kg)

NORMAL | FLYING

SQUIRTLE

Height: 1'08" (0.5 m)
Weight: 19.8 lbs. (9.0 kg)

WATER

STARMIE

Height: 3'07" (1.1 m)
Weight: 176.4 lbs. (80.0 kg)

WATER | PSYCHIC

STARYU

Height: 2'07" (0.8 m)
Weight: 76.1 lbs. (34.5 kg)

WATER

TANGELA

Height: 3'03" (1.0 m)
Weight: 77.2 lbs. (35.0 kg)

GRASS

TAUROS

Height: 4'07" (1.4 m)
Weight: 194.9 lbs. (88.4 kg)

NORMAL

TENTACOOL

Height: 2'11" (0.9 m)
Weight: 100.3 lbs. (45.5 kg)

WATER | POISON

TENTACRUEL

Height: 5'03" (1.6 m)
Weight: 121.3 lbs. (55.0 kg)

WATER | POISON

VAPOREON

Height: 3'03" (1.0 m)
Weight: 63.9 lbs. (29.0 kg)

WATER

VENOMOTH

Height: 4'11" (1.5 m)
Weight: 27.6 lbs. (12.5 kg)

BUG | POISON

VENONAT

Height: 3'03" (1.0 m)
Weight: 66.1 lbs. (30.0 kg)

BUG | POISON

VENUSAUR

Height: 6'07" (2.0 m)
Weight: 220.5 lbs. (100.0 kg)

GRASS | POISON

VICTREEBEL

Height: 5'07" (1.7 m)
Weight: 34.2 lbs. (15.5 kg)

GRASS | POISON

VILEPLUME

Height: 3'11" (1.2 m)
Weight: 41.0 lbs. (18.6 kg)

GRASS | POISON

VOLTORB

Height: 1'08" (0.5 m)
Weight: 22.9 lbs. (10.4 kg)

ELECTRIC

VULPIX

Height: 2'00" (0.6 m)
Weight: 21.8 lbs. (9.9 kg)

FIRE

WARTORTLE

Height: 3'03" (1.0 m)
Weight: 49.6 lbs. (22.5 kg)

WATER

WEEDLE

Height: 1'00" (0.3 m)
Weight: 7.1 lbs. (3.2 kg)

BUG | POISON

WEEPINBELL

Height: 3'03" (1.0 m)
Weight: 14.1 lbs. (6.4 kg)

GRASS | POISON

WEEZING

Height: 3'11" (1.2 m)
Weight: 20.9 lbs. (9.5 kg)

POISON

WIGGLYTUFF

Height: 3'03" (1.0 m)
Weight: 26.5 lbs. (12.0 kg)

NORMAL

ZAPDOS

Height: 5'03" (1.6 m)
Weight: 116.0 lbs. (52.6 kg)

ELECTRIC | FLYING

ZUBAT

Height: 2'07" (0.8 m)
Weight: 16.5 lbs. (7.5 kg)

POISON | FLYING

ORANGE ISLANDS

Everything is slightly different in the Orange Islands. From the Gym battles to the civil servants, Nurse Joy and Officer Jenny, the Orange Islands are a world away from the normalcy of the mainland. They are a large group of tropical islands (about 24 islands). Professor Ivy works in and around the Orange Islands.

There are many islands of interest. Kumquat Island is perhaps the most luxurious resort of the islands. Fantastic hotels, natural hot springs, and the pristine beaches make this island the top destination for anyone wanting rest and relaxation. The seven small islands in the Grapefruit Archipelago supply nearly all the grapefruit for the world regions. Sunburst Island is world famous for its glassblown works of art. The strange Meowth of Bounty worshippers of Golden Island mistake Team Rocket's Meowth for the one in prophecy. The largest island is Mandarin Island South; its largest principality is Trovitopolis—a large port on the western end of the island.

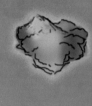

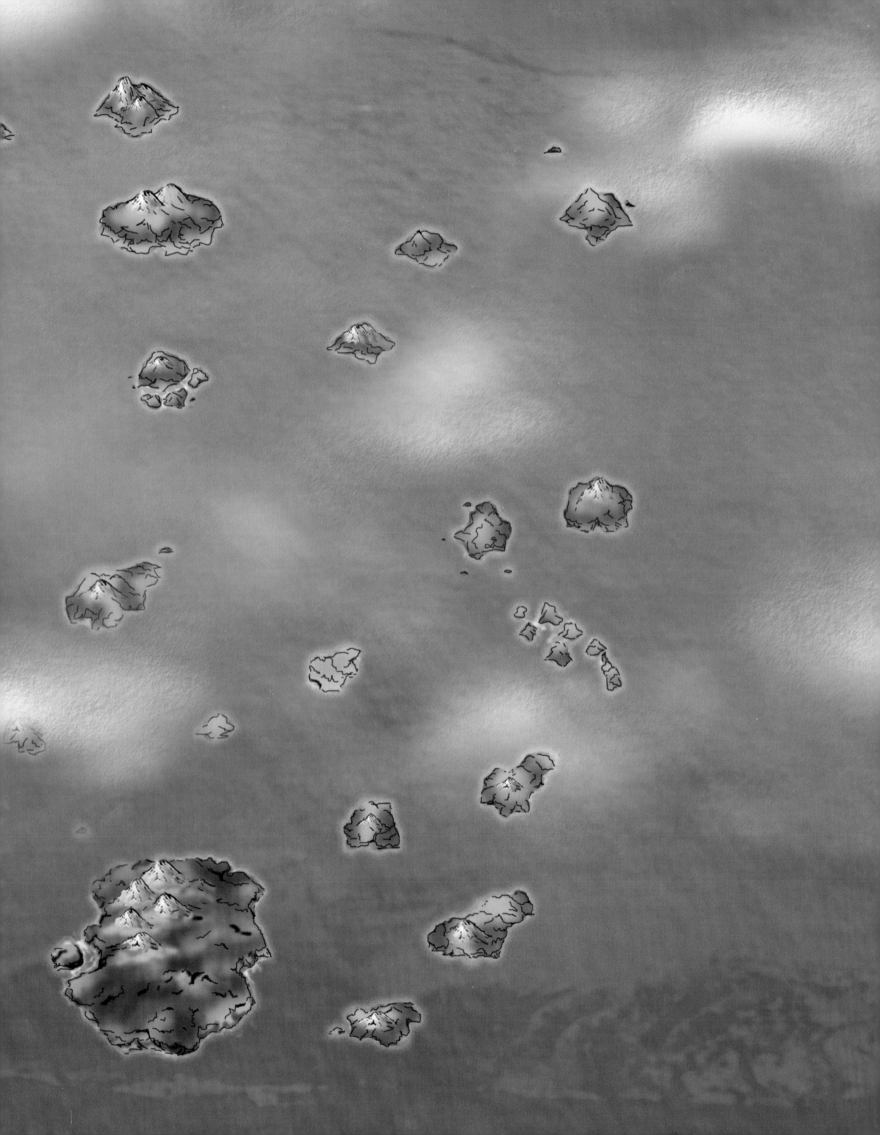

TRACEY SKETCHIT

Tracey is fascinated by Pokémon but, unlike many Trainers, his goal isn't to win battles or catch lots of Pokémon. In contrast, he's a Pokémon watcher, one dedicated to the study and observation of Pokémon, plus he's a talented sketch artist to boot!

After Ash and Misty left Brock behind on Valencia Island with Professor Ivy, they ended up finding a new friend in Tracey Sketchit. Like Brock, Tracey plays the role of Pokémon expert and middle man during Ash and Misty's squabbles, but Tracey is notable for being easygoing—almost to a fault. His single-minded interest in Pokémon often renders him oblivious to everything else around him. Tracey walked straight into a battle between Ash and several nasty Trainers, unaware of the danger, in order to study and sketch their Pokémon.

Tracey is a typical Pokémon watcher, one of many people with a special interest in the study and observation of Pokémon. Because they spend so much time observing, good Pokémon watchers can judge a Pokémon's health and strength with just a visual inspection.

Tracey's no Brock, but he does take an interest in girls. He's just more likely to sketch an attractive girl like Cissy, the Mikan Island Gym Leader, than he is to actually approach one.

Tracey's Pokémon

VENONAT

Tracey's Venonat is more useful to him as a tracker than as a battler—he often uses its Radar Eye to locate things.

MARILL

Together with Venonat, Marill is great at helping Tracey track down whatever he's searching for. Its supersensitive hearing can track Pokémon and other targets.

SCYTHER

Scyther was the head of its swarm until it was deposed in a battle for leadership. Tracey found the old Scyther injured and alone, but Scyther didn't appreciate Tracey catching it so he could get it to a Pokémon Center. Now it gets along very well with Tracey, but Scyther is still touchy about its pride.

PROFESSOR OAK'S ASSISTANT

Tracey outright idolizes Professor Oak; as soon as he learned that Ash knew Professor Oak, he cheerfully declared himself to be Ash and Misty's new traveling companion.

After meeting the Professor in person, Tracey was nervous about the Professor's opinion of his work and too petrified to admit he wanted to be Professor Oak's assistant. Eventually, inspired by Ash's own determination, Tracey worked up enough courage to request a position as the Professor's assistant.

Now Tracey is anything but shy around Professor Oak. Not only does Tracey assist with research and care for the Pokémon on Professor Oak's ranch, he also keeps an eye on the Professor, prodding him to follow his own advice and eat regular meals.

PROFESSOR IVY

Professor Ivy certainly doesn't resemble the other Pokémon Professors. She's young and very stylish. She also makes the briefest appearance of the other Professors. So what's Ivy's deal?

IVY LEAGUE

Professor Felina Ivy is the resident Professor of the Orange Islands. Since the island chain is so scattered, her research takes her by helicopter to many of the distant land masses. She specializes in the physiological differences between Pokémon in the various regions. For example, she tries to determine why a Vileplume may look different on one island as opposed to another island.

Professor Ivy's swimsuit-clad figure and introduction to Ash and friends is certainly unique and most unProfessorlike. But like other Professors, she is very smart and an accomplished author: "Pokémon Adaptive Variations as a Function of Regional Distribution"

BROCK'S MATCH

Brock decides that he wants to stay with Professor Ivy during the Orange Island journeys, but he appears back in Pallet Town during the reunion celebration. So what happened to his internship with Ivy? No one knows, but Brock responds with quaking, shaking fear every time her name is mentioned. "Don't mention that name!" is his only response.

Professor Ivy's Researched Pokémon

GYARADOS

Ivy rides to shore on a Gyarados, which she seems to be very close to.

RATICATE

Ivy tries to save a Raticate that gets caught in Vileplume's spore-spreading defensive maneuvers. Unfortunately, Ivy pays the price and is hospitalized but they both recover.

POLIWRATH

When Professor Ivy is first introduced, Poliwrath is in the lagoon.

MAGIKARP

What exactly is Ivy doing with the Magikarp in her lab? The hapless Magikarp has wires attached to it in several places.

VILEPLUME

The Vileplume on Valencia Island are somewhat different than the Vileplume in Ash's Pokédex. This is Ivy's field of study; the physical differences in Pokémon from different regions.

BUTTERFREE

Butterfree is not eating well, which worries Professor Ivy. This is Brock's chance to shine, as he concocts a berry-enhanced bowl of food for the Butterfree to impress Professor Ivy.

ORANGE ISLAND LEAGUE

The Orange Islands were not meant to be so involved. Professor Oak asked Ash and friends to find out about the mysterious GS Ball, but they found a tropical paradise complete with new Pokémon, new friends, and new battles!

The Orange Island Gyms are centered more around contests of skill, not battles. The philosophy of the Orange League is that Pokémon Trainers must know all aspects of their Pokémon, not just their prowess on the battlefield.

MIKAN ISLAND GYM
GYM LEADER: SISSY

Water Gun Challenge
Seadra uses Water Gun and knocks out the cans with ease, as does Ash's Squirtle. When they move on to moving targets, both Pokémon excel. The match ends in a draw.

Pokémon Wave Ride
With Sissy using Blastoise and Ash using Lapras, this relay turns into a hotly contested race for the finish line. Ash gets creative when he has Lapras use an Ice Beam and skids into first place.

NAVEL ISLAND GYM
GYM LEADER: DANNY

Geyser Freezing
Danny sends out Nidoqueen to compete against Ash's Lapras, but the Ice Beam attack Ash uses hits Nidoqueen.

Ice Sculpting
Ash calls out Pikachu, Bulbasaur, and Charizard to carve out an ice sculpture. Charizard starts to snooze again, but rouses itself and with Flamethrower, sculpts an awesome ice-luge, winning the round.

Race
Ash and Danny now have to race to the goal line from the icy mountaintop to the beach, with their Pokémon as passengers. It looks like Danny is about to win, when suddenly Ash and his team charge from the bushes and take the lead.

TROVITA ISLAND GYM
GYM LEADER: RUDY

  VS.

The two Electric-types go at it, but Electabuzz handily defeats Pikachu's electric attacks, absorbing their power. Electabuzz uses Quick Attack and ThunderPunch with devastating results.

VS.

The battle of the Grass-types starts with Bulbasaur using Razor Leaf, but the dancing, prancing Exeggutor deftly avoids it. When Exeggutor uses Egg Bomb, Bulbasaur counters with Sleep Powder and the match goes to Ash.

 VS.

Starmie has an Electric-type attack up its sleeve, but luckily, Squirtle learns Hydro Pump and takes Starmie out. Ash wins.

KUMQUAT ISLAND GYM
GYM LEADER: LUANA

   VS.

You know things don't look good when the two teammates start frying and electrocuting each other before the battle starts. At the beginning, Pikachu refuses to help its teammate out. However, Pikachu comes around and saves Charizard from utter defeat. Marowak tries to deliver a Body Slam to Pikachu, but Charizard catches it, saving Pikachu. Suddenly working like a well-oiled machine, Pikachu and Charizard combine Thunderbolt and Flamethrower to defeat Luana's team.

ORANGE LEAGUE FINALS
GYM LEADER: DRAKE

  VS.

Ditto is an interesting choice for Drake. It simply transforms its opponent's strengths into its own. In the end, Pikachu uses Quick Attack against Ditto, and when Ditto falls, Pikachu shocks it into submission.

  VS.

Rock-types are strong against electrical attacks, so Ash recalls Pikachu and sends out Squirtle. Drake is no slouch—when Squirtle uses Water Gun, Onix digs underground. Squirtle uses its newly learned Hydro Pump attack and knocks Onix out.

  VS.

When Gengar Confuses Tauros, Ash uses Lapras. Lapras avoids Gengar's Hypnosis, then uses its Water Gun attack. The match ends in a dramatic draw with both Pokémon knocked out.

 VS.

Ash sends out Tauros once again, and this time Drake sends out Venusaur. The field changes and the Trainers are now on sandy ground. Tauros' first attack, Fissure, misfires, and Venusaur counters with SolarBeam, but Tauros uses Take Down to knock Venusaur out.

A Thundershock does little, but Electabuzz follows it up with ThunderPunch and Bulbasaur goes flying. Electabuzz easily defeats Bulbasaur.

Electabuzz tries to devastate Charizard with ThunderPunch, followed by Thunder. Charizard uses Ember, and when Electabuzz tries to use Thunderbolt, Charizard takes it out with Seismic Toss.

  VS.

The mighty Dragonite seems like a formidable opponent, and when Charizard uses Flamethrower, Dragonite counters with Water Gun, which is super-effective. As both Pokémon fly, it is obvious Dragonite possesses superior aerial skills, and takes Charizard out.

THE FINAL BATTLE

Ash uses two of his last three Pokémon to tire Dragonite out. When Squirtle bravely tries and fails to take Dragonite out, Tauros comes in and weakens Dragonite further. When Tauros goes down, it's up to little Pikachu to finish Dragonite out, and it does, with a well-placed Thunderbolt to the head. Dragonite goes down. Ash is the new champion of the Orange League!

MEWTWO • (MYU-too)

Height: 6'07" (2.0 m)   **Weight: 269.0 lbs (122.0 kg)**

Mewtwo is unique in the entire world. Not a natural Pokémon, scientists created Mewtwo through genetic manipulation. They crafted it with breathtaking power, but failed to endow it with a compassionate heart.

Created for destruction, when Mewtwo became self-aware it swore to destroy those who made it. In a titanic struggle, Mewtwo gained respect for life through the collected efforts of Ash and Mew.

JOHTO

Johto is a very large area. Home of Professor Elm, Johto seems more eco-friendly than other regions; a region of wide forest dominates the landscape of Johto.

Johto is connected to Kanto in a couple ways: there is a ship that runs from Olivine City to Vermilion City, and a speed train runs from Saffron City to the mammoth Goldenrod City. Goldenrod City is a monstrous sprawling city: one of the largest cities in the world. Ash, Brock, and Misty get lost inside the urban sprawl; they find that even residents of Goldenrod City have trouble getting around, because many of the streets are dead ends.

Johto has other attractions: the Whirl Islands' Whirl Cup, Mahogany Town's ninja, and Ecruteak City's ancient history. In ancient times, Ho-Oh lived in a tower in Ecruteak City, but war came and the tower was burned down. During its destruction Entei, Raikou, and Suicune were created.

PROFESSOR ELM

Professor Elm is a nerdy, timid person who loves the sound of his own voice. He is still respected by others and his contributions to the Johto region are welcomed by all the Trainers.

He is also an author of the book *A Brilliant Analysis of the Hypersized Communicative Faculties of Pokémon.*

Professor Elm was at the top of his class and a favorite of Professor Oak's. He often argues with the Professor over research, but he still respects and admires Professor Oak greatly.

Professor Elm's lab is located in New Bark Town. The lab is spotless (unlike Professor Ivy's), but Elm spends so much time there you have to wonder what his living quarters look like. It's also one of the bigger labs used by the various Professors.

AS THE WHIRL TURNS

Professor Elm catches up with Ash and his friend and reveals some background information about the Whirl Islands. He also tells them about the Whirl Cup, a Water-type Pokémon competition, and provides a researcher's-eye view of Corsola.

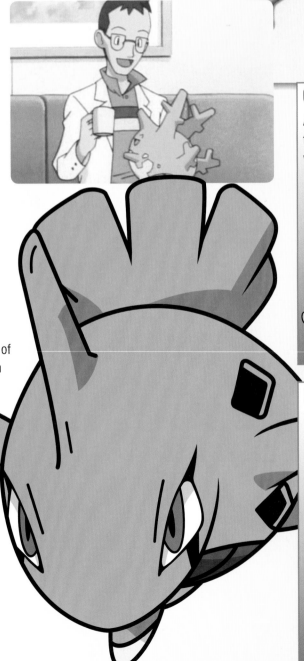

ELM'S EGG-SCITING HOBBIES

Professor Elm is the head of the Pokémon Preservation Council and, as one of his duties, he asks Ash and his friends to bring back an Egg from the Pokémon Marine Conservatory. This Egg eventually hatches into a Larvitar.

Professor Elm's Pokémon

CORSOLA

Although it only appears briefly in the Whirl Islands. Misty sees it and wants one, too!

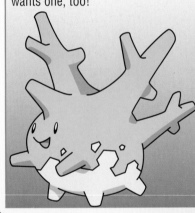

TOTODILE

Professor Elm hands out the first Pokémon in Johto. Plus, we learn that he gave a Totodile to Marina, a young Trainer.

CHIKORITA

Professor Elm bestows a Chikorita to Vincent, another young Trainer. This is also the first Pokémon he gives to Casey.

CYNDAQUIL

Cyndaquil is the Pokémon given to the young Trainer Jimmy.

CASEY SAKURA

CASEY

When Ash and Casey first met, Casey was a novice Trainer who challenged Ash to a battle after an argument over baseball. Ash smugly used Charizard to crush her, a defeat that brought her to tears—but the Electabuzz Baseball Team never gives up, and neither does their number one fan.

Casey is a Pokémon Trainer, but she thinks of herself first and foremost as a third-generation Electabuzz fan. She holds and throws a Poké Ball like a baseball, she swings a mean bat, and she talks in nonstop baseball references even when there's no one around to hear her or her enthusiastic rendition of the Electabuzz fight song.

She takes defeat hard but even when she's down, she's not out; her fighting Electabuzz spirit usually has her back up and swinging in no time. Casey's competitive streak can get the better of her, although she learned a valuable lesson when she pushed Chikorita too hard while trying to beat Ash in a Pokémon Bug Catching contest.

Her Dream Team is Beedrill, Elekid, Electabuzz, and Pikachu: four yellow Pokémon with stripes, an homage to the Electabuzz team colors.

Casey's Pokémon

BEEDRILL

MEGANIUM

PIDGEY

ELEKID

RATTATA

SAKURA

Sakura longed to go on a Pokémon journey, but her four older sisters were reluctant to grant permission.

When Ash and his friends met Sakura in Ecrutreak City, she was a sweet but meek young girl. That was hardly surprising, since she lived in the shadow of four older sisters—Satsuki, Sumomo, Tamao, and Koume, the Four Beautiful Tea Ceremony Sisters. They told Sakura she's not included in that count because she's not beautiful.

Sakura and Misty are particularly good friends; both know all too well how it feels to be invisible while their older sisters get all the attention.

Despite their teasing, Sakura's sisters love her and don't want her to leave home until she's ready. She almost decided to travel with Misty and the gang, but decided to stay home until she was strong enough to travel on her own. The second time Misty sees her in Ecruteak City, Sakura's Eevee is an Espeon and Sakura is tough enough to take on Team Rocket. It's clear to everyone how much Sakura has grown, and she finally gets to depart on her own solo journey.

Sakura's Pokémon

ESPEON

BEAUTIFLY

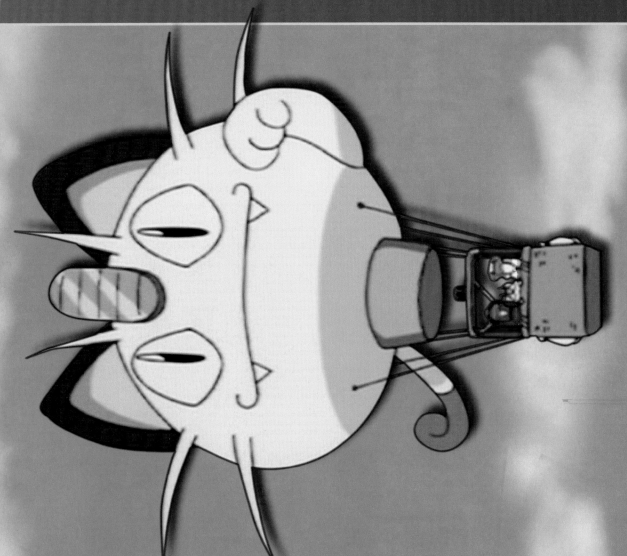

TEAM ROCKET'S MACHINES

Villains are lonely people; they always need a helping hand when pulling off their dastardly schemes. Unfortunately, Jessie and James are bumbling, ineffectual knuckleheads who couldn't pour water out of a shoe if the directions were on the heel. Somehow, though, they manage to create the most elaborate, nefarious contraptions in their spare time. These are just a few of their crazy inventions.

THE MEOWTH BALLOON

Incredibly unsafe, easily destroyed, this is Team Rocket's most identifiable mode of transportation. It often is modified with some sort of resistance, but never enough to keep them from blasting off. The balloon usually has the ability to capture Pikachu or other unsuspecting Pokemon through the use of an extendable clamping hand, or an electric-proof net. Never able to fully trick-out the Meowth balloon, it is a sturdy, eco-friendly reminder of just how persistent Jessie and James are.

ROBOT BUILDING

Upset from getting ripped off in another Team Rocket get-rich-quick scheme, a large mob surrounds the building in which they're located. With just a single button press, though, the building sprouts legs and arms and walks away. When they use the building in an attempt to capture Pokémon, however, some accurate attacks by Harrison and Ash destroy the building.

ARBO TANK

In their never-ending quest to show Giovanni how intelligent they are, Team Rocket has a bright idea: use a multi-ton tank as a getaway car! Still, not even Jessie and James could foresee Togepi and Sentret's takeover and subsequent joy ride inside their tank.

MAGIKARP SUBMARINE

This submarine is the primary mode of underwater transportation for Team Rocket. Pedal-powered, James and Meowth often pick up the slack for a plotting Jessie.

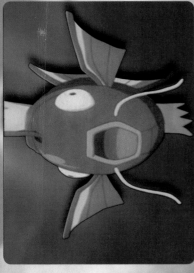

POKÉMON MECHAS

A number of mechas have been created and used by Team Rocket over the years. For example, as the crew discovers a wild Buneary, Team Rocket also finds it. They soon construct a wild and partially effective mech to battle our friends. The machine is resistant to electricity (sorry, Pikachu!) and has extendable claws that it uses to catch Pokémon, along with containers to store them. What it doesn't have is a warranty and, eventually, it needs one.

JOHTO GYM BATTLES!

The Johto region proved to be an extensive trek for Ash and his friends. Numerous side adventures didn't deter Ash from getting his required eight badges to compete in the Johto League Championships. Fresh from his Orange Islands triumph, Ash proves once again that he is on the road to becoming a Pokémon Master.

VIOLET CITY GYM

GYM LEADER: FAULKNER

Chikorita is definitely at a disadvantage against the Flying-type, Hoothoot, but it holds its own fairly well. In the end Hoothoot goes into a top-speed Tackle attack combo, and its game over for Chikorita.

The battle against Hoothoot is short and sweet, ending after one Thunderbolt. Hoothoot never even had a chance.

Faulkner calls out Dodrio. Dodrio's Drill Peck followed by its Tri-Attack almost does Pikachu in, but Pikachu's Thunder attack ends the round with a win for Ash.

Faulkner takes out his last Pokémon, but Pikachu needs a break. It gamely tries to use Thunderbolt, but Pikachu is discharged and Pidgeot's Whirlwind attack takes it out.

The match begins with both Pokémon taking to the air. Charizard uses Flamethrower, but Pidgeot uses Whirlwind to send the flames back. Charizard is injured and the match looks over, but Charizard comes through in the end and defeats Pigeot.

GOLDENROD CITY GYM

REMATCH

GYM LEADER: WHITNEY

Cyndaquil uses Tackle, but gets smashed repeatedly. It looks like Ash is going for a repeat of his earlier loss to Whitney.

Totodile digs huge trenches in the ground using its Water Gun attack. Miltank is befuddled and just as Totodile is about to deliver the final blow, Ash recalls it.

Pikachu hides in the trenches created by Totodile, and when Miltank gets stuck Pikachu slams it into the air. A full power Thunderbolt knocks Miltank out.

AZALEA TOWN GYM

GYM LEADER: BUGSY

The Fire-type Cyndaquil should be a no-brainer, but Cyndaquil is cold and its fire fails to ignite. Ash is forced to reevaluate the fight, and he recalls it.

Chikorita then uses Sweet Smell in conjunction with Tackle and takes Spinarak down.

Pikachu comes out swinging; Metapod tries Tackle, but Pikachu's speed and agility are too much. A well-placed Thunderbolt wins the round for Ash.

Scyther is a formidable opponent. Pikachu's Agility is no match for Scyther's speed. Scyther's Fury Cutter does Pikachu in.

Cyndaquil is Ash's last hope. Scyther tries to end the match with Fury Cutter, but Cyndaquil dodges and its fire comes back. Scyther uses Swords Dance, but Ash is to able to get Cyndaquil above Scyther, blasting it through the open space above.

ECRUTEAK CITY GYM

GYM LEADER: MORTY

Noctowl uses its Foresight, and follows up with Tackle. Gastly hits Noctowl with Lick, but Ash recalls Noctowl now that Gastly has been revealed.

Using Quick Attack, Pikachu gains a slight advantage, but after Gastly dodges its Thunderbolt, it counters with Night Shade and knocks Pikachu out.

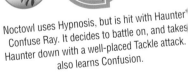

The weakened Gastly tries Night Shade again, but Cyndaquil dodges it, and uses Tackle to defeat it.

Haunter is faster than Gastly, and uses Mean Look, which forces Ash to stay with Cyndaquil until the end of the match. Cyndaquil uses Swift, then SmokeScreen to counter the Hypnosis but Hanuter grabs it out of the smoke and ends the round with Lick.

Noctowl uses Hypnosis, but is hit with Haunter' Confuse Ray. It decides to battle on, and takes Haunter down with a well-placed Tackle attack. also learns Confusion.

Gengar is twice as fast as Haunter. Noctowl its newly learned Confusion, while Gengar Night Shade. Ash has Noctowl use Confus through the whole Gym in order to pinpo Gengar, then uses Tackle to win the rour

CIANWOOD CITY GYM
GYM LEADER: CHUCK

Ash's assessment of the battle is partially right: Poliwrath is somewhat susceptible to Electric-type attacks. But the round goes sour when Poliwrath is relentless in its attacks.

Poliwrath uses Water Gun, which misses. Bayleef comes back with Razor Leaf, ending the round with a constricting Vine Whip and a Body Slam.

Machoke smacks Bayleef around, using Cross Chop against Bayleef's Vine Whip. During the tug-of-war with the Vine Whip, Ash decides to go toe-to-toe with Chuck's Pokémon, and Ash's confidence in Bayleef is inspiration. It stays focused and tosses Machoke, ending the match with a Body Slam and Razor Leaf attack.

MAHOGANY TOWN GYM
GYM LEADER: PRYCE

Dewgong tries to freeze Cyndaquil with an Ice Beam, but the flame on Cyndaquil's back melts the ice! Pryce sends Dewgong underwater. Cyndaquil follows with Swift, then Flamethrower, knocking Dewgong out.

Cyndaquil tries Flamethrower, but Piloswine uses Blizzard to freeze the pool of ice, and finishes Cyndaquil down with a Take Down.

Pikachu comes out next, but the slippery surface proves tough for Pikachu. Ash realizes that the ice is a problem, so he changes his strategy. Pikachu eventually slides under Piloswine and uses Thunder to weaken it. Pryce is afraid of hurting Piloswine, and throws in the towel, giving the Glacier Badge to Ash.

OLIVINE CITY GYM
GYM LEADER: JASMINE

Pikachu starts the party with Thunderbolt, which Magnemite easily avoids. Pikachu finally lets Magnemite hit it with Thunder Wave, and after absorbing the hit, uses Quick Attack to knock Magnemite out.

Pikachu is ineffective against Steelix. Pikachu's speed is a problem for Steelix, but after a short time a very tired Pikachu is knocked out with Iron Tail.

Cyndaquil uses Flamethrower right from the get-go, but Steelix uses Sandstorm and digs itself underground. After nearly getting knocked out, Cyndaquil superheats Steelix's Sandstorm and melts Steelix into a defeat.

BLACKTHORN CITY GYM
GYM LEADER: CLAIR

Snorlax starts with Hyper Beam, which Kingdra dodges. Snorlax wears Kingdra out, and ends the round with an Ice Punch.

Clair sends out Gyarados next, and the two exchange Hydro Pump and Hyper Beams. But Gyarados paralyzes Snorlax with its DragonBreath, and before Snorlax has a chance to snap out of it, Gyarados' Hyper Beam takes Snorlax out.

Gyarados leaves the water and attempts to use Bite on Pikachu, but Pikachu's Agility allows it to ride Gyardos' incoming Hydro Pump! The water intensifies Pikachu's Thunderbolt, leaving Gyarados unable to continue the battle.

Clair goes with Dragonair as her third and final Pokémon. All it takes is one Hyper Beam to knock Pikachu out.

Charizard is Ash's last hope. The playing field changes to an earth, wind, and fire environment. Charizard uses Flamethrower, while Dragonair ducks underwater and uses Hyper Beam. Fire Spin evaporates all the water in the arena, leaving the earth and sky as Dragonair's only refuge. Charizard uses a Seismic Toss/Fire Spin combo to knock out Dragonair, giving Ash the victory.

WHIRL CUP COMPETITION

There are other tournaments that specialize in a single type of Pokémon, but the Whirl Cup's history makes it something special. Held only once every three years, this Water-type Pokémon tournament is infused with the Whirl Islands' age-old traditions.

The Whirl Cup is six days of intense competition that will crown one Trainer as the Water Pokémon Alpha Omega, a title that legend says was once held by expert Water Pokémon Trainers who lived underwater. The winner also receives a Mystic Water Pendant, which can power up Water Pokémon attacks.

Water Pokémon have always been a vital part of life in the Whirl Islands. At the start of the Whirl Cup, Maya, the Sea Priestess who presides over the event, uses the Sea Spirit orb on the end of her staff to call forth the energy of all Water Pokémon. She also closes the Whirl Cup by using the Sea Spirit to invoke the harmony between people and Water Pokémon.

The coliseum for the finals is just up the coast from the Pokémon Center. Open to the sea on one side and adjacent to classical-looking ruins, it's a setting that captures the Whirl Islands' history and ties to the sea. The first round of the finals is all 1-on-1 battles, while later rounds are 2-on-2.

The Whirl Islands

The Whirl Islands are a chain of islands located in the sea between Johto's Cianwood City and Olivine City. From north to south, its four main islands are Silver Rock Isle, Red Rock Isle, Yellow Rock Isle, and the largest, Blue Point Isle.

Registration for the preliminaries takes place in Scarlet City's Pokémon Center, located on a cliff outside the city. Competitors can also bunk at the Pokémon Center during the competition.

Preliminary matches take place at different stadiums—although "stadiums" may be a grand word to describe these bare-bones match facilities.

WHIRL CUP RESULTS

FIRST ROUND (1-ON-1 BATTLES)

Ash and Totodile defeat Christopher and Kingdra.

Christopher

Christopher, a natural showman, likes to make an entrance by using a fishing rod to cast his Lure Ball into the water and release his Kingdra.

FIRST ROUND (1-ON-1 BATTLES)

Misty and Corsola defeat Harrison and Qwilfish.

Harrison

Harrison is a knowledgable Trainer, but he doesn't know what to do when his Qwilfish gets stuck in Corsola's horns during the match.

SECOND ROUND (2-ON-2 BATTLES)

Misty uses Poliwhirl and Psyduck to defeat Ash's Totodile and Kingler.

Misty plans to use Corsola as her second Pokémon, but Psyduck lets itself out instead. Things look grim until Kingler uses ViceGrip on Psyduck's head, which triggers Psyduck's Confusion attack.

THIRD ROUND (2-ON-2 BATTLES)

Trinity uses Gyarados and Chinchou to defeat Misty's Poliwhirl and Corsola.

Poliwhirl's quick defeat leaves Corsola with two opponents to battle. It beats Gyarados, but can't evade the attacks of Trinity's Chinchou.

Trinity

Elegantly composed and always sportsmanlike, Trinity's poise and experience wins Misty's admiration as well as their match.

FINALS

Semifinal Match: Trinity and Golduck defeat an unknown opponent.

Final Match: A male Trainer and his Feraligatr defeat Trinity's Golduck and wins the Whirl Cup.

THINK GREEN

A major Pokémon theme is the importance of nature and, just as importantly, balance. Preservation of the environment is portrayed as a good thing, but without condemnation of humanity, people can live in cities, manufacture goods, and mine coal as long as they're also considerate of the natural world around them. This underlying message is presented in several different ways, some explicit, some implicit.

NATURE WILL DEFEND ITS OWN

The Pokémon world has one major safeguard to fall back on: the Pokémon themselves. Some Pokémon can use their powers to protect or repair the environment; Celebi can use vines to quench a forest fire, while Suicune can purify water. There are also times, however, when Pokémon take matters directly into their own appendages and strike at threats to their natural habitat.

GETTING EVERYONE TO PITCH IN

No matter how bad things get, Pokémon has a message of hope: through hard work and dedication to the environment, things can be turned around. This message conveys an emphasis on direct personal action, because in the Pokémon world environmental protection is a task that often falls upon the individual, rather than the largely unseen government or any expectation that future technology will fix humanity's errors.

PORTRAYING THE WONDER OF NATURE

An ecological message can be more than just a reminder to preserve the environment—it's also important for people to understand why nature should be preserved. It should come as no surprise, then, that Pokémon depicts the nature world and its marvels as worthy of sincere appreciation.

When Ash first met his Treecko, it was struggling to save the tree where it lived. Ash and Pikachu immediately chipped in to help, but the tree was beyond saving. Although the tree died, it left behind a seed for the future and a vision for Ash and Treecko, an eloquent sequence that shows the cycles of nature and reminds the viewer that even a tree's life has importance.

CASE STUDY: LAKE LUCID

These days, Johto's Lake Lucid, a body of crystal-clear water surrounded by trees, is a haven for Water Pokémon. Lake Lucid wasn't always this way; pollution devastated the lake and it took decades of dedicated effort to restore the environment to good health.

Lake Lucid then: About 50 years ago, the lake was a toxic wonderland filled with pollution from factories and nearby towns. When Nurse Joy studied the lake, she didn't wear a gas mask and overalls just for looks—it was so dirty that even Muk wouldn't live there!

Lake Lucid now: With water so clean and clear that it's a haven for recuperating Water Pokémon, Lake Lucid is unrecognizable as the wasteland it was some 50 years ago. Even now, the lake is still protected by a watchful Nurse Joy—the granddaughter of the first Nurse Joy who worked to save the lake.

JOHTO SILVER CONFERENCE

This is what every Trainer in Johto dreams of: the Johto Silver Conference in Silver Town. To get here, a Trainer must earn eight Johto Gym Badges, but even that doesn't guarantee a spot in the Silver Conference tournament.

Silver Stadium lies at the heart of Silver Town, which is— unsurprisingly—not far from Mt. Silver.

Competitors stay in the well-appointed Athlete's Village, where rooms feature lake views and computer terminals with information on all the participating Trainers.

JOHTO SILVER CONFERENCE RULES

- FOR EVERY BATTLE, A COMPUTER RANDOMLY DETERMINES WHICH TRAINER WILL SEND OUT HIS OR HER POKÉMON FIRST.

- ALTHOUGH SPARRING IS PERMITTED, YOU MAY LOSE POINTS OR BE DISQUALIFIED IF YOUR POKÉMON ARE CAUGHT FIGHTING WHILE THE TOURNAMENT IS BEING HELD.

- THE SILVER CONFERENCE CONSISTS OF THE FOLLOWING THREE STAGES:

- THE ATHLETE SCREENING ROUND (1-ON-1 BATTLES)

- ROUND-ROBIN ROUND (3-ON-3 BATTLES)

- VICTORY TOURNAMENT (6-ON-6 BATTLES)

SILVER CONFERENCE STAGES

ATHLETE SCREENING ROUNDS

Before any Trainer can step foot in an actual stadium, he or she must make it past the athlete screening battles. These are held in small, barebones courts where Trainers compete in three 1-on-1 battles. A single loss doesn't automatically disqualify a Trainer from moving on to the next round, but the competition is tough—this stage reduces the number of Trainers from over 200 to just 48.

OPENING CEREMONIES

After the athlete screening round, the remaining 48 Trainers enter Silver Stadium for the opening ceremonies, which also marks the end of the torch run bringing Ho-Oh's Sacred Flame from the Ho-Oh Shrine to Silver Town.

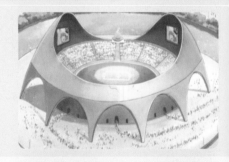

The torch bearer is injured by a collision with Team Rocket just as he enters Silver Stadium and Ash carries the torch in his place. The flame is the symbol of the Silver Conference and nothing can get underway until the Stadium's main torch is lit!

ROUND ROBIN SEMIFINAL

The 48 Trainers who pass the initial screening are then sorted into groups of three for a series of 3-on-3 battles. Each Trainer fights the other Trainers in their group once and only the Trainer with the most points will advance. A win earns 3 points, a draw is 1 point, and a loss is 0 points. After completion of the semifinals, there's a vacation day to allow Trainers to prepare for the Victory Tournament.

VICTORY TOURNAMENT

The Victory Tournament is what it all comes down to: 16 Trainers and full-on, 6-on-6 battles in front of a packed stadium. The battlefield can rotate between four different types (Grass, Rock, Water, and Ice) and a computer randomly selects the type at the beginning of each match.

VICTORY TOURNAMENT, FINAL 16

Ash defeats Gary on the Rock Field.

The battle between Ash and Gary comes down to Charizard versus Blastoise. Blastoise uses Rapid Spin to deflect Charizard's Flamethrower attack. In the end, Charizard edges out Blastoise through physical might.

ASH'S POKÉMON	GARY'S POKÉMON
Tauros	Nidoqueen
Heracross	Magmar
Muk	Blastoise
Bayleef	Arcanine
Snorlax	Scizor
Charizard	Golem

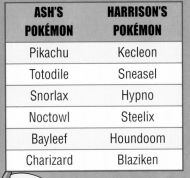

VICTORY TOURNAMENT, FINAL 8

Harrison defeats Ash on the Grass Field.

Ash's powerhouse, Charizard, takes on Harrison's equally tough Blaziken, a novel Pokémon in this competition. Blaziken manages to endure just a bit more than Charizard, securing Harrison the win.

ASH'S POKÉMON	HARRISON'S POKÉMON
Pikachu	Kecleon
Totodile	Sneasel
Snorlax	Hypno
Noctowl	Steelix
Bayleef	Houndoom
Charizard	Blaziken

Harrison

Harrison, from Hoenn's Littleroot Town, is a good-natured Trainer who is one of Ash's friendlier rivals. He even helped cover for Ash after Ash's Squirtle and Bulbasaur were caught fighting outside of a tournament match, a big Silver Conference no-no. The two Trainers first met at the Ho-Oh Shrine, where

Harrison caught a Sneasel that was blocking access to Ho-Oh's Sacred Flame. After his Silver Conference run ended, Harrison told Ash about Hoenn and the inspirational Professor Birch, setting the stage for Ash's next big Pokémon journey.

VICTORY TOURNAMENT, FINAL MATCH

Jon Dickson of Sento Cherry Town defeats Harrison and wins the Silver Conference.

Jon Dickson ends Harrison's winning streak, but Jon may have had an advantage since Harrison chose not to use his Blaziken. Harrison probably decided to give Blaziken a rest after its grueling fight with Ash's Charizard.

CELEBI • (SEL-ih-bee)

Height: 2'00" (0.6 m)   **Weight: 11.0 lbs (5.0 kg)**

Celebi is the spirit of the forest. A protector of nature and the environment, Celebi came from the future by crossing over time. As long as it appears, a bright and shining future awaits us.

Highly sought after by poachers because of its ability to manipulate time, Celebi's handling of time is at the heart of the strange relationship between Professor Oak and Ash Ketchum.

SUICUNE • (SWEE-koon)

Height: 6'07" (2.0 m) Weight: 412.3 lbs (187.0 kg)

The first of the Legendary Trio, Suicune represents the element of Ice. It also has unparalleled restorative powers; tears from a Suicune are said to have the ability to purify any water.

Like all the Legendary Trio, Suicune lives a secluded existence. It embodies the compassion of a pure spring, often helping those in dire need. Accompanied by the north wind, Suicune's most unique features are the two streamer-like appendages that run up the length of its body.

ENTEI • (EN-tay

Height: 6'11" (2.1 m)   **Weight: 436.5 lbs (198.0 kg)**

Entei embodies the passion of magma, and is thought to have been born in the eruption of a volcano. One of the three Legendary Trio, Entei has an intimidating and powerful presence.

Entei is physically powerful; its fiery red frame constantly smokes, adding another layer to its amazing mane. Its Fire-type attacks are to be respected and feared; its flames are hotter than a volcano's magma.

RAIKOU • (RYE-koo)

Height: 6'03" (1.9 m)   **Weight: 392.4 lbs (178.0 kg)**

Fast as lighting and representing the element of electricity, Raikou is one of the three Legendary Trio. Able to move over almost any terrain with its uncanny agility and leaping ability, Raikou embodies the speed of lightning.

Like some Electric-type Pokémon, Raikou's coat is yellow and black. Its mane trails down its back and has the appearance of thunderclouds. Proud and strong, its roar sends shock waves through the air, and is most often seen during lighting storms.

LUGIA • (LOO-gee-ah)

Height: 17'01" (5.2 m)   Weight: 476.2 lbs (216.0 kg)

The great guardian of the sea, Lugia's presence brings balance to the weather. Tied to the Titan Trio in mysterious ways, it can create and calm storms at will. Lugia's wings pack devastating power—a light fluttering of its wings can blow apart regular houses.

Capable of telepathic communication, Lugia are both kind and intelligent. They remain secluded from humanity, not because they fear them but because they fear harming them. This fear is well founded, as Lugia possess such incredible power over the winds and weather, they could easily ravage human civilization. Unlike most Legendary Pokémon, Lugia have been seen with their offspring.

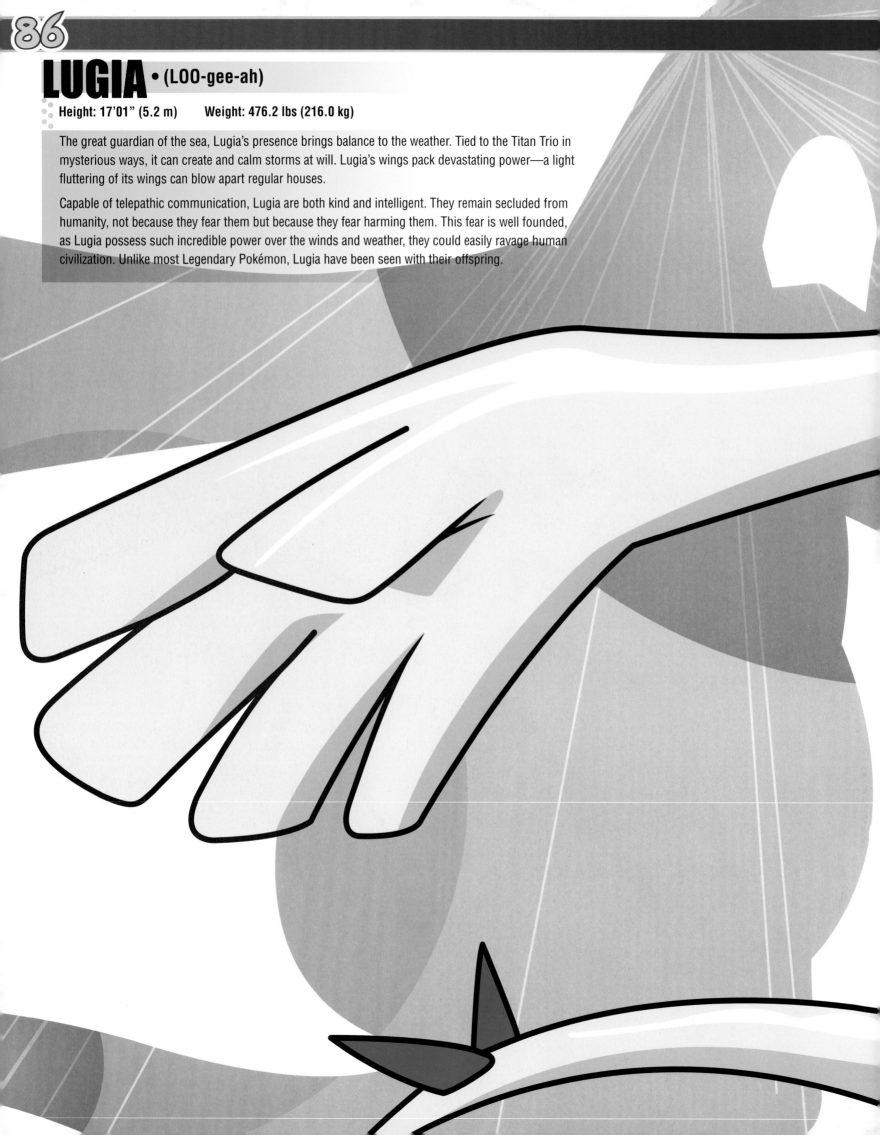

Loo-g-ah

HO-OH • (HOE-OH)

Height: 12'06" (3.8 m)   Weight: 438.7 lbs (199.0 kg)

A mysterious, magnificent bird, its feathers, which bring happiness, are a breathtaking array of seven different colors, which vary depending on the angle from which they are struck by light. This unique feather has a secondary effect: a rainbow follows Ho-Oh whenever it flies.

One of the most rare Legendary Pokémon, it could be that Ho-Oh is a singular Pokémon that has existed for generations. Considered to be the guardian of the sky, Ho-Oh has vast ancient powers.

JOHTO POKÉMON

This region is full of surprising new characters—and especially fierce ones,
like Tyranitar, Ursaring, and Lugia!

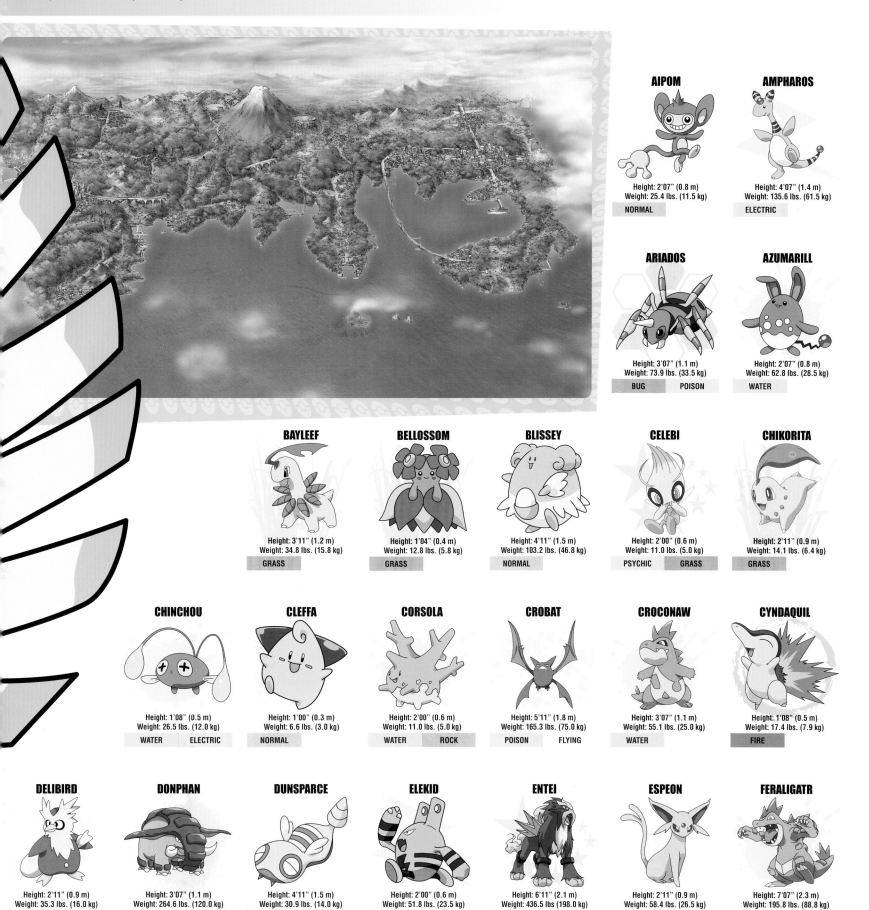

AIPOM
Height: 2'07" (0.8 m)
Weight: 25.4 lbs. (11.5 kg)
NORMAL

AMPHAROS
Height: 4'07" (1.4 m)
Weight: 135.6 lbs. (61.5 kg)
ELECTRIC

ARIADOS
Height: 3'07" (1.1 m)
Weight: 73.9 lbs. (33.5 kg)
BUG | POISON

AZUMARILL
Height: 2'07" (0.8 m)
Weight: 62.8 lbs. (28.5 kg)
WATER

BAYLEEF
Height: 3'11" (1.2 m)
Weight: 34.8 lbs. (15.8 kg)
GRASS

BELLOSSOM
Height: 1'04" (0.4 m)
Weight: 12.8 lbs. (5.8 kg)
GRASS

BLISSEY
Height: 4'11" (1.5 m)
Weight: 103.2 lbs. (46.8 kg)
NORMAL

CELEBI
Height: 2'00" (0.6 m)
Weight: 11.0 lbs. (5.0 kg)
PSYCHIC | GRASS

CHIKORITA
Height: 2'11" (0.9 m)
Weight: 14.1 lbs. (6.4 kg)
GRASS

CHINCHOU
Height: 1'08" (0.5 m)
Weight: 26.5 lbs. (12.0 kg)
WATER | ELECTRIC

CLEFFA
Height: 1'00" (0.3 m)
Weight: 6.6 lbs. (3.0 kg)
NORMAL

CORSOLA
Height: 2'00" (0.6 m)
Weight: 11.0 lbs. (5.0 kg)
WATER | ROCK

CROBAT
Height: 5'11" (1.8 m)
Weight: 165.3 lbs. (75.0 kg)
POISON | FLYING

CROCONAW
Height: 3'07" (1.1 m)
Weight: 55.1 lbs. (25.0 kg)
WATER

CYNDAQUIL
Height: 1'08" (0.5 m)
Weight: 17.4 lbs. (7.9 kg)
FIRE

DELIBIRD
Height: 2'11" (0.9 m)
Weight: 35.3 lbs. (16.0 kg)
ICE | FLYING

DONPHAN
Height: 3'07" (1.1 m)
Weight: 264.6 lbs. (120.0 kg)
GROUND

DUNSPARCE
Height: 4'11" (1.5 m)
Weight: 30.9 lbs. (14.0 kg)
NORMAL

ELEKID
Height: 2'00" (0.6 m)
Weight: 51.8 lbs. (23.5 kg)
ELECTRIC

ENTEI
Height: 6'11" (2.1 m)
Weight: 436.5 lbs. (198.0 kg)
FIRE

ESPEON
Height: 2'11" (0.9 m)
Weight: 58.4 lbs. (26.5 kg)
PSYCHIC

FERALIGATR
Height: 7'07" (2.3 m)
Weight: 195.8 lbs. (88.8 kg)
WATER

FLAAFFY

Height: 2'07" (0.8 m)
Weight: 29.3 lbs. (13.3 kg)

ELECTRIC

FORRETRESS

Height: 3'11" (1.2 m)
Weight: 277.3 lbs. (125.8 kg)

BUG	STEEL

FURRET

Height: 5'11" (1.8 m)
Weight: 71.6 lbs. (32.5 kg)

NORMAL

GIRAFARIG

Height: 4'11" (1.5 m)
Weight: 91.5 lbs. (41.5 kg)

NORMAL	PSYCHIC

GLIGAR

Height: 3'07" (1.1 m)
Weight: 142.9 lbs. (64.8 kg)

GROUND	FLYING

GRANBULL

Height: 4'07" (1.4 m)
Weight: 107.4 lbs. (48.7 kg)

NORMAL

HERACROSS
Height: 4'11" (1.5 m)
Weight: 119.0 lbs. (54.0 kg)

BUG	FIGHTING

HITMONTOP

Height: 4'07" (1.4 m)
Weight: 105.8 lbs. (48.0 kg)

FIGHTING

HO-OH

Height: 12'06" (3.8 m)
Weight: 438.7 lbs. (199.0 kg)

FIRE	FLYING

HOOTHOOT

Height: 2'04" (0.7 m)
Weight: 46.7 lbs. (21.2 kg)

NORMAL	FLYING

HOPPIP

Height: 1'04" (0.4 m)
Weight: 1.1 lbs. (0.5 kg)

GRASS	FLYING

HOUNDOOM

Height: 4'07" (1.4 m)
Weight: 77.2 lbs. (35.0 kg)

DARK	FIRE

HOUNDOUR

Height: 2'00" (0.6 m)
Weight: 23.8 lbs. (10.8 kg)

DARK	FIRE

IGGLYBUFF

Height: 1'00" (0.3 m)
Weight: 2.2 lbs. (1.0 kg)

NORMAL

JUMPLUFF

Height: 2'07" (0.8 m)
Weight: 6.6 lbs. (3.0 kg)

GRASS	FLYING

KINGDRA

Height: 5'11" (1.8 m)
Weight: 335.1 lbs. (152.0 kg)

WATER	DRAGON

LANTURN

Height: 3'11" (1.2 m)
Weight: 49.6 lbs. (22.5 kg)

WATER	ELECTRIC

LARVITAR

Height: 2'00" (0.6 m)
Weight: 158.7 lbs. (72.0 kg)

ROCK	GROUND

LEDIAN

Height: 4'07" (1.4 m)
Weight: 78.5 lbs. (35.6 kg)

BUG	FLYING

LEDYBA

Height: 3'03" (1.0 m)
Weight: 23.8 lbs. (10.8 kg)

BUG	FLYING

LUGIA
Height: 17'01" (5.2 m)
Weight: 476.2 lbs. (216.0 kg)

PSYCHIC	FLYING

MAGBY

Height: 2'04" (0.7 m)
Weight: 47.2 lbs. (21.4 kg)

FIRE

MAGCARGO

Height: 2'07" (0.8 m)
Weight: 121.3 lbs. (55.0 kg)

FIRE	ROCK

MANTINE

Height: 6'11" (2.1 m)
Weight: 485.0 lbs. (220.0 kg)

WATER	FLYING

MAREEP

Height: 2'00" (0.6 m)
Weight: 17.2 lbs. (7.8 kg)

ELECTRIC

MARILL

Height: 1'04" (0.4 m)
Weight: 18.7 lbs. (8.5 kg)

WATER

MEGANIUM

Height: 5'11" (1.8 m)
Weight: 221.6 lbs. (100.5 kg)

GRASS

MILTANK

Height: 3'11" (1.2 m)
Weight: 166.4 lbs. (75.5 kg)

NORMAL

MISDREAVUS

Height: 2'04" (0.7 m)
Weight: 2.2 lbs. (1.0 kg)

GHOST

MURKROW

Height: 1'08" (0.5 m)
Weight: 4.6 lbs. (2.1 kg)

DARK	FLYING

NATU

Height: 0'08" (0.2 m)
Weight: 4.4 lbs. (2.0 kg)

PSYCHIC	FLYING

NOCTOWL

Height: 5'03" (1.6 m)
Weight: 89.9 lbs. (40.8 kg)

NORMAL	FLYING

OCTILLERY

Height: 2'11" (0.9 m)
Weight: 62.8 lbs. (28.5 kg)

WATER

PHANPY

Height: 1'08" (0.5 m)
Weight: 73.9 lbs. (33.5 kg)

GROUND

PICHU

Height: 1'00" (0.3 m)
Weight: 4.4 lbs. (2.0 kg)

ELECTRIC

PILOSWINE

Height: 3'07" (1.1 m)
Weight: 123.0 lbs. (55.8 kg)

ICE	GROUND

PINECO

Height: 2'00" (0.6 m)
Weight: 15.9 lbs. (7.2 kg)

BUG

POLITOED
Height: 3'07" (1.1 m)
Weight: 74.7 lbs. (33.9 kg)

WATER

PORYGON2
Height: 2'00" (0.6 m)
Weight: 71.6 lbs. (32.5 kg)

NORMAL

PUPITAR

Height: 3'11" (1.2 m)
Weight: 335.1 lbs. (152.0 kg)

ROCK	GROUND

QUAGSIRE

Height: 4'07" (1.4 m)
Weight: 165.3 lbs. (75.0 kg)

WATER	GROUND

QUILAVA

Height: 2'11" (0.9 m)
Weight: 41.9 lbs. (19.0 kg)

FIRE

QWILFISH

Height: 1'08" (0.5 m)
Weight: 8.6 lbs. (3.9 kg)

WATER	POISON

RAIKOU

Height: 6'03" (1.9 m)
Weight: 392.4 lbs. (178.0 kg)

ELECTRIC

REMORAID

Height: 2'00" (0.6 m)
Weight: 26.5 lbs. (12.0 kg)

WATER

SCIZOR

Height: 5'11" (1.8 m)
Weight: 260.1 lbs. (118.0 kg)

BUG	STEEL

SENTRET

Height: 2'07" (0.8 m)
Weight: 13.2 lbs. (6.0 kg)

NORMAL

SHUCKLE

Height: 2'00" (0.6 m)
Weight: 45.2 lbs. (20.5 kg)

BUG	ROCK

SKARMORY

Height: 5'07" (1.7 m)
Weight: 111.3 lbs. (50.5 kg)

STEEL	FLYING

SKIPLOOM

Height: 2'00" (0.6 m)
Weight: 2.2 lbs. (1.0 kg)

GRASS	FLYING

SLOWKING
Height: 6'07" (2.0 m)
Weight: 175.3 lbs. (79.5 kg)

WATER	PSYCHIC

SLUGMA

Height: 2'04" (0.7 m)
Weight: 77.2 lbs. (35.0 kg)

FIRE

SMEARGLE
Height: 3'11" (1.2 m)
Weight: 127.9 lbs. (58.0 kg)

NORMAL

SMOOCHUM

Height: 1'04" (0.4 m)
Weight: 13.2 lbs. (6.0 kg)

ICE	PSYCHIC

SNEASEL

Height: 2'11" (0.9 m)
Weight: 61.7 lbs. (28.0 kg)

DARK	ICE

SNUBBULL

Height: 2'00" (0.6 m)
Weight: 17.2 lbs. (7.8 kg)

NORMAL

SPINARAK

Height: 1'08" (0.5 m)
Weight: 18.7 lbs. (8.5 kg)

BUG	POISON

STANTLER

Height: 4'07" (1.4 m)
Weight: 157.0 lbs. (71.2 kg)

NORMAL

STEELIX

Height: 30'02" (9.2 m)
Weight: 881.8 lbs. (400.0 kg)

STEEL	GROUND

SUDOWOODO

Height: 3'11" (1.2 m)
Weight: 83.8 lbs. (38.0 kg)

ROCK

SUICUNE

Height: 6'07" (2.0 m)
Weight: 412.3 lbs. (187.0 kg)

WATER

SUNFLORA

Height: 2'07" (0.8 m)
Weight: 18.7 lbs. (8.5 kg)

GRASS

SUNKERN

Height: 1'00" (0.3 m)
Weight: 4.0 lbs. (1.8 kg)

GRASS

SWINUB

Height: 1'04" (0.4 m)
Weight: 14.3 lbs. (6.5 kg)

ICE	GROUND

TEDDIURSA

Height: 2'00" (0.6 m)
Weight: 19.4 lbs. (8.8 kg)

NORMAL

TOGEPI
Height: 1'00" (0.3 m)
Weight: 3.3 lbs. (1.5 kg)

NORMAL

TOGETIC

Height: 2'00" (0.6 m)
Weight: 7.1 lbs. (3.2 kg)

NORMAL	FLYING

TOTODILE

Height: 2'00" (0.6 m)
Weight: 20.9 lbs. (9.5 kg)

WATER

TYPHLOSION

Height: 5'07" (1.7 m)
Weight: 175.3 lbs. (79.5 kg)

FIRE

TYRANITAR

Height: 6'07" (2.0 m)
Weight: 445.3 lbs. (202.0 kg)

ROCK	DARK

TYROGUE

Height: 2'04" (0.7 m)
Weight: 46.3 lbs. (21.0 kg)

FIGHTING

UMBREON

Height: 3'03" (1.0 m)
Weight: 59.5 lbs. (27.0 kg)

DARK

UNOWN

Height: 1'08" (0.5 m)
Weight: 11.0 lbs. (5.0 kg)

PSYCHIC

URSARING

Height: 5'11" (1.8 m)
Weight: 277.3 lbs. (125.8 kg)

NORMAL

WOBBUFFET

Height: 4'03" (1.3 m)
Weight: 62.8 lbs. (28.5 kg)

PSYCHIC

WOOPER

Height: 1'04" (0.4 m)
Weight: 18.7 lbs. (8.5 kg)

WATER	GROUND

XATU

Height: 4'11" (1.5 m)
Weight: 33.1 lbs. (15.0 kg)

PSYCHIC	FLYING

YANMA

Height: 3'11" (1.2 m)
Weight: 83.8 lbs. (38.0 kg)

BUG	FLYING

HOENN

Home of Professor Birch of Littleroot Town, Hoenn offers visitors spectacularly different environments all in one place. From sunny coastlines to bursting-with-life forests, Hoenn is in many ways an encapsulation of every experience of the mainland regions.

Hoenn is also home to Ash's friends May and Max. Their dad, the Gym Leader Norman, lives in Petalburg City. Slateport City is a very busy port town in the south of Hoenn. Two unique features dominate the landscape of Hoenn.

First, the active volcano, Mt. Chimney, is home to many hotsprings. Rising from the middle of Hoenn, Mt. Chimney is always smoking, on the verge of eruption. Second, the crater island city, Sootopolis City, rests inside a dormant underwater volcano. Only reachable by a ferry, Sootopolis City is an amazing tiered city marked by terraced dwellings reachable by stairs.

MAY

May's Pokémon

TORCHIC

May's first Pokémon, Torchic, was friendly, but ended up getting itself into trouble with other Pokémon often. As it evolved from Torchic into Combusken and from Combusken into Blaziken, it shed some of its temper but remains a tough, experienced fighter.

BLAZIKEN

COMBUSKEN

WURMPLE

Wurmple has had an interesting life; after evolving into a Silcoon, it was accidentally swapped with Jessie's Casoon. Finally, after a great deal of arguing, Silcoon was returned to May and evolved into a Beautifly.

BEAUTIFLY

SILCOON

BULBASAUR

Caught in the Forbidden Forest of Hoenn, May first discovered Bulbasaur while it was trying to pick flowers. Since then she has evolved it into an Ivysaur, then into a mighty Venusaur.

IVYSAUR

VENUSAUR

Although May is the daughter of Norman, Petalburg City's famous Gym Leader, she never intended to be a Pokémon Trainer *or* a Coordinator—what she really wanted was to see the world. During her travels, she developed an interest in Pokémon Contests and realized she had the makings of a great Coordinator.

May became a Pokémon Trainer when she was 10, but she wasn't even interested in Pokémon; food and travel have always been two of her biggest passions. Knowing little about Pokémon, she only chose Torchic as her first Pokémon because it seemed friendly. Things changed once she joined Ash on his travels and met Janet, a Pokémon Coordinator; intrigued by Pokémon Contests, May decided to become a Coordinator herself.

May wouldn't be a talented Coordinator if she didn't have some competitive mettle, but she's also a soft-hearted girl who's sometimes too easily swayed for her own good. After all, she became a Coordinator partly by chance instead of choice, and even as she grows in experience, she struggles to develop confidence in her own skills. But once she realizes she could be a top Coordinator if she just works hard, there's no looking back for the girl who will one day be known as the Princess of Hoenn.

There was a time when May would fall for everything from Harley's glib advice to the promises of Team Rocket's fake PokéBlock, but she's learned her lessons by now with help from her true friends and her rival, Drew.

THE WORLD IS HER OYSTER, MELON BREAD, AND CHICKEN NOODLE SOUP

May loves travel and adventure, but she's definitely a big-city girl. For one thing, she likes to shop—but more importantly, she loves to eat! Wherever she goes, she's sure to have guidebook tips on the best places to eat, even when the local specialties sound strange instead of savory.

SQUIRTLE

While at Professor Oak's, a Squirtle become enamored with May. Though intended to be a First Pokémon, Squirtle was given to May, and has since become very confident in Contests. It has evolved into a Wartortle.

WARTORTLE

MUNCHLAX

Munchlax was an unusual capture: it was caught from the inside after it gulped down May's Poké Ball. When Contest time rolls around, Munchlax isn't above putting a little extra swagger in its step.

SKITTY

Skitty is affectionate but hyperactive, and May has managed to put its energy to good use in her Contests. Skitty's Assist move in particular has saved her from more than one Contest battle crisis.

EEVEE

May received an Egg during her adventures in Kanto. It hatched into an Eevee which she soon introduced to Contests; just before the Wallace Cup, she made a special trip to Snowpoint City to evolve it into Glaceon.

GLACEON

Faced with a choice between finding her lost brother and boarding the last ferry to the last Contest before the Grand Festival, May decides to turn around and go find Max. Even though Ash offers to find him while May goes ahead, May knows she has to do the right thing, even if it costs her dream: there's always another Grand Festival, but she only has one brother.

MAY AND MAX HIT THE ROAD

Before she left home, May promised her mother and her father, Norman, that she'd look after her little brother Max. Max fancies himself the smarter of the two, and that's at least true when it comes to Pokémon trivia. He hates it when May treats him like a kid, but a big sister's responsibility never ends. Yet for all their squabbles, the genuine bond between them is never in question. After their Hoenn and Kanto journeys end, May goes on to Johto, while Max helps out his father in the Gym.

FLYING SOLO

After the Kanto Grand Festival, May decides to head for Johto on her own. That means no more looking after Max, but it also means she'll have to rely on herself without Ash and Brock to help out. It's the next step in her growth as a Coordinator and a person; when she revisits her old friends in Sinnoh at the Wallace Cup, she reports having a rough time trying to beat Harley and Drew—but she's won three Ribbons already, and she's strong enough to keep going even when times are tough.

MAX

Nerdy, know-it-all. That is Max in a nutshell. If you look beyond the oversized glasses and screechy voice you will find all the desire, commitment, and dedication that makes a Pokémon Trainer stand above all others. It is more important to know that one day Max will be a Trainer, and a formidable one.

FAMILY MATTERS

Although Max and May are brother and sister, it doesn't mean that he has the warmest feelings for her. After all, what kind of little brother would he be if he didn't tease her or complain about her once in a while? He certainly let loose on her with an embarrassing story about how she was mistaken for a Tentacruel in her fifth Ribbon Contest battle against Harley!

Max had a heartbreaking moment where he saw his own father lose to Ash in a hotly contested Gym Battle. After running away with the Balance Badge, Max goes on a tirade about Norman's loss to Ash. It is a coming-of-age realization for Max, whose father explains that losing is an important part of being a Gym Leader.

Max's parents, Caroline and Norman, want Max to travel with Ash, May and Brock to learn more about Pokémon through observation. They are worried that Max is too entrenched in the books about Pokémon, and not involved enough in field training. Maybe Max is shooting for a professorial position?

GOODBYE AND GOOD LUCK

At the end of their Kanto journey, May decides that she wants to travel through Johto alone, but agrees to escort Max back to the Petalburg Gym. Max is furious, not just at the thought of being abandoned, but also because he has become somewhat jealous of his sister's success. But when Ash agrees to battle him when he becomes a Trainer, Max calms down. He then goes back to Petalburg Gym to help his father train and to care for the Petalburg Gym Pokémon.

Max's Pokémon

What are Max's Pokémon? This is kind of a trick question, since Max is not allowed Pokémon because of his age. That doesn't mean that Max hasn't formed some significant bonds with certain Pokémon, including some Legendary Pokémon.

POOCHYENA

Max comes across a Poochyena that does not evolve, even though the rest of the pack has. He trains it to level it up, but Team Rocket steps in. During the battle, it finally evolves into Mightyena.

RALTS

Max finds a sick Ralts in the Izabe Forest, so Ash and his crew take it to the nearest Pokémon Center. Team Rocket intervenes, and in the ensuing getaway, a Gardevoir and Kirlia battle Max for the sick Ralts. Max does everything in his power to protect the Ralts, and finally makes it to the Pokémon Center. Max promises to return once he's a Trainer.

DEOXYS

When everything mechanical starts to malfunction, Pokémon Ranger Solana explains that it is an electromagnetic disturbance, caused by...Deoxys! Deoxys is scared and alone during its flight through space, and kidnaps Max and Meowth. Befriending Deoxys, Max is able to calm it, giving it hope that it will never truly be alone again.

PROFESSOR BIRCH

As Ash and his friends move from region to region in search of more badges, contests and battles, they encounter the resident Professors for each area. At the start of their adventures in Hoenn, Ash meets one of the most gregarious Professors, Professor Birch.

HOENN

Birch is responsible for delivering the first Pokémon to Trainers who come by his lab. He has Torchic, Treecko, and Mudkip under his care.

He also keeps a Poochyena on hand to help out with any problems that may arise.

He Knows His Stuff, Part I

Whether rolling around on the ground with a group of Seedot or trying to help Trainers identify Pokémon, Birch is more of a hands-on Professor compared to the others. He desperately tries to tell Jessie that her Silcoon is actually a Cascoon, but before she can learn from his wisdom it evolves into Dustox.

Professor Birch makes it well known that he "doesn't want to stay cooped up in his lab." This leads him outdoors with an opportunity to frequently cross paths with Ash and his friends.

His specialty in Pokémon research revolves around the habits of wild Pokémon, which means he must get closer to Pokémon than Professor Oak. To that end, he drives a jeep all around Hoenn, but not very carefully. He is also good friends with Norman, the Gym Leader of Petalburg City—May and Max's father.

SCALING NEW HEIGHTS

Professor Birch is no slouch when it come to field work. As a matter of fact, our friends catch him scaling the cliffs in Dewford Town looking for a Wingull nest. In addition, he uncovers lots of mysteries while working, like when he discovers Team Aqua for the first time while investigating Keanu's secret base!

He Knows His Stuff, Part II

Birch is one of the Professors Ash sees the most, usually explaining strange evolutions. For example, he explains that a DeepSeaTooth is needed for Clamperl to evolve into Huntail, while a DeepSeaScale evolves Clamperl into Gorebyss.

FIELD RESEARCH

Unlike the other Professors, Birch is most comfortable when out in the field. He combs the various forests, mountains, and towns of Hoenn researching Pokémon in the wild. However, his base and research lab is in Littleroot Town, which is located between Dewford Town and Slateport City.

DREW

Sometimes May's friend and sometimes her rival, Drew has grown to see May as genuine competition instead of just a rank novice. He was once a novice Coordinator just like everyone else, on the verge of tears after being beaten by Soledad in his Contest debut, but now he's a Coordinator from LaRousse City and a well-known figure on the Contest circuit.

Although Drew's criticisms of May are usually helpful in their own way, he's snapped at her on a few occasions. At first, he was frustrated with the way May's lack of confidence led her to believe Harley's constant lies. But at the Grand Festival in Kanto, Drew lashes out at both May and his Absol because May's up-and-coming presence puts him under pressure to stay one step ahead. Drew isn't big on coming in second; even after the Grand Festival in Hoenn, he skipped the afterparty to keep training.

He has a habit of handing out roses that add to his cool, aloof image—but he does become flustered in the face of his adoring public. And though Drew is a perfectionist, he doesn't bother to dress up for Contests because he wants the sole focus to be his Pokémon, not him.

May once described Drew as a guy who liked to make fun of her, not a friend, but their relationship has more than thawed; they even saved each other when they were both stranded on Mirage Island.

Drew's Pokémon

BUTTERFREE

MASQUERAIN

FLYGON

ABSOL

ROSERADE

HARLEY

Harley's demeanor is all sweetness and light, but cross this Slateport City Coordinator in any fashion and his true nature becomes all too apparent.

Some Coordinators try to wow a crowd with beauty, but Harley prefers to send a shiver down the audience's spine. Of course, he thinks his intimidating Pokémon are absolutely darling.

May made the unwitting mistake of not recognizing his Cacturne and saying his cookies "aren't half-bad," which infuriated Harley so much he took an instant photo of her for his little book of vengeance. Since then, he's been determined to beat her by any means, whether fair or foul. Time and time again, Harley played dirty tricks on May and then made a show of apologies so he could trick her again.

Harley's Pokémon

CACTURNE

BANETTE

OCTILLERY

ARIADOS

HOENN GRAND FESTIVAL

Slateport City hosts the Grand Festival, Hoenn's annual top-tier Pokémon Contest, where Coordinators and Pokémon put on shows of beauty and power to see who is truly worthy of the Ribbon Cup.

To enter the Grand Festival, Coordinators must supply their Hoenn Contest pass and their five prize ribbons. Once the ribbons are scanned in and registration is complete, each contestant receives a guide book with Grand Festival rules, stadium maps, and even restaurant locations. Contestants also get to stay in comfortable rooms with an ocean view.

PRELIMINARY ROUND

Held on outdoor contest stages, the preliminary appeals are scored on a scale of 1-100 and only the top 64 Coordinators advance to the main competition. Those are tough odds considering there are 247 preliminary round entries in the year May competes. These rounds are judged by auxiliary judges instead of the usual combination of Mr. Contesta, Mr. Sukizo, and Nurse Joy.

MAIN COMPETITION

Contestants take the stage for main competition appeals in the reverse order of their preliminary round standings. Three minutes are allotted for each appeal and each judge scores on a 1-20 point scale. The judges' individual scores are added up and the top 32 contestants advance to the next round. For the next day's five-minute double battle rounds, the top 32 are paired off based on their scores in the main competition appeals.

MAY DEFEATS HARLEY

Harley makes the first move, but May comes up with quick combinations like Vine Whip and Silver Wind to turn the game around and earn a clear victory.

DREW DEFEATS MAY

Drew unveils a Flygon he raised just for this tournament and, despite May's creative strategies, the power of Flygon's Steel Wing together with Roselia's Stun Spore is just too much for Combusken and Skitty.

MAY DEFEATS ANTHONY

Although Anthony's Pokémon hold their own against Bulbasaur and Combusken, when time runs out with both sides still standing, May takes the win due to her slight edge in the points.

Anthony

A shy but hard-working Coordinator, Anthony was lucky to make it to the main competition after Team Rocket stole his ribbons and Contest pass. Without his ribbons, he didn't have the heart to compete, but Ash and Officer Jenny helped apprehend Team Rocket and Anthony took the stage after all. He made a good showing with his Swalot, which he'd raised ever since it was a Gulpin.

ROBERT DEFEATS DREW

Robert

Robert and his Milotic have made several other appearances throughout the Hoenn Contest season; he's a classy Coordinator. Team Rocket tries to steal his identity as well—by conducting an actual kidnapping—but the attempt is cut short by Ash and his Snorunt. Even though Robert wins the Grand Festival, he doesn't even stick around for the closing ceremony party—he's already off to practice for his next competition.

POKÉMON CONTESTS & COORDINATORS

In Hoenn, contests were introduced as a new form of battling. Contestants, known as Contest Coordinators instead of Trainers, showcased their Pokémon's skills in beauty and grace competitions. Instead of competing for badges, coordinators competed for ribbons.

MAIN COORDINATORS

Piplup, Buneary, Pachirisu, Ambipom, Swinub | SINNOH | DAWN

Dawn, like May, wants to compete and win ribbons so that she can be the best Contest Coordinator ever. However, there are differences between the two: Dawn is more aggressive and more confident than May. She doesn't "wonder" what she should do, nor does she rely on luck or fate. Instead, she trains and enters each battle with knowledge and foresight.

Glameow, Misdreavus, Shellos, Finneon | SINNOH | ZOEY

Zoey is Dawn's rival, much like Drew is to May. She is a little more outgoing than others in Sinnoh and a lot more helpful. She suggested and facilitated the trade of Aipcm and Buizel between Ash and Dawn when she observed that Buizel was more attuned to battling. She also has expressed her distaste for people who seek out Gym Badges and Coordinator ribbons at the same time.

Roselia, Sunflora, Kricketune | SINNOH | NANDO

Nando is a wandering minstrel of sorts, playing a Mew-shaped harp wherever he goes. Keeping with his lifestyle, Nando has trouble making up his mind. Ultimately, he decides to becomes a Trainer and a Coordinator.

KENNY | SINNOH | Prinplup, Alakazam, Breloom

Kenny is a Coordinator who has a previous history with Dawn. The two were childhood friends and he even refers to her affectionately as "Dee-Dee." He also chose Piplup as his first Pokémon, although he had begun his quest for ribbons before her. When Kenny faced Dawn in Floaroma, he lost to her in a very tight battle.

DREW | HOENN | Roserade, Masquerain, Flygon, Absol, Butterfree

Drew is to May what Gary Oak is to Ash—a competitor, a friend, and a rival to the end. And like Gary Oak, Drew continues to inspire and assist May although his competitive nature flares from time to time. Drew has his own rival and longtime friend in Solidad, another Coordinator.

JESSIE | SINNOH AND HOENN | Dustox, Aipom (borrowed), Wobbuffet, Seviper, Yanmega

Jessie has a deep desire to win the coordinator contests, but she rarely does so in honest ways and usually competes masked. More effort goes into her disguises (Jessabelle, Jessalina, The Jester) than into her training. She has won two ribbons, one in an unofficial showdown using Ash's Aipom and another legitimate win in Solaceon Town using her Dustox.

MAY | HOENN | Blaziken, Beautifly, Wartortle, Glaceon, Venusaur, Munchlax, Skitty

May announced early on in Hoenn that she had no desire to become a Trainer. After watching a Pokémon Contest, however, she realized her true calling. Although outmatched in almost every event, she trained diligently and won all five of her ribbons with style.

SOLIDAD | HOENN | Slowbro, Lapras, Pidgeot, Butterfree

Solidad is a Pokémon Coordinator from Pewter City (and an apparent acquaintance of Brock's) who competed against May in the Kanto Grand Festival, which she won. She is also old friends with Drew and Harley. She is always willing to help or offer advice.

HARLEY | HOENN | Cacturne, Banette, Ariados, Octillery, Wigglytuff

Harley is a snobby, easily-offended coordinator whose issues with May stem from the fact that she didn't over-praise the cookies that Harley made for her on their first meeting. Plus, she she didn't even know what a Cacturne was! Since then, Harley has made it his life mission to antagonize, embarrass, and demean May in any way possible.

Introducing the Judges

RAOUL CONTESTA

Not much is known about Mr. Contesta, but he is the Pokémon Contest Director and head of the judging committee.

MR. SUKIZO

Another judge in the contest is Mr. Sukizo, the president of the Pokémon Fan Club. He joins Mr. Contesta and Nurse Joy on the panel, but says very little. His catch phrase is "Remarkable."

NURSE JOY

A Nurse Joy from the town in which the contest is being held is usually asked to serve as a contest judge as well.

CONTEST RULES

- Each contestant will use one Pokémon per round, uless it is a Double Performance. A Coordinator can change Pokémon between rounds.

- Pokémon will perform in a qualifying round.

- High scores in the qualifying round determine placement in the semi-finals.

- During a match, Pokémon are judged on skill, grace, and performance.

- Pokémon can use single, double, or triple combination attacks to lower an opponent's tally.

- There is a five-minute time limit.

- After five minutes, the Coordinator with the higher point tally is declared the winner.

HOENN GYM BATTLES!

When Ash heads into Hoenn, he doesn't know what to expect. The Gyms in Hoenn are staffed by expert warriors, specializing in Electric-types, Fighting-types, and Fire-types.

RUSTBORO CITY GYM
GYM LEADER: ROXANNE

Geodude uses Rollout followed by Mega Punch, which takes Treecko out.

Roxanne questions using an Electric-type Pokémon in a Rock Gym, but Pikachu has a trick up its sleeve. A massive Thunder attack changes the terrain of the Gym, and because the terrain has been altered, Geodude cannot perform his moves and Pikachu takes the match.

Nosepass uses Zap Cannon, but the electricity charges Pikachu, and it uses it against Nosepass (and a well-placed Iron Tail attack) for the win.

MAUVILLE CITY GYM
GYM LEADER: WATTSON

Jovial Wattson starts with Magnemite, which tries Swift on for size. Pikachu uses Dodge, then Thunderbolt, which surprisingly takes Magnemite down.

Voltorb is next, and uses Screech, before Pikachu uses one Thunderbolt and takes the victory.

Finally, Magneton uses Shock Cannon to take Pikachu out, but Pikachu takes down Magneton with a Thunder attack, giving Ash the Dynamo Badge!

Electric-type vs. Electric-type

Wattson is the fun-loving Gym Leader of Mauville City. He accepts Ash's challenge, and after a few tense battles, Ash beats him. However, the battles are one-sided—Pikachu easily wipes the floor with Wattson's Pokémon. After the match, however, Pikachu falls ill, and a trip to the local Pokémon Center reveals that Pikachu is suffering from overcharge again, making all its attacks super-powerful. Wattson, however, is so depressed after his defeat that he gives up the Mauville City Gym. Ash tries to return the badge to Wattson, who won't hear of it. Ash is rewarded the badge for helping the Electric-type Pokémon.

LAVARIDGE TOWN GYM
GYM LEADER: FLANNERY

The inexperienced Flannery seems like an easy target for Ash, but the ease turns to unease once Flannery settles in and uses Reflect to reduce Corphish's ViceGrip by half. Corphish's Crabhammer takes Magcargo out for good.

When Slugma tries using Smog again, Pikachu uses Thunderbolt, charging the cloud, then counters Yawn with Quick Attack, before applying Thunder for the win.

Surprisingly, Ash sends out the Grass-type Treecko against a Fire-type, which is a type disadvantage. The battle goes back and forth, but when Slugma burns Treecko, Ash calls it back.

Down to her last Pokémon, Flannery chooses Torkoal, and manages to take out Pikachu with a combination of Iron Defense and Flamethrower.

As Corphish charges Slugma with ViceGrip, it gets hit with a Yawn attack, putting it to sleep! Ash is forced to pick another Pokémon.

Ash takes out Treecko next, which gets eliminated by Overheat the minute it leaves the Poké Ball.

Ash's only Pokémon left is the napping Corphish. Torkoal starts with Overheat, then follows up with Flamethrower. This time Corphish gets around Iron Defense by spinning Torkoal to its feet with ViceGrip, then BubbleBeam. The battle goes in favor of Ash!

DEWFORD ISLAND GYM
GYM LEADER: BRAWLY

Machop starts with Karate Chop, but Treecko dodges it. Treecko uses the formation of the Gym as Ash defends against another two Karate Chops. Worrying about the geysers in the Gym, Ash recalls Treecko just in time.

Corphish succumbs to Hariyama's onslaught, as it's blown out of the water, then finished with a Seismic Toss.

Corphish comes out swinging, using Bubblebeam, then Crabhammer. Machop tries to block with Karate Chop, but a subsequent Crabhammer makes short work of Machop.

Hariyama starts with Arm Thrust, which Treecko deftly dodges. Treecko uses Pound attacks on Hariyama's legs, which weaken Hariyama. Eventually, Treecko wins.

PETALBURG CITY GYM

GYM LEADER: NORMAN

Facing Gym Leaders with his usual cockiness is usually no problem for Ash—but Ash has never faced the parent of one of his friends. Despite the warm welcome by all of Petalburg City, Ash still has to face May's dad, Norman, who avoided an even bigger battle earlier by surprising his wife with an anniversary present, and the Gym challenge goes on as planned!

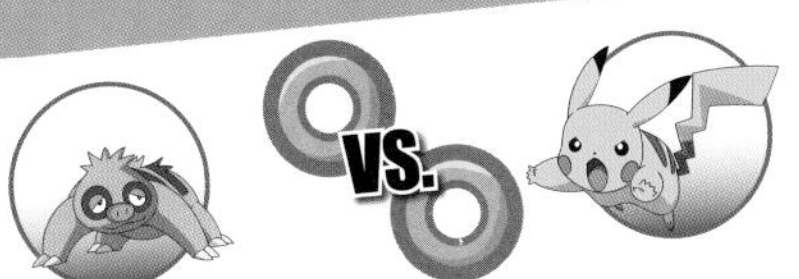

Pikachu can't get in one attack, as Slakoth dodges everything. Pikachu faces even more problems when Blizzard is used. Ash calls Pikachu back.

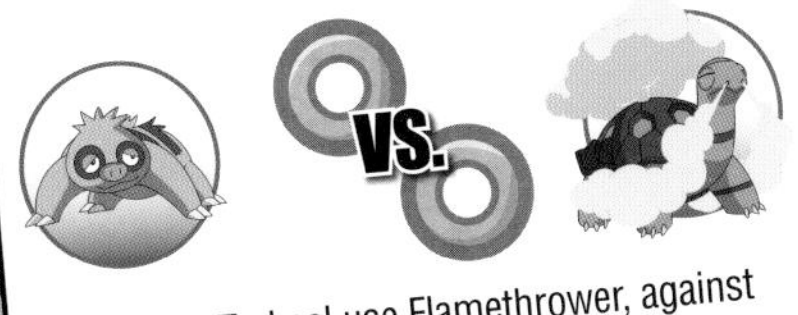

Ash has Torkoal use Flamethrower, against another Blizzard from Slakoth. Torkoal knocks out Slakoth.

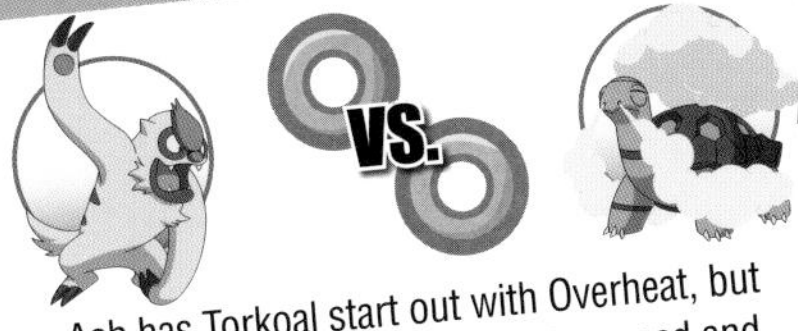

Ash has Torkoal start out with Overheat, but Vigoroth uses Scratch attack. Its speed and power knock out Torkoal with one attack.

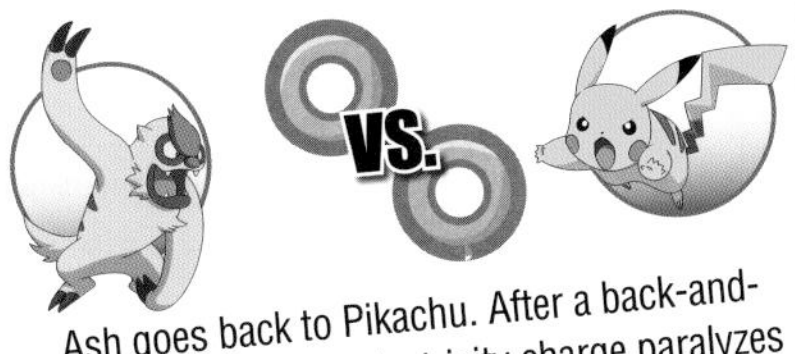

Ash goes back to Pikachu. After a back-and-forth battle, a static electricity charge paralyzes Vigoroth, and Pikachu ends the battle with Iron Tail. Unfortunately, Pikachu also succumbs, ending in a draw.

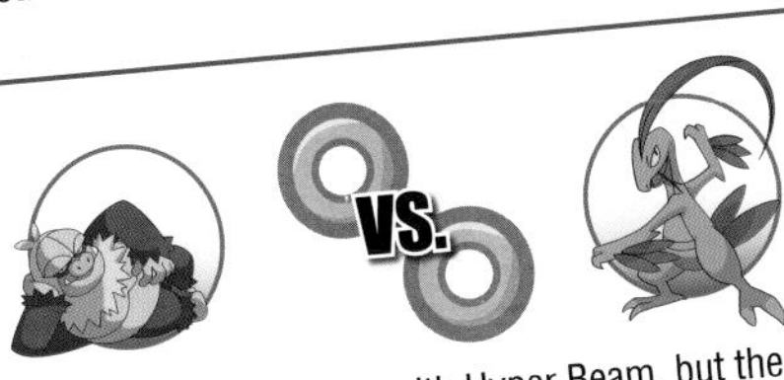

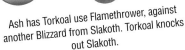

Grovyle uses Bullet Seed and Slaking counters with Hyper Beam, but the toughened Grovyle fights back and uses Overgrow, an ability that magnifies Grass-type attacks, and takes down Slaking with a Leaf Blade attack.

FORTREE CITY GYM

GYM LEADER: WINONA

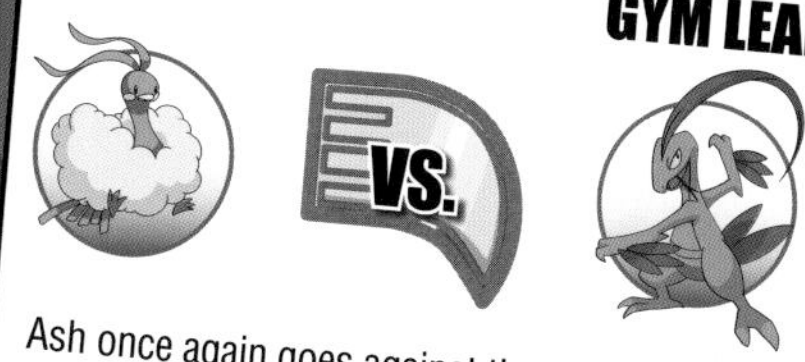

Ash once again goes against the grain and uses a type-disadvantaged Pokémon like Grovyle, which is weak against Flying-types like Altaria. In the end it works, as Grovyle uses Leaf Blade for the win!

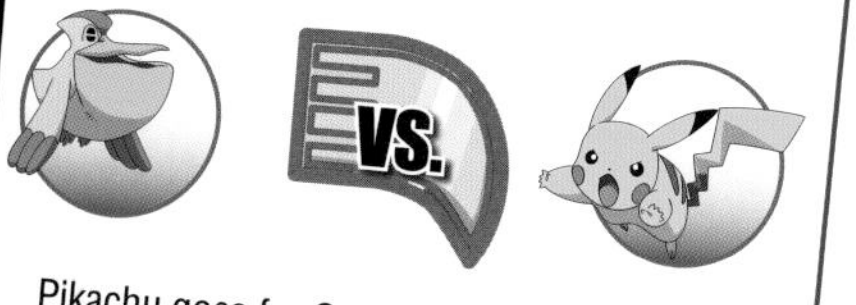

Pikachu goes for Quick Attack while Pelipper tries to keep its distance with Hydro Pump. Pikachu then electrifies the Hydro Pump, knocking both Pikachu and Pelipper out.

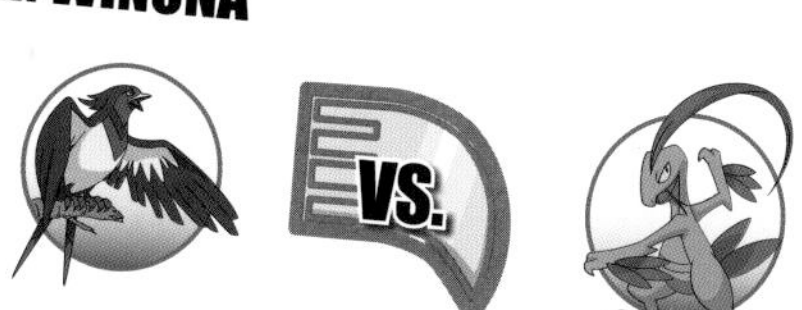

Winona sends out Swellow as her last Pokémon, while Ash chooses Grovyle, thinking his speed is an advantage. But all of Grovyle's jumping is no match for Swellow. Grovyle is hit with an Aerial Ace, an almost unavoidable attack, which does Grovyle in.

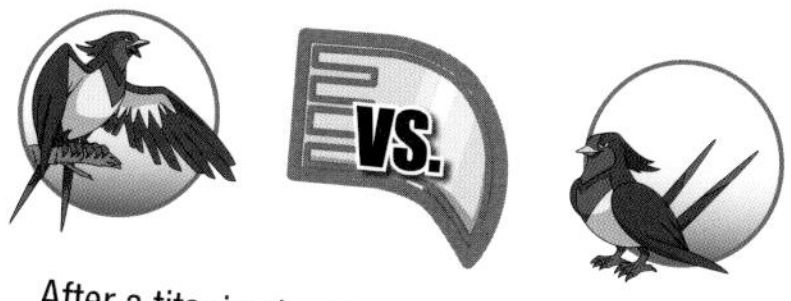

After a titanic clash in the air, Ash decides to have his Swellow use Wing Attack on the dusty ground, blinding Winona's Pokémon, allowing it to finish it off for the sixth Gym Badge.

MOSSDEEP CITY GYM

GYM LEADER: TATE AND LIZA

Ash finds that the Gym is run by two people, Tate and Liza, and after helping them defend against Team Rocket, they decide to battle for the Gym Badge. However, this is a double battle that uses 2-on-2 Pokémon battle, and Ash must find a way past the combination attacks of Solrock and Lunatone. Ash also must deal with the planets floating in the Gym, which will affect his battling style.

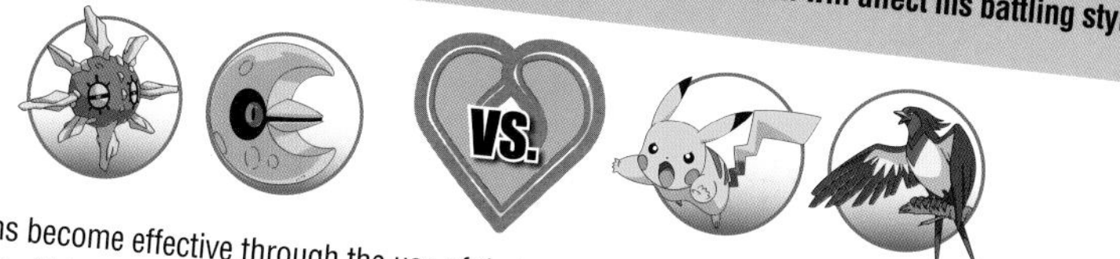

The twins become effective through the use of their teamwork, but Ash steps his game up using combos of his own. He has Pikachu and Swellow combine their attacks, and give each other a protective Thunder armor, which breaks through the Light Screen and paves their way to victory!

SOOTOPOLIS CITY GYM

GYM LEADER: JUAN

Battling at the Sootopolis City Gym takes a lot of strength and tenacity. Not only is there a Double Battle to deal with where you must defeat both of your opponents standing Pokémon to advance, but there is also a 3-on-3 battle where you use any of your surviving Pokémon from the previous rounds to take on Juan.

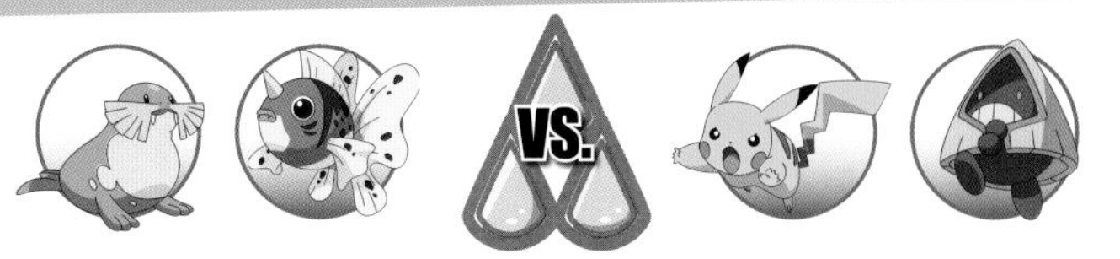

Pikachu and Snorunt use the ice to get closer to Juan's Pokémon. It seems to work but Pikachu's Iron Tail and Snorunt's Headbutt can't match Sealeo's Aurora Beam and Seaking's Hyper Beam. Snorunt is unable to battle.

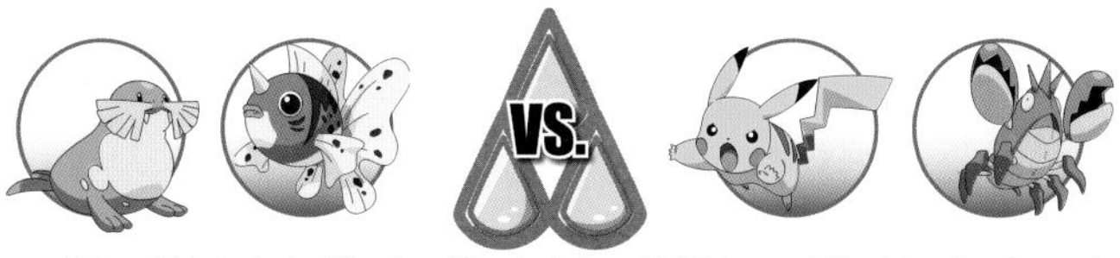

Ash brings out Corphish to help Pikachu. Pikachu's Iron Tail takes out Seaking, leaving only Sealeo. When Juan uses Ice Ball for the third time, Pikachu's Thunder breaks the ball allowing Corphish to knock Sealeo out with Crabhammer!

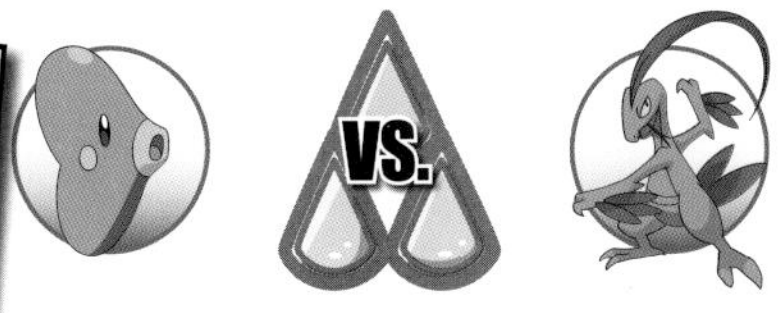

The battle switches to a more traditional one-on-one battle. When Grovyle uses Leaf Blade, Luvdisc's countering Sweet Kiss confuses Grovyle, who gets hit with a Water Gun and is knocked out.

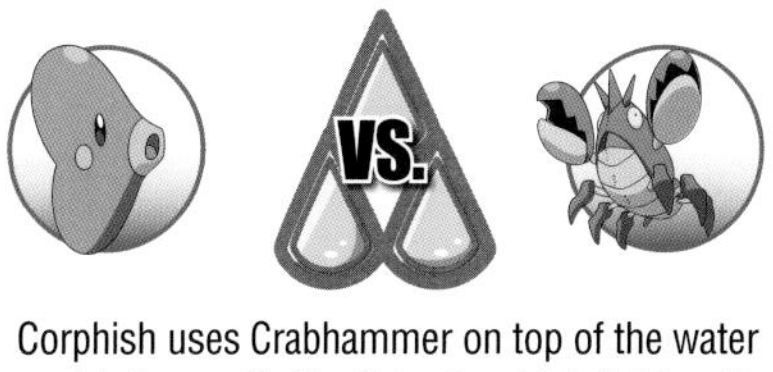

Corphish uses Crabhammer on top of the water and follows with ViceGrip. Corphish finishes it up with Crabhammer, which is super-effective.

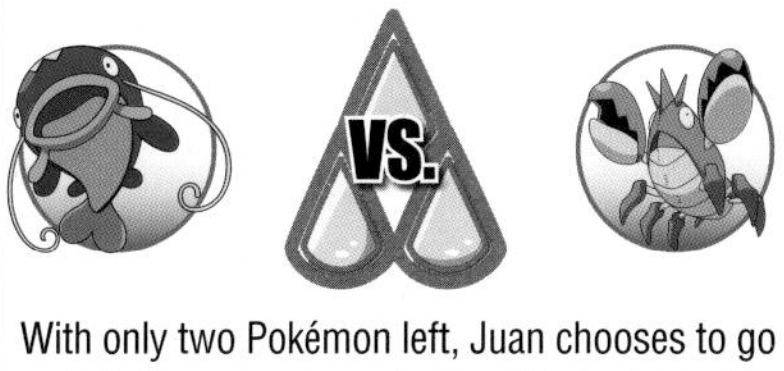

With only two Pokémon left, Juan chooses to go with Whiscash, who ends Corphish's night with a single Rock Smash!

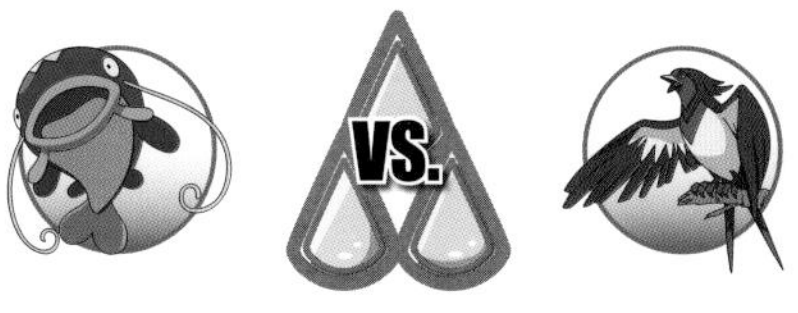

Whishcash uses Hyper Beam and the match seems lost, when suddenly Swellow comes back with an Aerial Ace and follows Whiscash into the water! Swellow follows with Aerial Ace to end the battle.

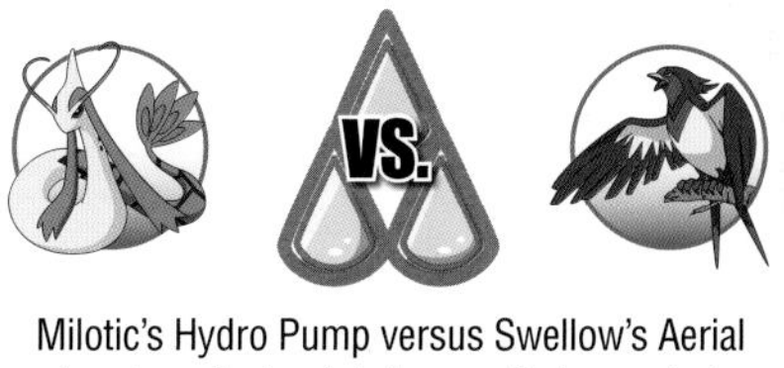

Milotic's Hydro Pump versus Swellow's Aerial Ace doesn't give Ash the results he wanted. Milotic's follow-up attack Twister knocks Swellow out.

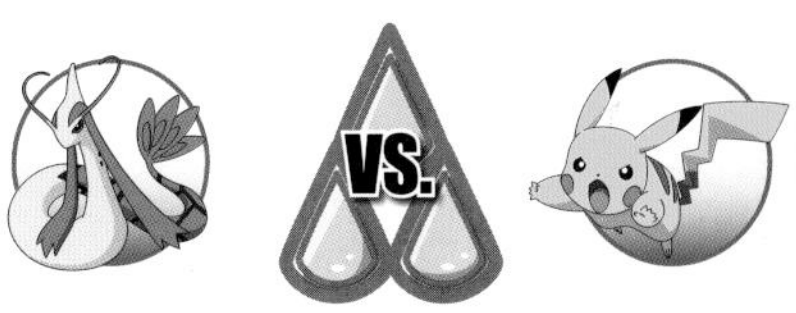

With both battlers down to their last Pokémon, it is up to Pikachu. Thunder seems to harm Milotic, but Milotic uses Recover. Pikachu rushes and flips Milotic into the water, where a full-tilt Thunder attack finishes it.

HOENN LEAGUE CHAMPIONSHIP

The Hoenn League Championship is Ever Grande City's star event and the gleam in every Hoenn Trainer's eye. As usual, a Trainer needs to earn eight badges for entry.

The Hoenn League Championship facilities are a sight to behold, featuring a main stadium surrounded by more stadiums, a Trainers' village, and its own Hoenn League Championship Pokémon Center.

OPENING CEREMONIES

To start off the tournament, a torch runner carries the flame of Moltres from Ever Grande City into the stadium, where it will be stored until the opening ceremonies. The ceremony itself, which features colorful balloons, the torchlighting, and appearances by the 256 qualifying competitors, doesn't begin until after the preliminary rounds have finished.

Tyson is the torch runner, but Ash is selected to light the main stadium's torch in recognition of his help in defeating Team Rocket's latest attempt at torch thievery.

PRESIDENT GOODSHOW AND THE TORCH COMMITTEE

Professor Charles Goodshow, President of the Pokémon League Torch Committee, is a jovial old fellow who truly loves his job. His duty is to make sure the torch relay and lighting goes smoothly for each tournament; to make sure nothing is derailed even if the torch is stolen or extinguished, he's been known to carry a special canister with another flame of Moltres burning inside.

The field type is selected randomly at the beginning of each match; one five-minute break is called as soon as a Trainer has three Pokémon knocked out, and the field type switches again before the battle resumes.

TOURNAMENT STRUCTURE

Cut-off for tournament registration is at 5 PM on the day before the preliminaries. With a field of over 600 entrants, the Hoenn League Championship's initial entry list will be chopped in half and then some before the tournament truly gets underway. Preliminary rounds trim down the field to 256 competitors through 1-on-1 battles where competitors register the Pokémon they plan to use.

After the preliminary rounds, Trainers must win all three double battle rounds of the Qualifying Tournament to join the 32 competitors advancing to the Victory Tournament. There's a day off following the completion of the Qualifying Tournament, allowing competitors to rest up and get in some last-minute training.

The Victory Tournament brings competitors to the main stadium for a full 6-on-6 battle on a stage that can rotate between Grass, Rock, Water, and Ice fields.

ASH DEFEATS KATIE

Katie is a strategy-minded Trainer from Lilycove City who takes an early lead against Ash. But luck starts to turn against her when Corphish knocks out her Golduck even while confused. Ash wins the day—although Katie makes him work for the win.

ASH DEFEATS MORRISON

Morrison is devastated to learn that he'll be paired up against his new buddy, and he almost loses the match by default when he can barely bring himself to call out his Pokémon. A quick lecture from Ash gets Morrison back into the game; although Ash still wins, the battle at least finishes as a fair fight.

Morrison

Morrison is a loud young Trainer from Verdanturf Town who easily matches Ash for sheer competitiveness. The two of them met before the Hoenn League Championship and they love to try and outdo each other. Just like Ash, he's also absent-minded when it comes to anything that doesn't involve Pokémon and battles—and Morrison doesn't have the advantage of Brock and Max to keep an eye on him. Morrison battles for fun, win or lose, and Ash is the first real friend he's ever battled.

TYSON DEFEATS ASH

In another close-fought battle between friendly rivals, even Tyson's powerhouse Metagross is taken down by Ash's quick strategizing. Tyson ekes out a win when both his Meowth and Ash's Pikachu are too exhausted to battle. Even though Tyson's Meowth is ready to collapse, Pikachu faints first.

Tyson

Hailing from Mauville City, Tyson is a calm, friendly Trainer with a passion for food. Like his personality, Tyson's battle strategy is carefully balanced, with a sound mix of offense and defense.

DEOXYS • (dee-OCKS-iss)

Height: 5'07" (1.7 m)   **Weight: 134.0 lbs (60.8 kg)**

Formed in a meteor while descending through the atmosphere, Deoxys is a mutated virus. Completely alien, this Psychic-type Pokémon can use any of four forms: Normal Forme, Attack Forme, Defense Forme, and Speed Forme.

Completely versatile, Deoxys can adapt its form to any situation. Each of its three modified forms change its appearance. In Attack Forme, Deoxys' tentacle arms merge to create a point and its head ends in a spike. In Defense Forme, its head and body merge, almost as if it were wearing a large helmet. The Speed Forme is more slender and the back of its head swoops out to a point to reduce wind resistance and drag.

JIRACHI • (jer-AH-chi)

Height: 1'00" (0.3 m) **Weight: 2.4 lbs (1.1 kg)**

Jirachi is asleep most of the time. It will only awake from its sleep if it is sung to with a voice of purity. Jirachi is a small white Steel-and-Psychic-type Pokémon.

Floating most of the time, Jirachi has stubby little legs and a unique third eye that appears very rarely from the curved semi-circle on its stomach. The only known Pokémon that can learn Doom Desire, Jirachi normally flees when in trouble. If forced to fight, it can use its exceedingly powerful Electric attacks.

GROUDON • (GRAU-don)

Height: 11'06" (3.5 m)   Weight: 2094.4 lbs (950.0 kg)

The mighty king of Magma, Groudon weighs in at an enormous 2094 pounds, making it the heaviest Legendary Pokémon in existence. Extremely powerful, Groudon rages with the burning strength of newly formed land.

Worshipped for its power by the nefarious Team Magma, Groudon can create land. Groudon is a savior to flood victims because of its ability to evaporate water and create ground. The opposite of majestic Kyogre, the two have battled with neither laying claim to victory.

KYOGRE • (kai-OH-gurr)

Height: 14'09" (4.5 m)   **Weight:** 776.0 lbs (352.0 kg)

Majestic servant of the sea, Kyogre is the mythological Pokémon that expanded the seas by covering the lands with rain. Very large, resembling a killer whale, Kyogre's most dominant features are its fins.

Sought greatly by Team Aqua, Kyogre can expand the oceans. Though large, Kyogre is nimble within the waves of its natural habitat—the sea.

LATIAS • (LAT-ee-ahs)

Height: 4'07" (1.4 m)   **Weight: 88.2 lbs (40.0 kg)**

Red with a white neck, Latias' appearance to humans are rare; a highly intelligent Pokémon, her body is made of glass-like down that refracts light to alter her appearance.

To maximize air speed and minimize drag, Latias can tuck her arms and legs close to the body appearing to have none at all. Latias telepathically communicate with others. She is also the only known Pokémon that learns Mist Ball.

LATIOS • (LAT-ee-ose)

Height: 6'07" (2.0 m)   **Weight: 132.3 lbs (60.0 kg)**

Latios' appearance is very similar to Latias, with the exception being size: Latios is blue and white and he is larger than his sister. Latios dislikes confrontation and would be more inclined to hide than fight! Latios will open its heart to a compassionate Trainer, however.

Using a form of telepathy, Latios can show friends images as if they are looking through his own eyes. If driven to fight, Latios will use its high-pitched speech to intimidate a foe. Both Latias and Latios are exceedingly compassionate and willing to sacrifice themselves for the safety of other Pokémon and humans.

REGICE • (REDGE-ee-ice)

Height: 5'11" (1.8 m)   **Weight:** 385.8 lbs (175.0 kg)

Completely composed of Ice, Regice's body is so cold, not even magma can melt it. Wrapped in super-cold air, anyone who approaches Regice has a high probability of freezing. Its face, like all the Regis, is a series of small dots that form a shape: Regice's looks like a plus sign.

REGISTEEL • (REDGE-ee-rock)

Height: 5'07" (1.7 m)   **Weight:** 507.1 lbs (230.0 kg)

Sleek and spherical, Registeel's body is still flexible despite being made of metal. Registeel's face appears to be a series of dots arranged like a hexagon with a dot in the center.

REGIROCK • (REDGE-ee-steel)

Height: 6'03" (1.9 m)   **Weight:** 451.9 lbs (205.0 kg)

Regirock is—surprise—made of large rocks and small boulders. If damaged in battle, Regirock will use whatever rocks are near it to repair itself. Because of this, Regirock has a pieced-together appearance. The dots for its face resemble a capital letter "H."

ray-KWAZ

RAYQUAZA • (ray-KWAZ-uh)

Height: 23'00"(7.0 m) **Weight: 455.2 lbs (206.5 kg)**

Rayquaza has lived for hundreds of millions of years in the ozone layer. This Dragon-and-Flying-type has never touched the ground. Its constant movement has prevented it from being discovered until recently.

Very aggressive, Rayquaza is a powerful Pokémon. Large and sleek, it lacks wings or other propulsion, but it still flies. It does have rudder-like fins that appear periodically down its long green serpent-like body. It has no legs, but has short three-fingered hands that deliver its amazing Dragon Claw, and a large mouth to expel its awesome Hyper Beam.

HOENN POKÉMON

After traveling through the regions of Kanto and Johto, Hoenn is your next stop—home to the mighty Kyogre and Groudon!

ABSOL

Height: 3'11" (1.2 m)
Weight: 103.6 lbs. (47.0 kg)

DARK

AGGRON

Height: 6'11" (2.1 m)
Weight: 793.7 lbs. (360.0 kg)

STEEL	ROCK

ALTARIA

Height: 3'07" (1.1 m)
Weight: 45.4 lbs. (20.6 kg)

DRAGON	FLYING

ANORITH

Height: 2'04" (0.7 m)
Weight: 27.6 lbs. (12.5 kg)

ROCK	BUG

ARMALDO

Height: 4'11" (1.5 m)
Weight: 150.4 lbs. (68.2 kg)

ROCK	BUG

ARON

Height: 1'04" (0.4 m)
Weight: 132.3 lbs. (60.0 kg)

STEEL	ROCK

AZURILL

Height: 0'08" (0.2 m)
Weight: 4.4 lbs. (2.0 kg)

NORMAL

BAGON

Height: 2'00" (0.6 m)
Weight: 92.8 lbs. (42.1 kg)

DRAGON

BALTOY

Height: 1'08" (0.5 m)
Weight: 47.4 lbs. (21.5 kg)

GROUND	PSYCHIC

BANETTE

Height: 3'07" (1.1 m)
Weight: 27.6 lbs. (12.5 kg)

GHOST

BARBOACH

Height: 1'04" (0.4 m)
Weight: 4.2 lbs. (1.9 kg)

WATER	GROUND

BEAUTIFLY

Height: 3'03" (1.0 m)
Weight: 62.6 lbs. (28.4 kg)

BUG	FLYING

BELDUM

Height: 2'00" (0.6 m)
Weight: 209.9 lbs. (95.2 kg)

STEEL	PSYCHIC

BLAZIKEN

Height: 6'03" (1.9 m)
Weight: 114.6 lbs. (52.0 kg)

| FIRE | FIGHTING |

BRELOOM

Height: 3'11" (1.2 m)
Weight: 86.4 lbs. (39.2 kg)

| GRASS | FIGHTING |

CACNEA

Height: 1'04" (0.4 m)
Weight: 113.1 lbs. (51.3 kg)

| GRASS |

CACTURNE

Height: 4'03" (1.3 m)
Weight: 170.6 lbs. (77.4 kg)

| GRASS | DARK |

CAMERUPT

Height: 6'03" (1.9 m)
Weight: 485.0 lbs. (220.0 kg)

| FIRE | GROUND |

CARVANHA

Height: 2'07" (0.8 m)
Weight: 45.9 lbs. (20.8 kg)

| WATER | DARK |

CASCOON

Height: 2'04" (0.7 m)
Weight: 25.4 lbs. (11.5 kg)

| BUG |

CASTFORM

Height: 1'00" (0.3 m)
Weight: 1.8 lbs. (0.8 kg)

| NORMAL |

CHIMECHO

Height: 2'00" (0.6 m)
Weight: 2.2 lbs. (1.0 kg)

| PSYCHIC |

CLAMPERL

Height: 1'04" (0.4 m)
Weight: 115.7 lbs. (52.5 kg)

| WATER |

CLAYDOL

Height: 4'11" (1.5 m)
Weight: 238.1 lbs. (108.0 kg)

| GROUND | PSYCHIC |

COMBUSKEN

Height: 2'11" (0.9 m)
Weight: 43.0 lbs. (19.5 kg)

| FIRE | FIGHTING |

CORPHISH

Height: 2'00" (0.6 m)
Weight: 25.4 lbs. (11.5 kg)

| WATER |

CRADILY

Height: 4'11" (1.5 m)
Weight: 133.2 lbs. (60.4 kg)

| ROCK | GRASS |

CRAWDAUNT

Height: 3'07" (1.1 m)
Weight: 72.3 lbs. (32.8 kg)

| WATER | DARK |

DELCATTY

Height: 3'07" (1.1 m)
Weight: 71.9 lbs. (32.6 kg)

| NORMAL |

DEOXYS

Height: 5'07" (1.7 m)
Weight: 134.0 lbs. (60.8 kg)

| PSYCHIC |

DUSCLOPS

Height: 5'03" (1.6 m)
Weight: 67.5 lbs. (30.6 kg)

| GHOST |

DUSKULL

Height: 2'07" (0.8 m)
Weight: 33.1 lbs. (15.0 kg)

| GHOST |

DUSTOX

Height: 3'11" (1.2 m)
Weight: 69.7 lbs. (31.6 kg)

| BUG | POISON |

ELECTRIKE

Height: 2'00" (0.6 m)
Weight: 33.5 lbs. (15.2 kg)

| ELECTRIC |

EXPLOUD

Height: 4'11" (1.5 m)
Weight: 185.2 lbs. (84.0 kg)

| NORMAL |

FEEBAS

Height: 2'00" (0.6 m)
Weight: 16.3 lbs. (7.4 kg)

| WATER |

FLYGON

Height: 6'07" (2.0 m)
Weight: 180.8 lbs. (82.0 kg)

| GROUND | DRAGON |

GARDEVOIR

Height: 5'03" (1.6 m)
Weight: 106.7 lbs. (48.4 kg)

| PSYCHIC |

GLALIE

Height: 4'11" (1.5 m)
Weight: 565.5 lbs. (256.5 kg)

| ICE |

GOREBYSS

Height: 5'11" (1.8 m)
Weight: 49.8 lbs. (22.6 kg)

| WATER |

GROUDON

Height: 11'06" (3.5 m)
Weight: 2094.4 lbs. (950.0 kg)

| GROUND |

GROVYLE

Height: 2'11" (0.9 m)
Weight: 47.6 lbs. (21.6 kg)

| GRASS |

GRUMPIG

Height: 2'11" (0.9 m)
Weight: 157.6 lbs. (71.5 kg)

| PSYCHIC |

GULPIN

Height: 1'04" (0.4 m)
Weight: 22.7 lbs. (10.3 kg)

| POISON |

HARIYAMA

Height: 7'07" (2.3 m)
Weight: 559.5 lbs. (253.8 kg)

| FIGHTING |

HUNTAIL

Height: 5'07" (1.7 m)
Weight: 59.5 lbs. (27.0 kg)

| WATER |

ILLUMISE

Height: 2'00" (0.6 m)
Weight: 39.0 lbs. (17.7 kg)

| BUG |

JIRACHI

Height: 1'00" (0.3 m)
Weight: 2.4 lbs. (1.1 kg)

| STEEL | PSYCHIC |

KECLEON

Height: 3'03" (1.0 m)
Weight: 48.5 lbs. (22.0 kg)

| NORMAL |

KIRLIA

Height: 2'07" (0.8 m)
Weight: 44.5 lbs. (20.2 kg)

| PSYCHIC |

KYOGRE

Height: 14'09" (4.5 m)
Weight: 776.0 lbs. (352.0 kg)

| WATER |

LAIRON

Height: 2'11" (0.9 m)
Weight: 264.6 lbs. (120.0 kg)

| STEEL | ROCK |

LATIAS
Height: 4'07" (1.4 m)
Weight: 88.2 lbs. (40.0 kg)

| DRAGON | PSYCHIC |

LATIOS

Height: 6'07" (2.0 m)
Weight: 132.3 lbs. (60.0 kg)

| DRAGON | PSYCHIC |

LILEEP
Height: 3'03" (1.0 m)
Weight: 52.5 lbs. (23.8 kg)

| ROCK | GRASS |

LINOONE

Height: 1'08" (0.5 m)
Weight: 71.6 lbs. (32.5 kg)

NORMAL

LOMBRE

Height: 3'11" (1.2 m)
Weight: 71.6 lbs. (32.5 kg)

WATER | GRASS

LOTAD

Height: 1'08" (0.5 m)
Weight: 5.7 lbs. (2.6 kg)

WATER | GRASS

LOUDRED

Height: 3'03" (1.0 m)
Weight: 89.3 lbs. (40.5 kg)

NORMAL

LUDICOLO

Height: 4'11" (1.5 m)
Weight: 121.3 lbs. (55.0 kg)

WATER | GRASS

LUNATONE

Height: 3'03" (1.0 m)
Weight: 370.4 lbs. (168.0 kg)

ROCK | PSYCHIC

LUVDISC

Height: 2'00" (0.6 m)
Weight: 19.2 lbs. (8.7 kg)

WATER

MAKUHITA

Height: 3'03" (1.0 m)
Weight: 190.5 lbs. (86.4 kg)

FIGHTING

MANECTRIC

Height: 4'11" (1.5 m)
Weight: 88.6 lbs. (40.2 kg)

ELECTRIC

MARSHTOMP

Height: 2'04" (0.7 m)
Weight: 61.7 lbs. (28.0 kg)

WATER | GROUND

MASQUERAIN

Height: 2'07" (0.8 m)
Weight: 7.9 lbs. (3.6 kg)

BUG | FLYING

MAWILE

Height: 2'00" (0.6 m)
Weight: 25.4 lbs. (11.5 kg)

STEEL

MEDICHAM

Height: 4'03" (1.3 m)
Weight: 69.4 lbs. (31.5 kg)

FIGHTING | PSYCHIC

MEDITITE
Height: 2'00" (0.6 m)
Weight: 24.7 lbs. (11.2 kg)

FIGHTING | PSYCHIC

METAGROSS

Height: 5'03" (1.6 m)
Weight: 1212.5 lbs. (550.0 kg)

STEEL | PSYCHIC

METANG

Height: 3'11" (1.2 m)
Weight: 446.4 lbs. (202.5 kg)

STEEL | PSYCHIC

MIGHTYENA

Height: 3'03" (1.0 m)
Weight: 81.6 lbs. (37.0 kg)

DARK

MILOTIC

Height: 20'04" (6.2 m)
Weight: 357.1 lbs. (162.0 kg)

WATER

MINUN

Height: 1'04" (0.4 m)
Weight: 9.3 lbs. (4.2 kg)

ELECTRIC

MUDKIP

Height: 1'04" (0.4 m)
Weight: 16.8 lbs. (7.6 kg)

WATER

NINCADA

Height: 1'08" (0.5 m)
Weight: 12.1 lbs. (5.5 kg)

BUG | GROUND

NINJASK

Height: 2'07" (0.8 m)
Weight: 26.5 lbs. (12.0 kg)

BUG | FLYING

NOSEPASS

Height: 3'03" (1.0 m)
Weight: 213.8 lbs. (97.0 kg)

ROCK

NUMEL

Height: 2'04" (0.7 m)
Weight: 52.9 lbs. (24.0 kg)

FIRE | GROUND

NUZLEAF

Height: 3'03" (1.0 m)
Weight: 61.7 lbs. (28.0 kg)

GRASS | DARK

PELIPPER

Height: 3'11" (1.2 m)
Weight: 61.7 lbs. (28.0 kg)

WATER | FLYING

PLUSLE

Height: 1'04" (0.4 m)
Weight: 9.3 lbs. (4.2 kg)

ELECTRIC

POOCHYENA

Height: 1'08" (0.5 m)
Weight: 30.0 lbs. (13.6 kg)

DARK

RALTS

Height: 1'04" (0.4 m)
Weight: 14.6 lbs. (6.6 kg)

PSYCHIC

RAYQUAZA

Height: 23'00" (7.0 m)
Weight: 455.2 lbs. (206.5 kg)

DRAGON | FLYING

REGICE

Height: 5'11" (1.8 m)
Weight: 385.8 lbs. (175.0 kg)

ICE

REGIROCK

Height: 5'07" (1.7 m)
Weight: 507.1 lbs. (230.0 kg)

ROCK

REGISTEEL

Height: 6'03" (1.9 m)
Weight: 451.9 lbs. (205.0 kg)

STEEL

RELICANTH

Height: 3'03" (1.0 m)
Weight: 51.6 lbs. (23.4 kg)

WATER | ROCK

ROSELIA

Height: 1'00" (0.3 m)
Weight: 4.4 lbs. (2.0 kg)

GRASS | POISON

SABLEYE

Height: 1'08" (0.5 m)
Weight: 24.3 lbs. (11.0 kg)

DARK | GHOST

SALAMENCE

Height: 4'11" (1.5 m)
Weight: 226.2 lbs. (102.6 kg)

DRAGON | FLYING

SCEPTILE

Height: 5'07" (1.7 m)
Weight: 115.1 lbs. (52.2 kg)

GRASS

SEALEO
Height: 3'07" (1.1 m)
Weight: 193.1 lbs. (87.6 kg)

ICE | WATER

SEEDOT
Height: 1'08" (0.5 m)
Weight: 8.8 lbs. (4.0 kg)

GRASS

SEVIPER
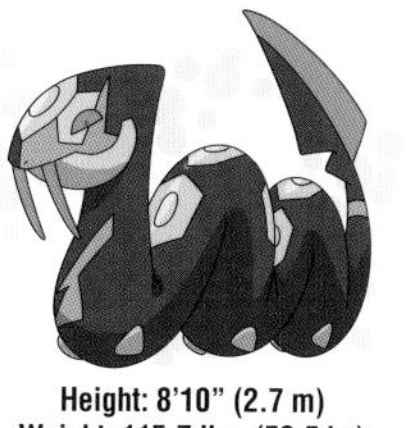
Height: 8'10" (2.7 m)
Weight: 115.7 lbs. (52.5 kg)
POISON

SHARPEDO
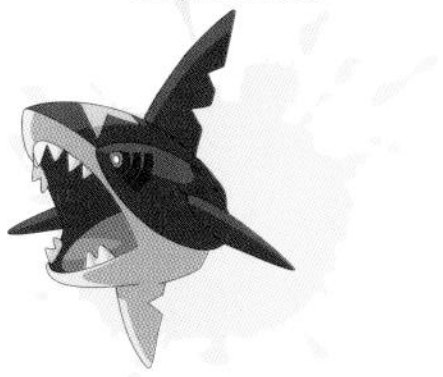
Height: 5'11" (1.8 m)
Weight: 195.8 lbs. (88.8 kg)
WATER DARK

SHEDINJA
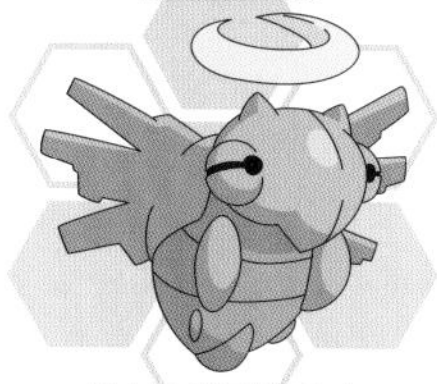
Height: 2'07" (0.8 m)
Weight: 2.6 lbs. (1.2 kg)
BUG GHOST

SHELGON
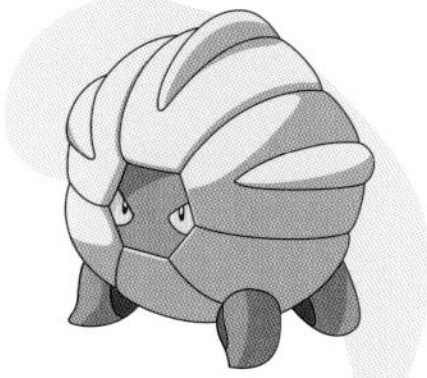
Height: 3'07" (1.1 m)
Weight: 243.6 lbs. (110.5 kg)
DRAGON

SHIFTRY
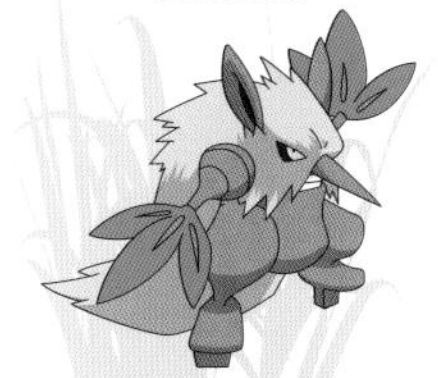
Height: 4'03" (1.3 m)
Weight: 131.4 lbs. (59.6 kg)
GRASS DARK

SHROOMISH
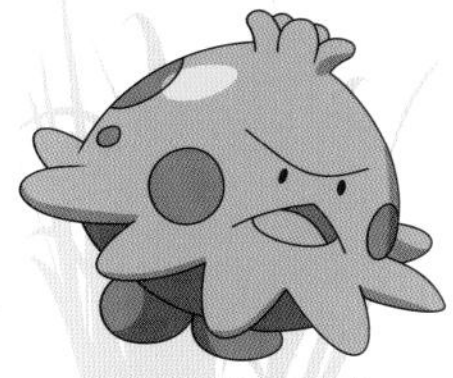
Height: 1'04" (0.4 m)
Weight: 9.9 lbs. (4.5 kg)
GRASS

SHUPPET
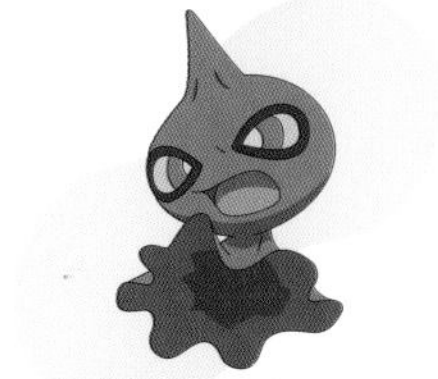
Height: 2'00" (0.6 m)
Weight: 5.1 lbs. (2.3 kg)
GHOST

SILCOON
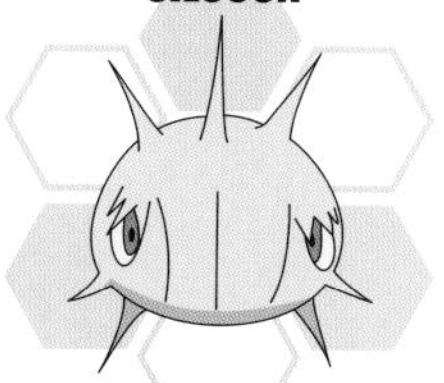
Height: 2'00" (0.6 m)
Weight: 22.0 lbs. (10.0 kg)
BUG

SKITTY
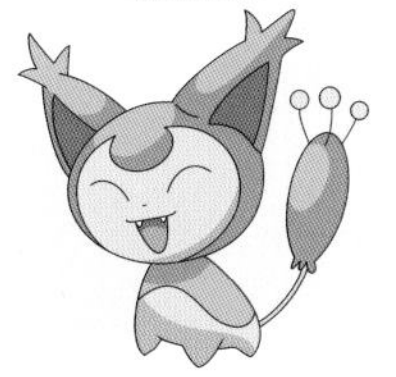
Height: 2'00" (0.6 m)
Weight: 24.3 lbs. (11.0 kg)
NORMAL

SLAKING
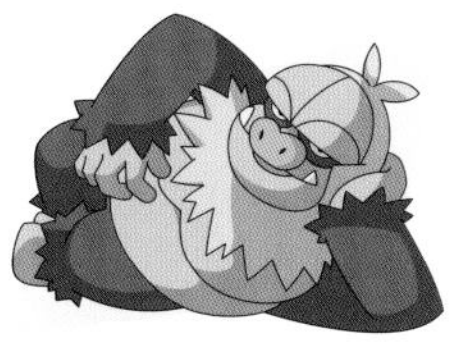
Height: 6'07" (2.0 m)
Weight: 287.7 lbs. (130.5 kg)
NORMAL

SLAKOTH
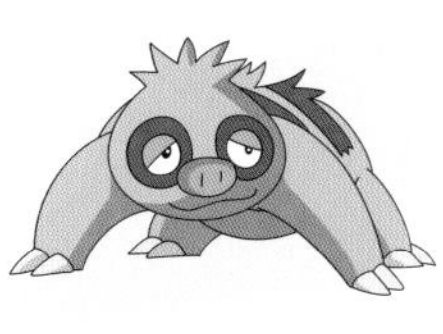
Height: 2'07" (0.8 m)
Weight: 52.9 lbs. (24.0 kg)
NORMAL

SNORUNT
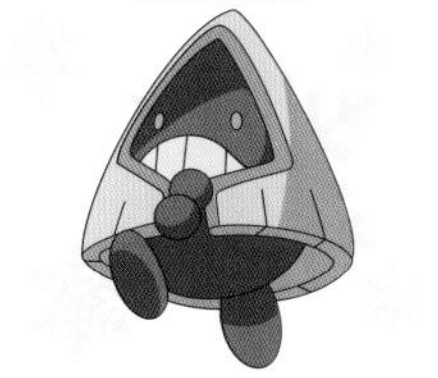
Height: 2'04" (0.7 m)
Weight: 37.0 lbs. (16.8 kg)
ICE

SOLROCK
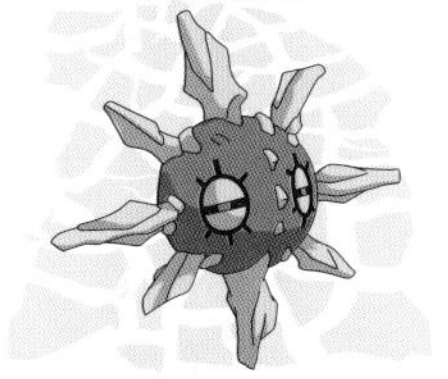
Height: 3'11" (1.2 m)
Weight: 339.5 lbs. (154.0 kg)
ROCK PSYCHIC

SPHEAL
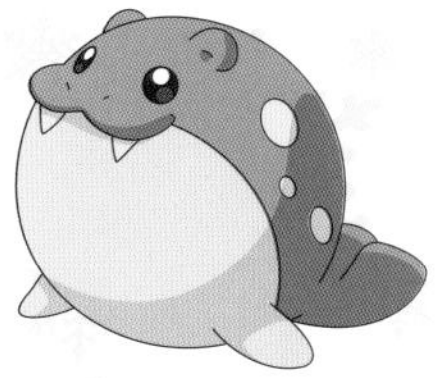
Height: 2'07" (0.8 m)
Weight: 87.1 lbs. (39.5 kg)
ICE WATER

SPINDA
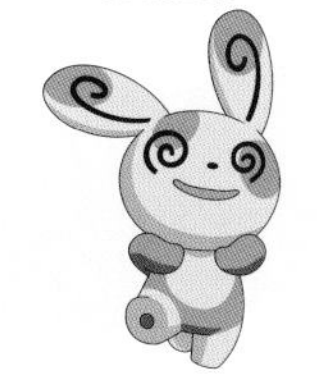
Height: 3'07" (1.1 m)
Weight: 11.0 lbs. (5.0 kg)
NORMAL

SPOINK
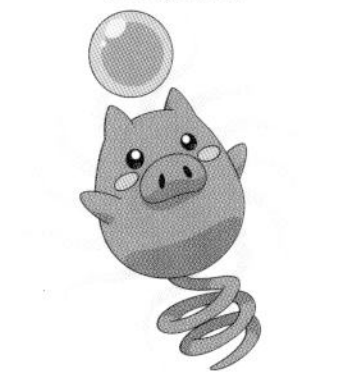
Height: 2'04" (0.7 m)
Weight: 67.5 lbs. (30.6 kg)
PSYCHIC

SURSKIT
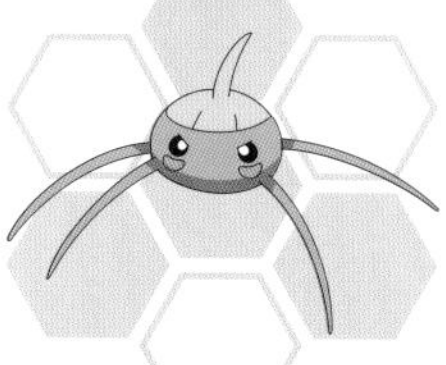
Height: 1'08" (0.5 m)
Weight: 3.7 lbs. (1.7 kg)
BUG WATER

SWABLU
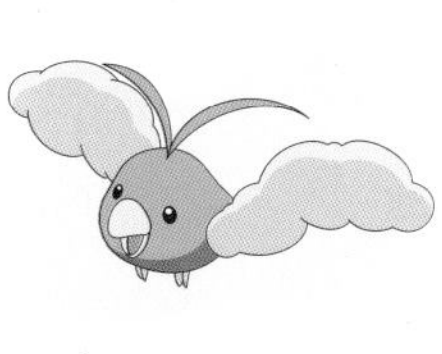
Height: 1'04" (0.4 m)
Weight: 2.6 lbs. (1.2 kg)
NORMAL FLYING

SWALOT
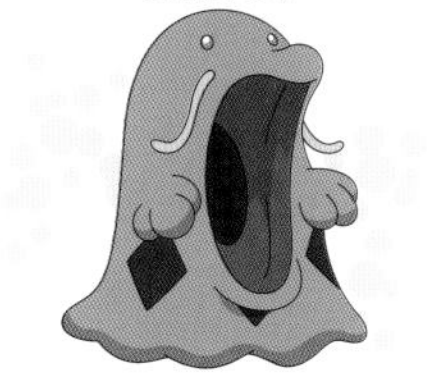
Height: 5'07" (1.7 m)
Weight: 176.4 lbs. (80.0 kg)
POISON

SWAMPERT
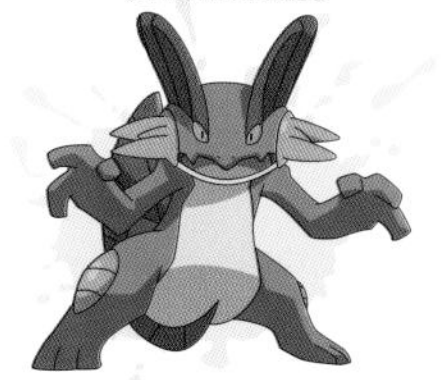
Height: 4'11" (1.5 m)
Weight: 180.6 lbs. (81.9 kg)
WATER GROUND

SWELLOW
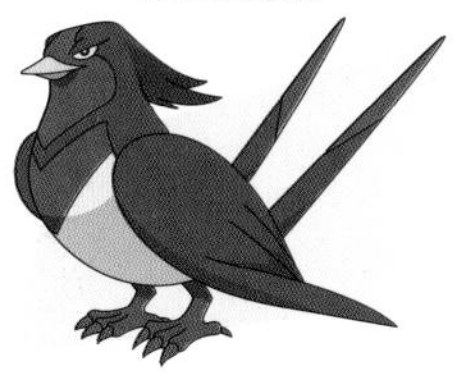
Height: 2'04" (0.7 m)
Weight: 43.7 lbs. (19.8 kg)
NORMAL FLYING

TAILLOW
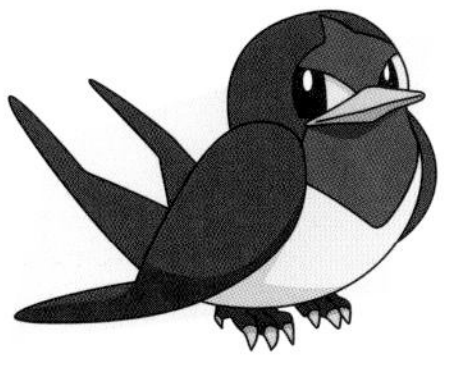
Height: 1'00" (0.3 m)
Weight: 5.1 lbs. (2.3 kg)
NORMAL FLYING

TORCHIC
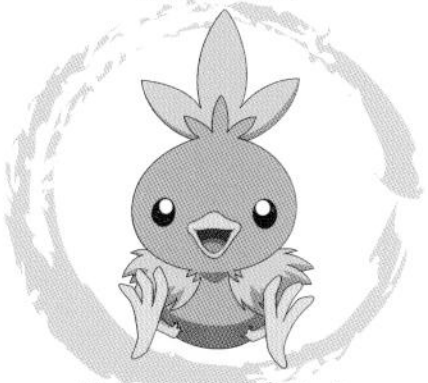
Height: 1'04" (0.4 m)
Weight: 5.5 lbs. (2.5 kg)
FIRE

TORKOAL
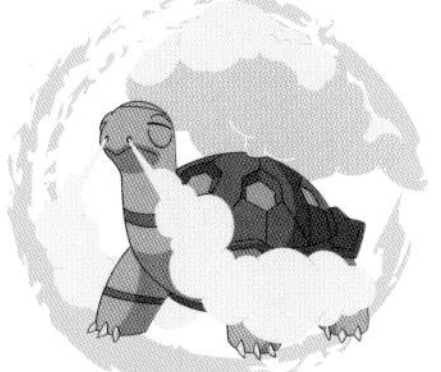
Height: 1'08" (0.5 m)
Weight: 177.2 lbs. (80.4 kg)
FIRE

TRAPINCH
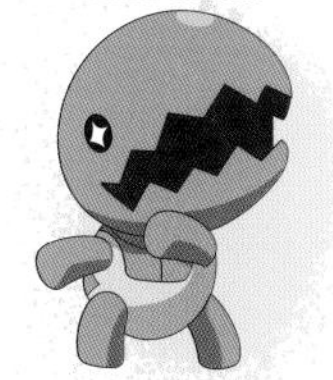
Height: 2'04" (0.7 m)
Weight: 33.1 lbs. (15.0 kg)
GROUND

TREECKO
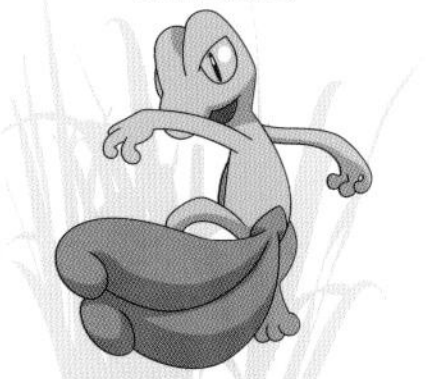
Height: 1'08" (0.5 m)
Weight: 11.0 lbs. (5.0 kg)
GRASS

TROPIUS
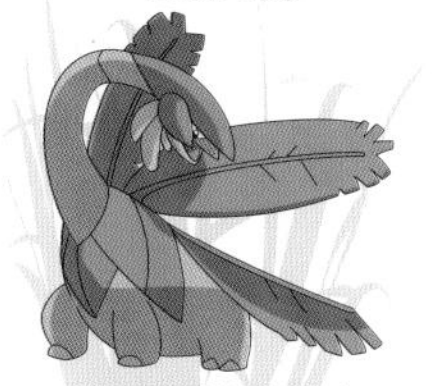
Height: 6'07" (2.0 m)
Weight: 220.5 lbs. (100.0 kg)
GRASS FLYING

VIBRAVA
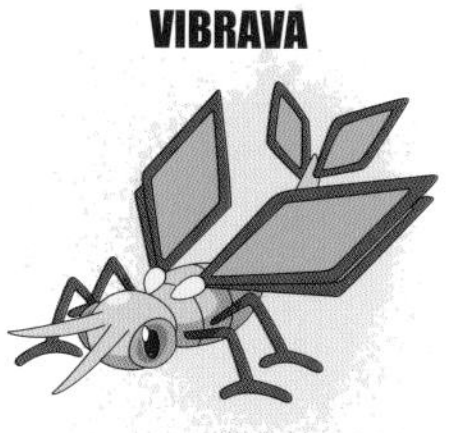
Height: 3'07" (1.1 m)
Weight: 33.7 lbs. (15.3 kg)
GROUND DRAGON

VIGOROTH
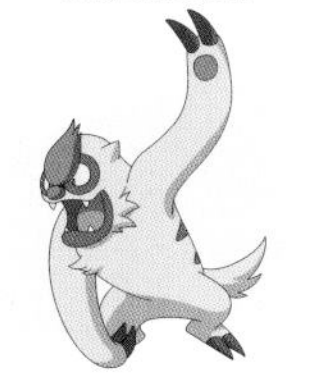
Height: 4'07" (1.4 m)
Weight: 102.5 lbs. (46.5 kg)
NORMAL

VOLBEAT
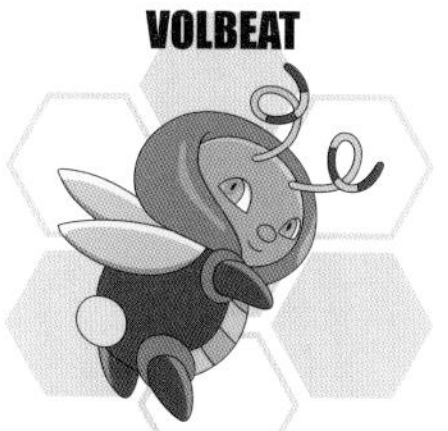
Height: 2'04" (0.7 m)
Weight: 39.0 lbs. (17.7 kg)
BUG

WAILMER
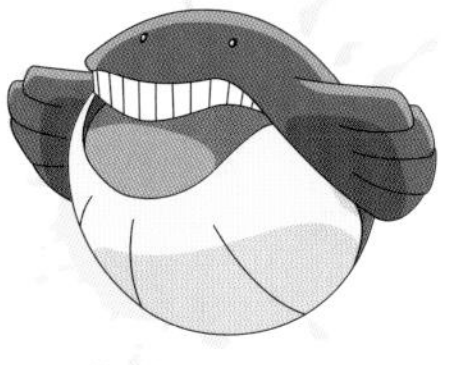
Height: 6'07" (2.0 m)
Weight: 286.6 lbs. (130.0 kg)
WATER

WAILORD
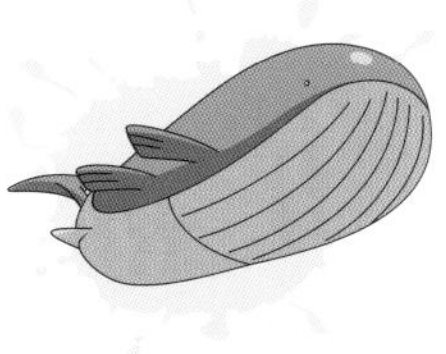
Height: 47'07" (14.5 m)
Weight: 877.4 lbs. (398.0 kg)
WATER

WALREIN
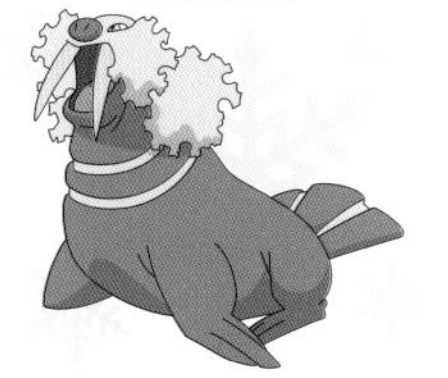
Height: 4'07" (1.4 m)
Weight: 332.0 lbs. (150.6 kg)
ICE WATER

WHISCASH
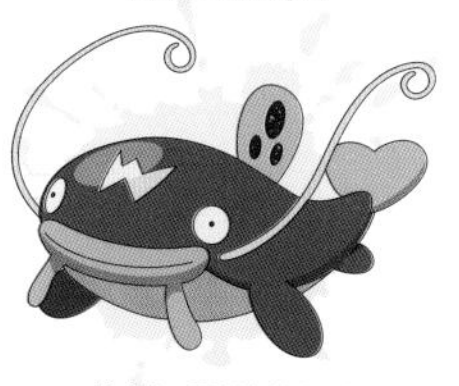
Height: 2'11" (0.9 m)
Weight: 52.0 lbs. (23.6 kg)
WATER GROUND

WHISMUR
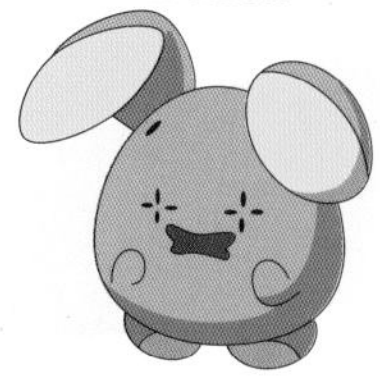
Height: 2'00" (0.6 m)
Weight: 35.9 lbs. (16.3 kg)
NORMAL

WINGULL
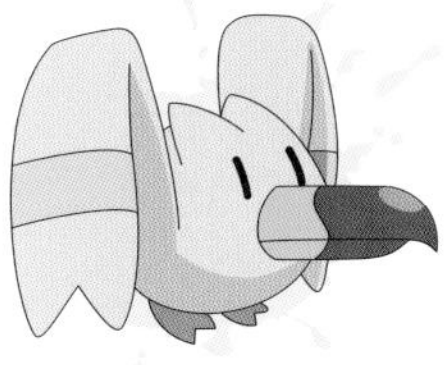
Height: 2'00" (0.6 m)
Weight: 20.9 lbs. (9.5 kg)
WATER FLYING

WURMPLE
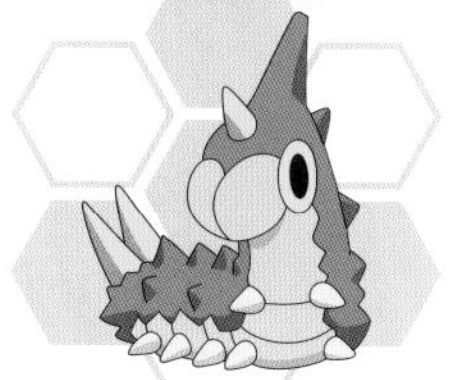
Height: 1'00" (0.3 m)
Weight: 7.9 lbs. (3.6 kg)
BUG

WYNAUT
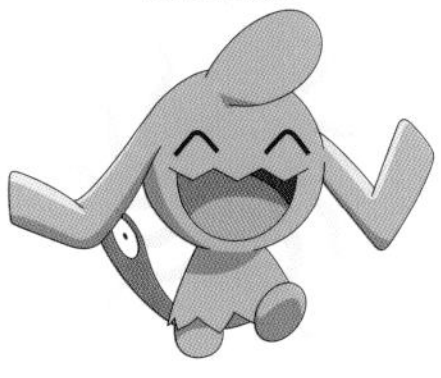
Height: 2'00" (0.6 m)
Weight: 30.9 lbs. (14.0 kg)
PSYCHIC

ZANGOOSE
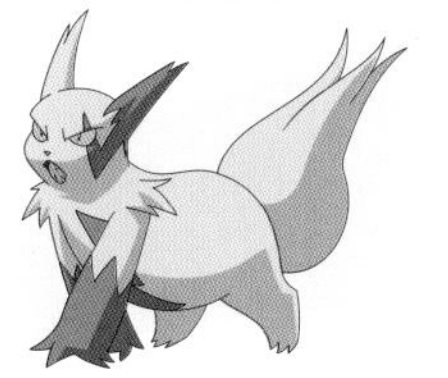
Height: 4'03" (1.3 m)
Weight: 88.8 lbs. (40.3 kg)
NORMAL

ZIGZAGOON
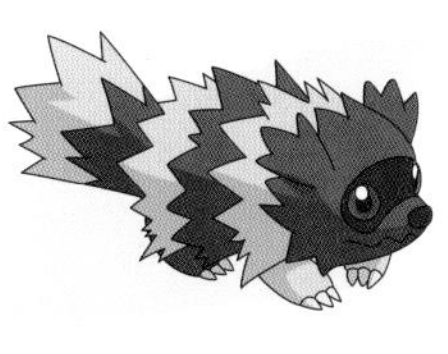
Height: 1'04" (0.4 m)
Weight: 38.6 lbs. (17.5 kg)
NORMAL

SINNOH

Sinnoh is a vast region bisected by Mt. Coronet. Professor Rowan is the resident Pokémon Professor, hailing from Sandgem Town. Sinnoh is an amazing place, and is the only region visited by Ash to have a substantial area covered in snow.

Though a large majority of Sinnoh is land, fresh-water lakes are prevelant within the region proper. Three rather important lakes are Verity in the west, Acuity in the north, and Valor in the east. These three lakes are home to Mesprit, Uxie, and Azelf. The entire northwest of the region is dominated by the Eterna Forest. Many Trainers, including Ash, have gotten lost in this massive forest.

Jubilife is the largest city in Sinnoh, and it is very modern. Hearthome City is an active city with many things to do. People from all over the world of Pokémon come to Hearthome to test their skill in the Tag Battle.

DAWN

After her 10th birthday, this spirited young girl left her home in Sinnoh's Twinleaf Town to see the world and become a great Pokémon Coordinator. She first met Ash after she and her Piplup helped save Ash's Pikachu, and since then she's traveled with Ash and Brock on their Sinnoh adventures, competing in Pokémon Contests along the way.

Pokétch

Dawn earned her Pokétch after helping stop Team Rocket pass out a wave of fake Pokétch. One of her newest Pokétch applications is the Coin Toss application, which she uses to help decide which way to go—or who gets to go first in a Pokémon battle!

THE SURPRISING VOICE OF REASON

Dawn hasn't had quite as many adventures as Ash and Brock, but that often comes as an asset! For one thing, Dawn hasn't had nearly as much experience with Team Rocket and their various schemes. So when Team Rocket suggests that the "twerps" help them train Cacnea, Ash and Brock cheerfully agree to help—while Dawn is openly skeptical of any plan that helps makes the villains even stronger.

A SENSE OF STYLE

Dawn likes to dress up—so much so that her mother had to stop her from bringing a suitcase full of clothes on her journey! Being a Coordinator may involve looking good on stage, but Dawn is determined to stay stylish at all times, even if it means having Piplup use BubbleBeam to help fix her bedhead.

A CRISIS OF CONFIDENCE

Normally, Dawn is upbeat and cheerful—her catchphrase is "No need to worry!" But after two Contests in a row where she fails to advance beyond the first round, she starts to doubt whether she should even continue competing in Contests at all. Even the advice and encouragement of her rivals Zoey and Kenny aren't enough to keep her spirits up, though Dawn tries to hide her turmoil behind her usual happy demeanor. In Veilstone City, Dawn meets Maylene, a Gym Leader suffering from a similar crisis of confidence, and Dawn challenges her to a Gym battle. Dawn loses the match, but both she and Maylene regain their fighting spirit.

DAWN'S BIG SECRET

All of Dawn's childhood friends call her "Dee-Dee," for reasons that Dawn is determined to keep a secret. Ash has asked Dawn's friends to explain the story behind the name, but so far, nobody's telling…

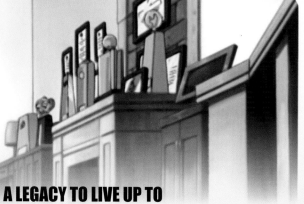

A LEGACY TO LIVE UP TO

Dawn's mother Johanna was a prize-winning Coordinator, and Dawn dreams of following in her footsteps. As a good luck charm, Dawn carries her mother's first Contest Ribbon with her on her journey.

A Full-Fledged Heroine

Not only is Dawn the latest Trainer to join Ash on his travels, she represents a new development in the world of Pokémon. Ash lives for his quest to become a Pokémon Master, and although we've met his mother Delia, little else is known about his past. Ash was joined by Brock and Misty, both characters who have families and Gym Leader responsibilities to deal with. With May, Ash was joined by a new and more nuanced character: not only did she have a Gym Leader father to deal with, but she also had to handle the responsibility of looking after her little brother Max.

But perhaps more so than any of Ash's other travel companions, Dawn is a fully realized character. Like Brock, Misty, and May, Dawn has a family—her mother, Johanna—that weighs on her mind. As with May, we also see snippets of Dawn's history in flashbacks, including embarrassing moments from her childhood. But what sets Dawn apart is that we also see her childhood friends, including Leona, her friend since kindergarten.

Dawn's Pokémon

PIPLUP

Piplup, Dawn's first Pokémon, is proud, sassy, and doesn't always follow Dawn's directions. Dawn met Piplup after it ran out of Professor Rowan's research center, and even though they didn't get along, they had to work together to escape some wild Ariados.

PACHIRISU

Pachirisu was so cute that Dawn just had to catch it after spotting it in the wild. But after an exhausting chase and capture, Dawn discovered that Pachirisu was too hyperactive to listen to any of her commands, and she reluctantly released it. Fortunately, she and Pachirisu were reunited, and this Electric-type Pokémon remains as energetic as ever—although its lack of control over its Discharge move still comes as a shock.

BUNEARY

Buneary was Dawn's first Pokémon capture, and it certainly wasn't an easy one. But it's more than happy to travel with Dawn and her friends, as it seems to have a real crush on Ash's Pikachu.

AMBIPOM

After Ash realized that his Aipom loved being in Contests, he traded it to Dawn in exchange for her Buizel. Aipom evolved into Ambipom and made its Contest debut with Dawn in the Solaceon Town Contest, but the pair didn't make it past the first round.

PROFESSOR ROWAN

The Sinnoh region may seem intimidating until you realize the man behind the research there is Professor Rowan. Although he may seem menacing and forceful, he is actually one of the most knowledgeable researchers around—second only to Oak.

Rowan specializes in the evolutionary processes and habits of Pokémon. He tries to demonstrate that Pokémon can mostly be linked to each other through evolution.

Professor Rowan is responsible for handing out the starting Pokémon to Trainers in the Sinnoh region from his lab outside Sandgem Town. However, he also provides a Pokédex to Dawn as well. Dawn's Pokédex is quite unique to say the least—it's pink!

Rowan's Pokémon

STARLY AND STARAPTOR

Starly is one of the Pokémon seen in Rowan's lab. The researchers under Rowan are conducting evolution research on Starly and Staraptor before Rowan returns. Eventually, Staraptor is the one that brings Chimchar back.

HAIKU? GESUNDHEIT!

Dawn recognizes Professor Oak as a purveyor of fine Pokémon poetry and the author of some original works. Professor Rowan, however, derides Oak for spending more time on his poetry than on his research. Apparently, they have a history that goes way back and Professor Rowan seems to be the more senior researcher of the two.

> Professor Rowan and Professor Oak share a lab fixture that may explain their commitment to an environmentally sound Pokémon world: both labs contain windmills!

ZOEY

A Coordinator from Snowpoint City who is Dawn's friend as well as her rival, Zoey first met Dawn by chance in the Jubilife Contest. Zoey, who already had a ribbon by that time, quickly fell into the role of Dawn's cool older friend (though Zoey's exact age is unknown). She's not afraid to stand up for herself or for Dawn. When Jessie challenges Dawn to a double battle, hoping to score an easy win on a novice, Zoey senses Jessie's trick and takes up the challenge herself.

Although Zoey always seems to have it together, she can admit that she gets nervous during Contests or upset about a loss. She doesn't measure her performance strictly in terms of ribbons, though, and she won't let herself, or her friends, succumb to second-guessing after a loss. So after Dawn's disappointing performance in the Solaceon Contest, Zoey heads over to dispel Dawn's blues and get her back on the right track.

Zoey is serious about Contests, and she expects everyone else to be dedicated, too. She doesn't believe it's possible to excel at both Contests and Gym Battles. But after Nando defeats her in a Contest, she realizes that even a Coordinator can learn from Gym battling. She's the one who suggests that Ash trade his Contest-loving Aipom for Dawn's battle-loving Buizel.

GLAMEOW

Like Dawn's other role model, her mother Johanna, Zoey also has a Glameow. Her Glameow can uncurl its tail and use it to strike, a move that catches opponents by surprise.

Zoey's Pokémon

MISDREAVUS

She has used Misdreavus in the Jubilife Contest and the Wallace Cup. She does use it during the appeals round, with its highly effective Shock Wave attack.

FINNEON

Not much is known about Finneon at this point. It has only been used in the Wallace Cup.

Rowan actually gives Ash Aipom's Poké Ball, which he received from Professor Oak, and he delivers a package from Delia Ketchum that contains new clothes. You'd think he'd have more important work to do.

KENNY

A regular kid from Twinleaf Town, Kenny is a Pokémon Coordinator who's known Dawn since their nursery school days. He enjoys having a chance to reveal Dawn's embarrassing childhood moments to her new friends, too.

Even though Kenny loves to tease Dawn and occasionally puts on a cocky attitude, he's still a young boy who's not always as tough as he wants to appear. When he's trapped in the Solaceon Ruins along with Ash and Brock, he's terrified by the strangeness of the place until Ash reminds him to put on a brave face for his Pokémon.

Kenny's Pokémon

PRINPLUP
Prinplup gets along fine with its Trainer, but it's a proud Pokémon and not always friendly towards everyone else.

BRELOOM
After Kenny's Breloom uses Energy Ball in a friendly battle against Ash, Ash asks Kenny to help teach the move to his Turtwig.

ALAKAZAM
Kenny uses it in the appeals round of Floaroma Contest.

NANDO

This self-styled Pokémon Bard adds a musical touch to almost everything he does, from conversations to Contests. He's exceedingly thoughtful and polite; in Pokémon battles, he even gives his Pokémon gentle requests instead of commands.

Despite his demeanor, he could be said to be a rival of both Ash and Dawn; unable to decide between pursuing Pokémon Contests or Gym battles, he battled both Trainers and was inspired to compete in Contests *and* Gym battles. Nando's plan seems to be paying off, as he's won at the Eterna Gym and earned two ribbons—the second ribbon was earned by defeating Zoey in the finals of the Hearthome Contest.

SHELLOS
After Dawn caught her Buizel, Zoey stuck around to do some more fishing and came up with this Shellos. She's used it as an effective Contest partner for Glameow.

Two Degrees of Separation
Prior to the Jubilife Contest, both Zoey and Kenny competed in a Contest where Zoey beat Kenny and came out the winner—that's how Zoey won her first ribbon. The two Coordinators didn't know each other before the Contest; although Zoey and Kenny have Dawn in common, up until now, Dawn has yet to meet up with both of them at the same time.

Nando's Pokémon

ROSELIA
Nando's Roselia evolved from a Budew during a battle with Ash's Pikachu.

SUNFLORA
Nando and his Sunflora were mistakenly framed for stealing the Adamant Orb from the Eterna Historical Museum, but Sunflora helped track down the real perpetrators: Team Rocket.

KRICKETUNE
When teamed with Sunflora's Grasswhistle, Kricketune can use Sing to put on a musical performance that will wow a Contest audience.

PAUL

On and off the battlefield, rival Pokémon Trainers are often friends, or at least good sports. Even Ash's first real rival, Gary Oak, is Ash's friend and ally as well. But Paul, a Trainer who treats Pokémon more like a game than a matter of living, feeling creatures, isn't here to be polite to anyone—least of all Ash. Paul is here to win.

Hailing from Veilstone City, Paul is a pragmatic, cold-hearted Trainer who believes in strength, victory, and not much else. He's no cheater, but to him, a win is a win regardless of whether it was won by kindness or cruelty. And kindness isn't in Paul's vocabulary: he expects 100% performance from his Pokémon at all times, never hesitating to criticize or release Pokémon who fail to fulfill expectations. Even at the moment of capture, Paul thinks only about what power a Pokémon has to offer, using his Pokédex to check the Pokémon he catches and keeping only Pokémon that meet his requirements. There's no room for weakness on his team.

WHEN A LIFE TOUCHES ANOTHER LIFE...

Cynthia, the top Trainer in Sinnoh, has seen Paul's behavior firsthand. But, unlike Ash, she doesn't react with outrage. She sees her younger self in Paul, a Trainer whose only thought is to become stronger, and gently urges him to think of his Pokémon not as tools but like people, each with their own unique personality. Although Ash and his friends remind Paul of Cynthia's lesson, it remains to be seen whether her words will have any effect.

ELEKID

Raised by Paul from an Elekid, Electabuzz has an attitude like its Trainer and an ongoing feud with Pikachu.

TURTWIG

Paul's very first Pokémon was a Turtwig. It's reached its final evolved form: a massive Torterra.

Most Trainers want their Pokémon to avoid being hurt. But if he can get an advantage out of it, Paul orders his Pokémon to take damage during a battle; it's one of his ruthless but effective strategies.

Ash is determined to beat Paul and prove friendship and cooperation are the best ways to train Pokémon, but to his chagrin, his best results against Paul are only draws. Ash can barely even get Paul's attention, which only causes Ash's frustration to build. But on some level, Paul *has* been paying attention to Ash— Ash's Pokémon, that is. He couldn't care less about Ash's speeches on trust and friendship; instead, he's more interested in Pikachu's Volt Tackle.

MAGMAR

This Magmar seems to have replaced Chimchar. Paul used it in his Veilstone Gym battle, exploiting Magmar's type advantage against Gym Leader Maylene's Lucario.

...SOMETHING NEW IS BORN?

Paul's Electabuzz seems to take after him; even when it was an Elekid. It doesn't get along with Ash's Pikachu, but in Veilstone City, Electabuzz had a chance to witness Ash's devotion toward his Pokémon. And as for Chimchar, Ash's support and kindess hasn't erased the memories of its brutal times with Paul. Chimchar still has some unfinished business to settle with its former Trainer.

Paul's Pokémon

URSARING

Caught in the Bewilder Forrest, Ursaring packs a mighty Hyper Beam. It takes on its former teammate Chimchar in a battle so brutal, it traumatizes Chimchar into unleashing its true power.

MURKROW

Paul caught his Murkrow during his travels outside the Sinnoh region. It evolves into Honchkrow in a battle with Gym Leader Maylene in Veilstone City.

HONCHKROW

WEAVILE

This Weavile is another Pokémon Paul caught during his travels in the Sinnoh region.

GLISCOR

In a city on the route back to Veilstone City, Paul heard about a tough Gliscor and decided to catch it.

Chimchar

Is this the one that Paul let get away? Paul knew his Chimchar had amazing potential; when he first saw it in the wild, it unleashed an almost uncontrollable power to defeat a gang of Zangoose that had it cornered and scared. Thinking this power would be useful for the Pokémon League, Paul asked Chimchar to come with him. Chimchar believed it could become strong this way, but Paul's harsh training methods—far beyond anything he used on his other Pokémon—never managed to reawaken that power in Chimchar.

During the Hearthome City Tag Battle Tournament, Chimchar froze up when again confronted with a Zangoose—so Paul, disgusted, deliberately turned his back on his own Pokémon. Fortunately for Chimchar, after the battle it found a new, gentler Trainer in Ash. Paul has even seen Ash unlock Chimchar's true power, though it's still uncontrolled and dangerous.

MINDING HIS MANNERS

Paul may be mean, but he's not mean enough to think he can treat *everyone* that way. When it comes to Nurse Joy and other authority figures, such as Gym Leader Roark, Paul sometimes even says "thank you." And even though it may have been arrogant of Paul to challenge Cynthia, the Sinnoh Champion, he didn't give her attitude. After she decisively defeated him in battle, she made a number of suggestions to that which he reluctantly followed.

On the other hand, Paul will turn on anyone he doesn't respect, even a Gym Leader. After an easy victory over Veilstone Gym Leader Maylene, Paul didn't hesitate to insult her to her face.

Paul's most candid conversation to date is not with Ash, but with Brock. When Brock approached Paul with serious concerns about Chimchar's health, Paul explained how he met Chimchar and why he pushes Chimchar to the breaking point.

Reggie

Reggie is the complete opposite of his younger brother Paul. Mild-manned and pleasant, Reggie is a Pokémon breeder who is now back in Veilstone City. Like his brother Paul, Reggie traveled to other regions before returning to Sinnoh.

These display cases full of badges don't belong to Paul—they're Reggie's! Kanto, Johto, Hoenn, Sinnoh, and the Battle Frontier: Reggie's seen and battled it all.

Paul can leave some of his Pokémon with Reggie, then call to have Reggie send over whatever Pokémon he needs for a battle. Paul isn't any more outwardly friendly towards his brother than he is with anyone else, but he did tell Reggie about Ash and Pikachu's Volt Tackle.

TEAM ROCKET AND THE "TWERPS"

Team Rocket has bedeviled Ash and his friends since the beginning, but these Pokémon thieves can put their criminal instincts aside and work with the "twerps" when it's necessary. Especially James and Meowth, who are more kind-hearted than they look. Although Team Rocket usually doesn't take long to break the truce, they've cooperated with Ash and his friends on more occasions than one would think.

UNITED TO DEFEAT A COMMON FOE

Shortly after Ash and his friends land on Mandarin Island in the Orange Islands, Pikachu and Togepi suddenly turn on Ash and Misty. Meowth acts strangely and runs from Team Rocket, too. Butch and Cassidy are using a Drowzee to control all the Pokémon in the area; Jessie and James try to beat them and get Meowth back, but to no avail. Ash and his friends help patch up Jessie and James, then convince them to join the fight against Butch and Cassidy.

After Butch and Cassidy are busted, Team Rocket is up for a special award and the gratitude of the locals, but playing the hero would be bad for their reputation, so they skip out on the accolades.

SOMETIMES IT'S JUST THE RIGHT THING TO DO

When Brock helps Jaco the Pokémon breeder forge a working relationship with his Electrike, their hard work and dedication touches James and Meowth. The two Team Rocket members even stop Jessie in the middle of an attempt to steal Electrike, refusing to let her destroy the deepening partnership between Electrike and Jaco.

James and Meowth even volunteer to help Jaco and Electrike train; with their experience getting blasted by Pikachu, they're happy to provide moving targets for Electrike's Thunder attacks. They still can't resist the chance to try and steal Pikachu, but when Electrike evolves into Manectric and blasts them off with Thunder, they're just pleased that it's finally mastered its electric attack.

SOMETIMES THERE'S JUST NO OTHER CHOICE

When angry Ursaring (on a mating-season rampage) force both heroes and bad guys to scatter and regroup, Jessie finds herself with Brock and Ash, while James and Meowth end up with Misty. Everyone has to call a temporary truce if they want to make it out of the forest, and although Team Rocket's members can't quite put their criminal ways aside, seeing the way the other half lives causes Team Rocket to reflect on their own lives.

Team Rocket is awed by Brock's delicious cooking, and Jessie is also startled by Brock's generosity when their group bunks down for the night.

WE'RE JUST HERE FOR MORAL SUPPORT

When Ash and Pikachu first took on Lt. Surge at the Vermillion City Gym, Pikachu received a sound drubbing at the hands of Lt. Surge's Raichu. Pikachu remained determined to defeat Raichu under its own power. This courage is so touching to Team Rocket that they secretly root for Pikachu to win the rematch.

Team Rocket pulled for Chimchar in the Hearthome Tag Tournament; they'd seen how harshly Paul treated his Chimchar, and it was too much for even them to condone. Later, Meowth sees Chimchar struggle to adjust to Ash's kindness, and has a moonlight heart-to-heart with the troubled Fire-type.

Can You Keep a Secret?

Sometimes Team Rocket is absolutely, 100% sincere about asking for cooperation. When James' Chimecho falls ill, he takes it to his Nanny and Pop-Pop for treatment. He can't bear to tell the kindly couple what he does for a living, so he passes himself off as a company president. But May's sick Munchlax is also recuperating under Nanny and Pop-Pop's care, so James earnestly begs the twerps to help maintain his charade.

WANTED DANGEROUS
SINNOH'S MOST WANTED

Team Galactic and Team Rocket aren't the only threats to peace in Sinnoh—there are criminals both big and small, but one of the biggest of them all is the ruthless mercenary known as Pokémon Hunter J.

POKÉMON HUNTER J

Even the combined efforts of Officer Jenny and the Pokémon Rangers have yet to stop Pokémon Hunter J and her heartless business. No one knows her true identity, but they know her work: she's a Pokémon Hunter, a mercenary who captures Pokémon with the sole intent of selling them to willing buyers. She doesn't stop at capturing wild Pokémon, either—if she sees a Pokémon she needs or thinks she can sell at a good price, she'll take it and add it to her sales catalog regardless of whether it already has an owner.

What makes J particularly dangerous is that she's a pro at what she does. She takes the same business-like approach towards her clients as she does her targets. She never fawns over a client and won't hesitate to cut off any clients who break a deal. As for her targets, she treats valuable Pokémon with care, but shows no mercy toward anything without a resale value. Being a member of her crew is no guarantee of safe conduct, either; she once jettisoned an entire hangar of her ship, together with all the crew onboard.

Good vs. Evil

Ash and his friends have run into J more times than they care to think about. First, she grabbed Pikachu and they had to get it back along with a Trainer's stolen Gardevoir. Then she came after a group of Shieldon that Gary was studying, so they had to help. Finally, she was hired to steal a Riolu, and it took the help of Top Ranger Kellyn to assist Ash and his friends in getting Riolu back. Fortunately, although they haven't managed to stop her yet, Ash and his allies have thwarted her plan every time they've crossed paths.

TRICKS OF THE TRADE

Pokémon Hunter J's operation includes a fleet of vehicles and a giant airship that can cloak itself to avoid detection, but not all of her equipment is on such a large scale.

Pokémon Hunter J doesn't do all the dirty work herself—she has an ample crew of subordinates who help run the ship and grab Pokémon. These minions have Golbat of their own, too.

Her visor doubles as a data display, letting her view maps and live information that help track her targets.

The gauntlet on her left wrist fires a beam that can freeze Pokémon in stasis. Once a Pokémon is frozen, it can be transferred to a case for easier transport and storage.

Pokémon Hunter J's Pokémon

DRAPION, ARIADOS, & SALAMENCE

POKÉMON RANGERS

Just about anywhere you go, you'll find Officer Jenny and her fellow police officers working hard to keep the peace. When it comes to protecting nature and Pokémon, however, you can't do better than the dedicated, highly trained members of the Pokémon Rangers.

WHO ARE THE POKÉMON RANGERS?

Whether the mission is stopping a forest fire or nabbing a Pokémon poacher, you can always rest easy when a Pokémon Ranger is on the case. Their job is to deal with natural disasters or incidents, including issues related to Pokémon. The Ranger Union that oversees Ranger missions also responds to outside requests for assistance, so Rangers sometimes work in conjunction with local authorities such as Nurse Joy or Officer Jenny. But for the most part, Rangers work independently to handle every part of a mission, from initial investigation to resolving the problem and even apprehending criminals.

Because Rangers often operate alone—sometimes even undercover—and can't rely on always having Pokémon around, they have to be confident in their own abilities. Rangers need to be smart, knowledgable about Pokémon, and physically tough. A large part of their success is also due to the key item in every Ranger's arsenal: the Capture Styler.

THE CAPTURE STYLER

Pokémon Rangers use the power of Pokémon to help accomplish their tasks, but not by catching and training Pokémon. Instead, Rangers can "capture" wild Pokémon with a Capture Styler and ask for their help. Usually, this means having a Pokémon use one of its moves or Abilities. As soon as the task at hand is complete, the Pokémon is released with the Ranger's heartfelt thanks.

This makes the Capture Styler essential to a Ranger's job. And because Ranger missions can take them just about anywhere, the Capture Styler is hermetically sealed so that it functions under any and all conditions. It even functions in the face of geomagnetic disturbances that can disrupt Poké Balls and similar devices.

How Does a Capture Styler Work?

By successfully using the Capture Styler on a Pokémon, a Ranger opens the Pokémon's heart and helps it understand the Ranger's friendly intentions. As such, capturing can also be used to help soothe an agitated Pokémon.

In order to calm a Deoxys in pain, Solana must capture it and have it use Recover on itself. The Capture Styler can only be used on a Deoxys in Normal Forme, which means waiting for just the right moment to make the capture.

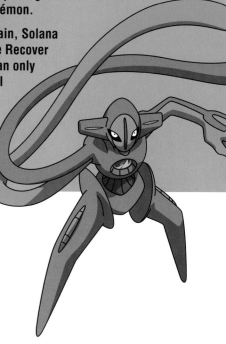

How to Use the Capture Styler

With a flick of the switch, the Capture Styler can be set to Capture Mode and used to capture a wild Pokémon. The Capture Styler's antenna extends when the capture is ready to start. Then, the Capture Styler shoots out a spinning Capture Disc. Using the Styler, the Ranger directs the Capture Disc so that it rapidly encircles the target Pokémon. Once the Capture Disc has made several uninterrupted loops around the target, the capture is complete! The Ranger can now ask the Pokémon to help out.

A true multipurpose gadget, the Capture Styler can also analyze a Pokémon's status and abilities. Rangers use it to determine what Pokémon might be useful in a given situation, or check the health of the Pokémon they encounter.

Vatonage Styler

Unlike the regular Capture Styler, a handheld device usually carried in a holster, the Vatonage Styler is mounted on the forearm. Instead of holding the Styler and making circling motions, the Vatonage Styler lets a Ranger control the Capture Disc by gesturing while wearing a special glove.

RANGER ROLL CALL

SOLANA

This wonder woman has crossed paths with Ash and his friends several times, first in Kanto and now in Sinnoh. Capable and no-nonsense, she's a typical Ranger who's faced some very atypical missions, including helping an injured Celebi and solving the mystery of a distraught Deoxys. Solana takes her work seriously and isn't always thrilled when Ash and his friends try to tag along on one of her big missions, but she's always glad for the help.

Partner Pokémon

Some Rangers travel with a partner Pokémon. Solana's partner Pokémon, Plusle, assists by using Helping Hand to cheer on other Pokémon.

JACKIE

Jackie's rank is 9, and his Capture Styler also differs slightly from the ones seen previously. Unlike other Rangers, Jackie is not tied to a location, but can travel anywhere to solve a case.

KELLYN

Kellyn isn't just any Pokémon Ranger—he's a Top Ranger, which means he has the special skills it takes to use the Vatonage Styler. Both he and Solana work together with Ash during an operation to stop Pokémon Hunter J and return a kidnapped Riolu to its home kingdom.

INSIDE THE POKÉMON LEAGUE

The Pokémon League doesn't often cross Trainer's minds, but it's the organizing body behind the system of Gyms and region-wide tournaments that every Trainer aspires to challenge. In addition, the League is also involved in the process of raising Pokémon to distribute to starting Trainers.

TOURNAMENT ORGANIZATION

The Pokémon League tournaments represent the pinnacle of achievement for Trainers everywhere, and it's important to make sure that everything goes off without a hitch. The League is involved in all aspects from the promulgation of rules and selection of referees to the torch relay that starts a tournament.

POKÉMON JUDGES

Being a referee for Pokémon battles involves more than just waving a few flags, and Hoenn's Bomba Island is where aspiring battle judges learn what it takes. There, the Pokémon Battle Judge Training School puts would-be judges through a rigorous curriculum; knowing how to call a match requires expert knowledge

of Pokémon types, moves, and other characteristics, which allows a judge to gauge whether a Pokémon is down for the count. Only the best of the best will be qualified and selected to referee actual Pokémon League tournaments.

Where Do First Pokémon Come From?

New Trainers begin their adventures with one of three first Pokémon from their region. But where do these first Pokémon come from, and why are they all at the same strength? It's normally a well-kept secret, but the Pokémon League distributes Eggs to individuals who raise them as first Pokémon—one such individual is Mr. Swampy, who raises Mudkip Eggs in a secluded part of Hoenn.

POKÉMON LEAGUE CERTIFICATION

In Kanto's Dark City, two unofficial Gyms—the Yas Gym and Kaz Gym—battled for supremacy in the belief that the winning Gym would receive official certication and make a fortune. Their activities gave all Pokémon Trainers a bad reputation in town, since the Gyms weren't content to just recruit passing Trainers to their cause. The Gyms' Trainers and Pokémon would brawl in the streets, unacceptable behavior for any respectable Gym.

A disguised Nurse Joy was one of the Pokémon League's official inspectors, and there was no chance she'd approve the Yas or Kaz Gyms. However, she gave them a chance to make amends: if they joined forces to repair all the damage they'd caused and learned how to be responsible Trainers, they might get a chance to start their Gym certification bid from scratch.

GYM INSPECTION AND CERTIFICATION

To get to a Pokémon League tournament, a Trainer needs badges. And to get badges, a Trainer needs to win challenges at an official Gym. That means the League has to oversee Gym approvals and certifications to make sure the process runs smoothly.

Gym Inspection

Once a Gym is certified and operational, it still has to face the might of the Pokémon Inspection Agency. The PIA has the power to shut down Gyms that are unclean, unsafe, or just not up to their standards.

SINNOH GYM BATTLES

The rules for Gym battles in Sinnoh aren't much different from the rules anywhere else; the standard Gym battle is a 3-on-3 match where only the challenger may substitute Pokémon. Win badges from eight Gyms, and you'll be eligible to compete in the Sinnoh League. Ash is determined to get those badges, and these are the Gyms he's visited so far.

REMATCH OREBURGH GYM
GYM LEADER: ROARK

Gym Leaders 101

Being a Gym Leader means more than schooling Trainers on the battlefield. Ash wants to win against Roark to prove Paul's methods are wrong, and Ash takes on the Oreburgh Gym rematch with this in mind. Sensing something amiss, Roark approaches Ash during a training session and reminds him to focus on the Gym battle, not his battle to prove Paul wrong.

Pikachu utilizes his speed and Iron Tail to frustrate Onix until Onix uses Rock Tomb to imprison Pikachu. Never one to give up, Ash uses Thunderbolt to escape and Iron Tail to finish it.

The fight is fairly even, with Geodude using Roll Out and Aipom using Swift. In the end, Aipom gets the best of Geodude, surprising Roark.

Rampardos was originally a very special Cranidos—the first fossil Pokémon revived by the Fossil Restorer machine, and Roark's Pokémon ever since he was a kid.

Rampardos makes quick work of an already tired Aipom. One hit and Aipom is unable to battle.

Pikachu and Rampardos put each other to the test, meeting in the middle of the ring with a Volt Tackle and Headbutt. In the end, Rampardos was just too strong, flinging Pikachu against the rocky terrain of the Gym, securing the win.

Rampardos' knowledge of Fire-type moves puts Turtwig at a big disadvantage, but Turwig is well trained and strong. It uses Razor Leaf to secure the win and Ash's first badge in the Sinnoh region.

HEARTHOME GYM
GYM LEADER: FANTINA

The giant Drifblim on the Hearthome Gym roof is certainly distinctive, but who knows what might lie inside? Ash still doesn't know, because no one was in when he came running up for his Hearthome Gym Challenge. The Gym Leader is out on a journey; Ash will have to battle her when he returns.

ETERNA GYM
GYM LEADER: GARDENIA

The open roof of the Eterna Gym proves pivotal in this battle, as Cherubi turns a stalemate into a victory when the sun comes out and provides Cherubi with more power.

Staravia outflies Cherubi's Leaf Blade attack and, using the brightness of the sun as cover, uses an ultra-fast Aerial Ace to send Cherubi packing.

Having fought once in the Eterna Forest, Ash knows Gardenia's Turtwig is as fast as his Staravia. And although Staravia does much better, it still finds itself on the losing end of a Leech Seed attack.

This matchup isn't so much about skill or tactics, but about Ash's Turtwig's toughness. It battles through the same Leech Seed attack to win the match.

Still suffering from the previous battle's Leech Seed attack, Turtwig succumbs in one blow to Gardenia's Roserade.

Aipom starts the battle with the flair of a Pokémon Contest entrance, and backs it up with a massive and beautiful Swift for the win.

VEILSTONE GYM
GYM LEADER: MAYLENE

Gym Leaders 101

Both Gym Leaders and challengers have something to give each other. Maylene became unnerved by the realization that winning or losing a Gym battle can have a huge effect on a challenger. For Brock, what's important is the cumulative effect of all those battles and the lessons they teach: in his opinion, challengers actually help shape a Gym Leader into someone better than they were before.

Staravia proves its strength once again, as it comes back from the brink of defeat with Aerial Ace to defeat Machoke.

Meditite dodges everything Staravia throws at it, and in the end has to return when it is too confused to continue the battle.

Chimcar suffers the same fate as Staravia, but Ash manages to retrieve it as well.

Having been cleared of its Confusion by the Poké Ball, Staravia takes Meditite out with its newly learned Brave Bird attack.

Fresh off the first use of Brave Bird by Ash's Staravia, he tries it again but Maylene's Lucario is powerful and ready. Its Metal Claw attack sends Staravia back to the Poké Ball for good.

Lucario is much too powerful for Chimchar, as its Bone Rush and Force Palm make quick work of the feisty, fiery Pokémon.

In a titanic clash, Lucario and Buizel put on a show for the ages. Back and forth with interminable will, in the end they blast the roof off the Veilstone Gym and are both unable to battle. The match ends in a draw, but Maylene awards the Cobble Badge anyway because of the effort of Ash's Pokémon.

HEARTHOME TAG BATTLE TOURNAMENT

Hearthome City is the "City Where Hearts Meet" and if it takes a tag battle tournament to make Trainers' hearts meet, so much the better!

Hearthome City is famous for the Hearthome Tag Battle tournament, a three-day tournament that brings Trainers together in Hearthome Stadium.

The prize for each winner is the Soothe Bell, a bell with a beautiful sound that puts everyone's mind at ease who hear it.

Each contestant receives a numbered registration card. At the start of the tournament, all the Trainers are gathered in the Hearthome Stadium and the random pairings are displayed so they can find their tournament partner. Battles begin later that afternoon, giving Trainers some time to practice with their partner.

TOURNAMENT RULES:

- EACH TRAINER BATTLES WITH THE SAME PARTNER FOR THE ENTIRE TOURNAMENT.
- THE TOURNAMENT IS A TAG BATTLE EVENT, WITH EACH TRAINER USING ONE POKÉMON PER BATTLE.
- THERE ARE NO SUBSTITUTIONS AND NO TIME LIMITS DURING BATTLES.

The tournament MC is none other than Hearthome's own mayor, Enta.

Ash, Dawn, and Brock all enter the tournament. For Ash and Brock, the tournament is just another fun event, but for Dawn—who enters at Zoey's suggestion—it just might be a way to get her mind off her Hearthome Contest disappointment. Two of them will find new friendships and excitement in tag battle teamwork, but for one of them, the tag battle tournament turns out to be a bittersweet experience.

DAWN'S PARTNER: CONWAY

Conway is all about statistics and strategy: he's analyzed every league battle to develop a formula for battle victory. He's not nearly as confident with girls as he is with numbers, but despite his deliberate, geeky demeanor, he's a great partner for Dawn. His Slowking is optimized with defensive moves like Safeguard and Protect so Dawn can concentrate on attacking while Conway watches her back.

BROCK'S PARTNER: HOLLY

Holly is a cool older girl who makes it clear to Brock that she's just not that into him. But once she sees that Brock is more than just a skirt-chaser, she comes to respect him as a person and a tag battle partner. After Paul's Torterra deals her Farfetch'd a one-hit KO during the quarterfinal battles, Holly is deeply apologetic to Brock for letting him down; she leaves right after the tournament, vowing to become a better Trainer.

ASH'S PARTNER: PAUL

Paul and Ash are all too well acquainted by now, and Paul certainly isn't interested in playing nice for the sake of the tournament—he's only competing so he can train his Pokémon, especially Chimchar.

HEARTHOME TAG BATTLE TOURNAMENT RESULTS

Notable Battles: Day One

Dawn and Conway use Piplup and Slowking to defeat a female Trainer's Scyther and male Trainer's Koffing.

Brock and Holly use Sudowoodo and Wingull to defeat two male Trainers' Yanma and Bagon.

Ash and Paul use Pikachu and Chimchar to defeat two male Trainers' Magmar and Rhydon.

Notable Battles: Day Two

Ash and Paul use Turtwig and Chimchar to defeat two male Trainers' Metagross and Zangoose.

Seeing Chimchar freeze in terror when confronted by Zangoose, Paul turns away in disgust and abandons it for good. After the battle, Ash takes in Chimchar as one of his own Pokémon.

Quarterfinal Battle: Day Three

Ash and Paul use Staravia and Torterra to defeat Brock's Croagunk and Holly's Farfetch'd. With Farfetch'd knocked out almost immediately, it's up to Brock and Croagunk to save the day. Croagunk single-handedly takes on Torterra, but Torterra's power proves to be too much.

Final Battle: Day Three

Ash and Paul use Chimchar and Elekid to defeat Dawn's Buizel and Conway's Heracross, winning the tournament.

During the battle, Elekid evolves into Electabuzz. Now that Paul has given up on Chimchar, this is the only tournament reward he cares about—later he even tosses his Soothe Bell prize at Ash, having no use for it.

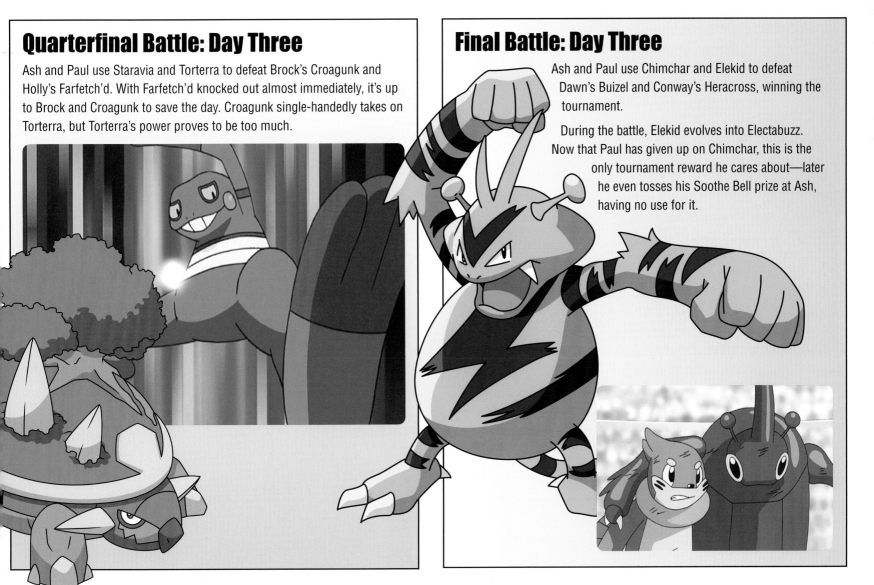

SINNOH POKÉMON CONTESTS

Pokémon Contests everywhere share the same basic structure, but there are a few extra details a Coordinator needs to know if they want to shine in the Sinnoh region.

WHAT'S THE SAME?

No matter where you are, the principle is the same: Pokémon Contests are judged on a contestant's ability to showcase their Pokémon in battles and individual appeals. Trainers from other regions will find the judging panel in Sinnoh to be a familiar sight. The panel members are: Mr. Contesta, Pokémon Contest Director and head of the judging committee; Mr. Sukizo, Head of the Pokémon Fan Club, and a "remarkable" man of few words; the Nurse Joy from the Contest town or city.

WHAT'S CHANGED?

Handling the Contest MC duties in Sinnoh is Marian, who's just as lively as Contest MCs everywhere else.

As always, a Coordinator needs a Contest pass in order to enter competitions. These passes don't transfer between regions, but a Sinnoh Contest pass can be acquired at any Sinnoh Region Contest Hall. Once a Coordinator's ID information is downloaded from their Pokédex and the Contest pass is printed, the newly registered Coordinator also receives a ribbon case, rulebook, Ball Capsule, and envelope containing starter seals.

Sinnoh's Unofficial Contests

Contests aren't just for Sinnoh's big towns and cities! Other towns also host "unofficial" Contests—in other words, Contests where the prize isn't a ribbon that's valid towards entry in the Grand Festival. Dawn enters one such Contest on the way to Floaroma Town: the Contest is part of a village festival, and the prize is a year's worth of fruit.

All it takes is an audio/video truck, some outdoor bleachers, two judges, and voila! Instant Contest.

Jessie enters the Contest with Ash's Aipom, which he reluctantly lent her for the Contest after she saved its life. Aipom loves the Contest spotlight and it's doing so well with Jessie that Ash is afraid it might never want to return to him!

After the village Contest's first round, two Coordinators are selected for the final round—a standard five-minute Contest battle. This time, Jessie and Aipom easily defeat Dawn and her untried Pachirisu.

Dress to Impress

Coordinators in Kanto and Hoenn are happy to compete in their everyday clothes, but in Sinnoh, Coordinators dress to the nines for every Contest. Some Coordinators, like Dawn, stick with the same basic outfit for each contest and alter their accessories, but Zoey prefers to wear different outfits for each Contest.

JUBILIFE CONTEST

Located in the heart of Jubilife City, the Jubilife Contest Hall is also conveniently close to a Pokémon Center.

The Jubilife Contest is Dawn's Contest debut, but Zoey's fourth Contest. It's also the Sinnoh Contest debut of Ash, indulging his Aipom's interest in Contests and Jessie, who takes the stage as her alter ego, the not-so-great Coordinator Jessilina.

Colorful seals can be placed on the Ball Capsule. Each seal creates a different special effect when the Poké Ball is thrown using the Ball Capsule.

For once in her life, Jessie fights fair, only to see Carnivine wither before the force of Zoey's Glameow and its attacks. Zoey wins the match, making this her second Ribbon.

FLOAROMA CONTEST

Scenic Floaroma Town is a testament to the wonders of the natural world. What better place for an event that showcases the natural beauty of Pokémon? But flowers are the last thing on the mind of Kenny, Dawn's childhood acquaintance, who enters this Contest for a chance to see her again.

In a battle between evolution stages that goes right down to the wire, Dawn's Piplup defeats Kenny's Prinplup.

Dawn is declared the winner. Kenny will just have to wait a little longer to earn his first ribbon.

HEARTHOME CONTEST

In Hearthome City, the Contest format is in a double performance format. Dawn faces twice the competition from her rivals as well, since both Nando and Zoey are in town to enter the Contest. The Contest comes down to Zoey and Nando in the finals, with Nando surprising Zoey with a victory, earning his second Ribbon!

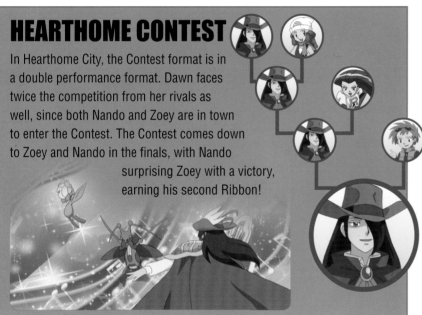

SOLACEON CONTEST

The Solaceon Contest draws a big crowd, as if there wasn't already enough pressure on Dawn to prove her Hearthome Contest defeat was just a fluke.

Convinced James and Meowth have a top-secret strategy to guarantee her the win, Jessie sails onstage and wins with confidence, not realizing she's just won her first Ribbon fair and square.

WALLACE CUP

Unlike most Contests, in the Wallace Cup, 16 contestants move on to the second round instead of eight.

Sootopolis Gym Leader, Champion Master of Hoenn, Top Contest Coordinator and Contest Master: Wallace is the cream of the Coordinator crop. Originally hailing from Hoenn, he's traveled both Hoenn and Kanto to promote his Wallace Cup Contest event. Now the Wallace Cup has come to the shores of Sinnoh's Lake Valor, where Wallace will sit in as a special judge.

Coordinator 101

Friendship is the key to success. Wallace has an important reminder for all Trainers—for a Pokémon to truly shine, it's the relationship between Trainer and Pokémon that's most important. Part of building that relationship is taking time out to interact with Pokémon beyond just training; play time is important too!

Ribbons Are a Girl's Best Friend

May still has the half of a ribbon she won at Terracotta Town in a draw with Ash, and Dawn always carries her mother's first Ribbon with her. Both of them draw on these Ribbons for strength during their competitions—though for Dawn, a constant reminder of all she has to live up to can be a source of pressure as well as inspiration!

JOIN THE EVOLUTION

As we grow, travel, and learn, we begin to change: become wiser, stronger, and more capable. The same holds true for Pokémon. During the course of a Pokémon's life , it can change if it so chooses. The change is both in its physical appearance and its abilities—some even alter their type.

The number of stage and the kind of Evolution is dependent upon the Pokémon, but for the most part, Pokémon have three stages. The first form of Pokémon is its earliest. When Professors hand out first Pokémon, they are always in their first stage. Through hard, consistent training, a Pokémon at an unannounced time begins to glow and change. When it is done, it is larger, looks more mature, and possesses one or more different moves.

Not all Evolutions happen in the same way, or for the same reasons. Some Pokémon will change to one of several completely different forms based on the time of day when it begins the evolution process. Likewise, if it evolves in one area versus another it could be totally different. Some stones cause Pokémon to evolve. There is no set way or time as a Trainer to know, you just have to be ready, flexible, and know your Pokémon inside and out.

It is important to note that all Pokémon evolve and not all Pokémon, if they can evolve, want to. Pikachu is a good example. Pikachu could evolve into a Raichu, and has had an opportunity, but didn't want to. Ash, to his credit, supported Pikachu's decision.

Some Pokémon have a pre-evolved form. This is a baby form. The Pokémon is not ready to train or be trained. James' Mime Jr. or Brock's Bonsly are examples of this. They usually don't know much, but have one or two safety abilities: Mime Jr.'s Mimic or Bonsly's Fake Tears. It is enough to carry them through the world long enough for them to evolve into their normal adult form.

IT CAME FROM OUTER SPACE

The Pokémon world is teeming with life, but some of that life may have originated beyond the planet. Might there be other Pokémon yet to be discovered, somewhere out amongst the stars?

DEOXYS

If there's a top candidate for extraterrestrial Pokémon, Deoxys must be it—sightings of this rare Pokémon are tied to meteorite activity.

Deoxys provided a great deal of insight into its species; using Meowth as a voicebox, it told Max that its long journey was cold, lonely, and frightening.

Even after the meteorite landed, Deoxys remained alone in the meteorite. It didn't emerge full-fledged until the meteorite's core was transformed by a combination of solar wind activity and the meteorite's own energy. Due to the painful geomagnetic energy emanating from the meteorite, it had to flee its "cradle" and take refuge in an extradimensional space it created.

Meteorite Mysteries

Meteorites are objects of particular interest in the Pokémon world. In Sinnoh, Veilstone City is known for its meteorites—without them, the city wouldn't even exist! Before there was a city, there was a cluster of meteorites that were recognized as "guardians" since ancient times. Veilstone City was created by the people who flocked to the area, drawn by curiosity.

CLEFAIRY

Are Clefairy from outer space? If not, there must be a very good explanation for why the Clefairy have a spaceship that resembles a UFO. The spaceship doesn't run on pixie dust, either; the banks of equipment inside show it's clearly a sophisticated machine.

LUNATONE

Mary and Ken, also known as the Pokémon Mystery Club, have evidence that Lunatone is definitely an extraterrestrial. When a meteor struck the Hoenn region, these two aggressive investigators tracked down the crash site and witnessed a Lunatone emerge from the broken shards of the meteorite.

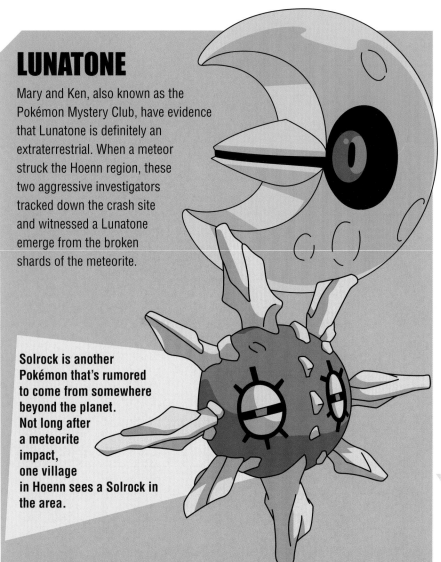

Solrock is another Pokémon that's rumored to come from somewhere beyond the planet. Not long after a meteorite impact, one village in Hoenn sees a Solrock in the area.

Clefairy's extraterrestrial connections may still be a secret to many, but it's no great secret that Clefairy can be found near Mt. Moon. Somewhere on the mountain is a huge meteor called the "Moon Stone."

On nights with a full moon, Clefairy and Clefable gather to dance around the Moon Stone as a form of prayer. It may be related to the Moon Stone's origins outer space.

Cleffa, the pre-evolved form of Clefairy, seem to appear whenever there's a meteor shower. Some say it rides to earth on shooting stars; its body is shaped like a star, too!

WORKING SIDE-BY-SIDE

All across the world, people have partnered with Pokémon to accomplish vital tasks and jobs. For all the Trainers who focus on battles, there are likely just as many who work alongside their Pokémon in every sense of the word! From the Pokémon firefighting squads to Machoke that help with manual labor, from Nurse Joy and Chansey to Officer Jenny and Growlithe—there are many examples of these fruitful partnerships.

WHISTLE WHILE YOU WORK: LEDYBA

Lots of flowering plants depend on other creatures to spread their pollen, and that's where Arielle and her six Ledyba come in. Farmers can ask Arielle and her Pokémon to pollinate orchards like this stand of apple tree, ensuring that the trees will bear fruit.

Arielle uses a mixture of verbal commands and whistle notes to direct her Ledbya. The whistle has been passed down through generations of her family, but it's not the whistle that's special. Arielle raised her Lebyda from their infancy, and it's this lifelong relationship that allows them to work together so well.

BRIDGING TROUBLED WATERS: BIBAREL

When you need a stone bridge built, this Bibarel is your best bet. Other Pokémon can cut stone, but no regular Pokémon can do it with this trained Bibarel's precision and know-how. Under the direction of Isis, an engineer, Bibarel uses its sharp teeth to swiftly cut rough blocks of stone down to exact specifications. It may not have an engineering degree, but Bibarel trained under a master before working with Isis.

THE ANSWER IS BLOWING ON THE WIND: HOPPIP

Mariah the weather forecaster uses all kinds of scientific instruments, but her seven Hoppip are a special help. Hoppip are so light that a strong wind can blow them miles away, and Mariah sometimes has to keep them in a netted enclosure so they don't fly off! But they're more than just a quick way to check wind speed—they can also sense imminent changes in the wind, and Mariah studies their behavior patterns in the hope that it will help meteorologists make weather predictions.

THE CUTTING EDGE: FARFETCH'D AND MAGMAR

Sylvester and his father are in the business of making purifying charcoal, a fuel that also cleanses the air and water. To do it, they rely on two things: top-quality wood from Ilex Forest, and help from Farfetch'd and Magmar.

The wood needs to be cut just so, and Farfetch'd can use its Cut move to chop a log into a perfect stack of wood. Then, Magmar turns up the heat to burn the wood into charcoal.

EXPRESS AIR MAIL: PIDGEY

For over 50 years, the carrier Pidgey of the Pidgey Carrier Express have delivered mail throughout the city and out to nearby islands that lack ferry service.

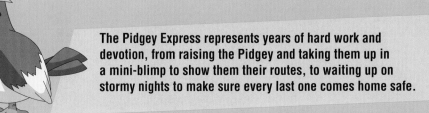

The Pidgey Express represents years of hard work and devotion, from raising the Pidgey and taking them up in a mini-blimp to show them their routes, to waiting up on stormy nights to make sure every last one comes home safe.

GIRATINA • (gear-uh-TEE-na)

Height: 22'07" (6.9 m)   **Weight: 1433.0 lbs (650.0 kg)**

Giratina is one of the most enigmatic Pokémon ever. Even its existence is a mystery – it is said to come from a world that mirrors our own. Its impressive height and ragged, horned wings make it a terrifying sight, and its six-legged body can appear in ancient cemeteries

PALKIA • (PAL-kee-uh)

Height: 13'09" (4.2 m)   **Weight: 740.8 lbs (336.0 kg)**

Palkia has the ability to distort space. It is said to live in a gap in the spatial dimension parallel to ours. Because of this, it is nearly impossible to get factual information about this Pokémon.

It has a long neck and formidable tail. Inset on its shoulders are two enormous pink spheres that resemble pearls.

PAL-kee-uh

DIALGA • (dee-AL-guh)

Height: 17'09" (5.4 m)   Weight: 1505.8 lbs (683.0 kg)

The Legendary Dialga has the power to control time. It is said that time began moving when Dialga was born. Dialga, like Palkia, lives in a parallel dimension, making it very difficult to study.

Dialga is dark blue with metallic gray accents. In its chest rests, what appears to be, a gigantic blue diamond. Along its back and head grow sail-back fins. One of the largest Pokémon in existence, Dialga's Roar is stunningly powerful.

dee-AL-guh

MANAPHY • (man-UH-fee

Height: 1'00" (0.3 m)   **Weight: 3.1 lbs (1.4 kg)**

Manaphy, also known as the Prince of the Sea, acts as the leader of Pokémon from the ocean.

Very empathetic, it can change the perception of people through its Heart Swap technique, forcing people to look at things from other perspectives.

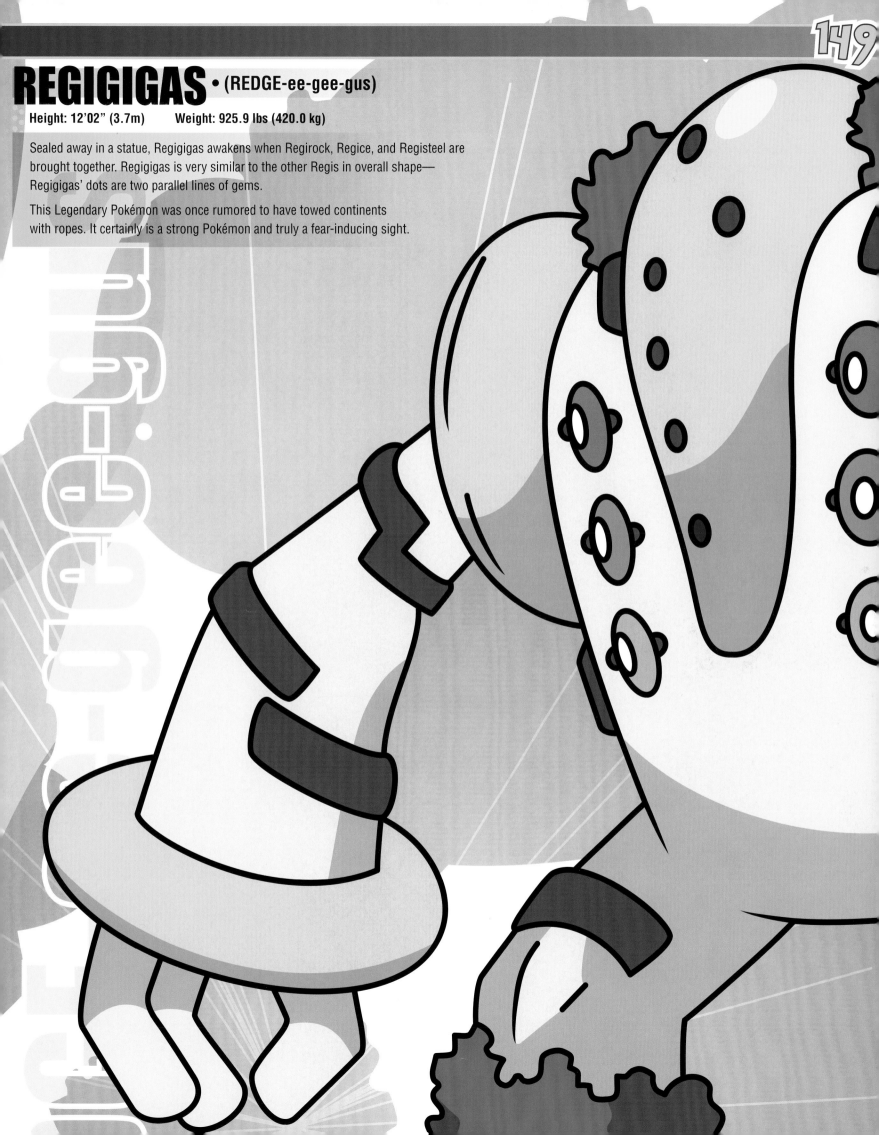

REGIGIGAS • (REDGE-ee-gee-gus)

Height: 12'02" (3.7m)   **Weight:** 925.9 lbs (420.0 kg)

Sealed away in a statue, Regigigas awakens when Regirock, Regice, and Registeel are brought together. Regigigas is very similar to the other Regis in overall shape—Regigigas' dots are two parallel lines of gems.

This Legendary Pokémon was once rumored to have towed continents with ropes. It certainly is a strong Pokémon and truly a fear-inducing sight.

AZELF • (AZ-elf)

Height: 1'00" (0.3 m)   **Weight:** 0.7 lbs (0.3 kg)

Azelf is known as "The Being of Willpower." It sleeps at the bottom of a lake to keep the world in balance. Small and blue, with three small red gems—two on its tails and one on its forehead.

UXIE • (YUKE-see)

Height: 1'00" (0.3 m)   **Weight:** 0.7 lbs (0.3 kg)

Uxie is known as "The Being of Knowledge." It is said that it can wipe out the memory of those who look into its eyes. Uxie's two tails have two red gems, while another sits in its forehead.

MESPRIT • (MES-prit)

Height: 1'00" (0.3 m)   **Weight:** 0.7 lbs (0.3 kg)

Mesprit is known as "The Being of Emotion." It taught humans the nobility of sorrow, pain, and joy. Mesprit also has two red jewels on its tails and one on its forehead.

HEATRAN • (HEE-tran)

Height: 5'07" (1.7 m)   **Weight: 948.0 lbs (430.0 kg)**

Born from fire, Heatran loves to dig into the walls and caverns of magma caves. It has immeasurably sharp claws extending from each of its feet. Heatran is a rarely seen Pokémon. This is not surprising, as it lives in active volcano craters.

DARKRAI • (DAR-cry)

Height: 4'11" (1.5 m)
Weight: 111.3 lbs (50.5 kg)

Dark and ominious, Darkrai lives up to its name. Legends say that on moonless nights, Darkrai lures people to sleep and gives them horrible nightmares.

Made of shadow and able to travel very fast, it can speak to humans. It has a flowing white mane.

CRESSELIA • (cres-SEL-ee-uh)

Height: 4'11" (1.5 m)   **Weight: 188.7 lbs (85.6 kg)**

Cresselia is light blue with a yellow underbelly.
She has glowing rings around her side and back.
These wings sometimes look like a veil
because of the shiny particles in them.

SINNOH POKÉMON

Just north of Kanto and Johto is Sinnoh. Sinnoh is home to some of the most mysterious Pokémon—Giratina and Darkrai!

ABOMASNOW

Height: 7'03" (2.2 m)
Weight: 298.7 lbs. (135.5 kg)

GRASS	ICE

AMBIPOM

Height: 3'11" (1.2 m)
Weight: 44.8 lbs. (20.3 kg)

NORMAL

AZELF

Height: 1'00" (0.3 m)
Weight: 0.7 lbs. (0.3 kg)

PSYCHIC

BASTIODON

Height: 4'03" (1.3 m)
Weight: 329.6 lbs. (149.5 kg)

ROCK	STEEL

BIBAREL

Height: 3'03" (1.0 m)
Weight: 69.4 lbs. (31.5 kg)

NORMAL	WATER

BIDOOF

Height: 1'08" (0.5 m)
Weight: 44.1 lbs. (20.0 kg)

NORMAL

BONSLY

Height: 1'08" (0.5 m)
Weight: 33.1 lbs. (15.0 kg)

ROCK

BRONZONG

Height: 4'03" (1.3 m)
Weight: 412.3 lbs. (187.0 kg)

STEEL	PSYCHIC

BRONZOR

Height: 1'08" (0.5 m)
Weight: 133.4 lbs. (60.5 kg)

STEEL	PSYCHIC

BUDEW

Height: 0'08" (0.2 m)
Weight: 2.6 lbs. (1.2 kg)

GRASS	POISON

BUIZEL

Height: 2'04" (0.7 m)
Weight: 65.0 lbs. (29.5 kg)

WATER

BUNEARY

Height: 1'04" (0.4 m)
Weight: 12.1 lbs. (5.5 kg)

NORMAL

BURMY (PLANT CLOAK)

Height: 0'08" (0.2 m)
Weight: 7.5 lbs. (3.4 kg)

BUG

BURMY (SANDY CLOAK)

Height: 0'08" (0.2 m)
Weight: 7.5 lbs. (3.4 kg)

BUG

BURMY (TRASH CLOAK)

Height: 0'08" (0.2 m)
Weight: 7.5 lbs. (3.4 kg)

BUG

CARNIVINE

Height: 4'07" (1.4 m)
Weight: 59.5 lbs. (27.0 kg)

GRASS

CHATOT

Height: 1'08" (0.5 m)
Weight: 4.2 lbs. (1.9 kg)

NORMAL	FLYING

CHERRIM

Height: 1'08" (0.5 m)
Weight: 20.5 lbs. (9.3 kg)

GRASS

CHERUBI

Height: 1'04" (0.4 m)
Weight: 7.3 lbs. (3.3 kg)

GRASS

CHIMCHAR

Height: 1'08" (0.5 m)
Weight: 13.7 lbs. (6.2 kg)

FIRE

CHINGLING

Height: 0'08" (0.2 m)
Weight: 1.3 lbs. (0.6 kg)

PSYCHIC

COMBEE

Height: 1'00" (0.3 m)
Weight: 12.1 lbs. (5.5 kg)

BUG	FLYING

CRANIDOS

Height: 2'11" (0.9 m)
Weight: 69.4 lbs. (31.5 kg)

ROCK

CRESSELIA

Height: 4'11" (1.5 m)
Weight: 188.7 lbs. (85.6 kg)

PSYCHIC

CROAGUNK

Height: 2'04" (0.7 m)
Weight: 50.7 lbs. (23.0 kg)

POISON	FIGHTING

DARKRAI

Height: 4'11" (1.5 m)
Weight: 111.3 lbs. (50.5 kg)

DARK

DIALGA

Height: 17'09" (5.4 m)
Weight: 1505.8 lbs. (683.0 kg)

STEEL	DRAGON

DRAPION

Height: 4'03" (1.3 m)
Weight: 135.6 lbs. (61.5 kg)

| POISON | DARK |

DRIFBLIM

Height: 3'11" (1.2 m)
Weight: 33.1 lbs. (15.0 kg)

| GHOST | FLYING |

DRIFLOON

Height: 1'04" (0.4 m)
Weight: 2.6 lbs. (1.2 kg)

| GHOST | FLYING |

DUSKNOIR

Height: 7'03" (2.2 m)
Weight: 235.0 lbs. (106.6 kg)

| GHOST |

ELECTIVIRE

Height: 5'11" (1.8 m)
Weight: 305.6 lbs. (138.6 kg)

| ELECTRIC |

EMPOLEON

Height: 5'07" (1.7 m)
Weight: 186.3 lbs. (84.5 kg)

| WATER | STEEL |

FINNEON

Height: 1'04" (0.4 m)
Weight: 15.4 lbs. (7.0 kg)

| WATER |

FLOATZEL

Height: 3'07" (1.1 m)
Weight: 73.9 lbs. (33.5 kg)

| WATER |

FROSLASS

Height: 4'03" (1.3 m)
Weight: 58.6 lbs. (26.6 kg)

| ICE | GHOST |

GABITE

Height: 4'07" (1.4 m)
Weight: 123.5 lbs. (56.0 kg)

| DRAGON | GROUND |

GALLADE

Height: 5'03" (1.6 m)
Weight: 114.6 lbs. (52.0 kg)

| PSYCHIC | FIGHTING |

GARCHOMP

Height: 6'03" (1.9 m)
Weight: 209.4 lbs. (95.0 kg)

| DRAGON | GROUND |

GASTRODON (EAST SEA)

Height: 2'11" (0.9 m)
Weight: 65.9 lbs. (29.9 kg)

| WATER | GROUND |

GASTRODON (WEST SEA)

Height: 2'11" (0.9 m)
Weight: 65.9 lbs. (29.9 kg)

| WATER | GROUND |

GIBLE

Height: 2'04" (0.7 m)
Weight: 45.2 lbs. (20.5 kg)

| DRAGON | GROUND |

GIRATINA

Height: 14'09" (4.5 m)
Weight: 1653.5 lbs. (750.0 kg)

| GHOST | DRAGON |

GLACEON

Height: 2'07" (0.8 m)
Weight: 57.1 lbs. (25.9 kg)

| ICE |

GLAMEOW

Height: 1'08" (0.5 m)
Weight: 8.6 lbs. (3.9 kg)

| NORMAL |

GLISCOR

Height: 6'07" (2.0 m)
Weight: 93.7 lbs. (42.5 kg)

| GROUND | FLYING |

GROTLE

Height: 3'07" (1.1 m)
Weight: 213.8 lbs. (97.0 kg)

| GRASS |

HAPPINY

Height: 2'00" (0.6 m)
Weight: 53.8 lbs. (24.4 kg)

| NORMAL |

HEATRAN

Height: 5'07" (1.7 m)
Weight: 948.0 lbs. (430.0 kg)

| FIRE | STEEL |

HIPPOPOTAS

Height: 2'07" (0.8 m)
Weight: 109.1 lbs. (49.5 kg)

| GROUND |

HIPPOWDON

Height: 6'07" (2.0 m)
Weight: 661.4 lbs. (300.0 kg)

| GROUND |

HONCHKROW

Height: 2'11" (0.9 m)
Weight: 60.2 lbs. (27.3 kg)

| DARK | FLYING |

INFERNAPE

Height: 3'11" (1.2 m)
Weight: 121.3 lbs. (55.0 kg)

| FIRE | FIGHTING |

KRICKETOT

Height: 1'00" (0.3 m)
Weight: 4.9 lbs. (2.2 kg)

| BUG |

KRICKETUNE

Height: 3'03" (1.0 m)
Weight: 56.2 lbs. (25.5 kg)

| BUG |

LEAFEON

Height: 3'03" (1.0 m)
Weight: 56.2 lbs. (25.5 kg)

| GRASS |

LICKILICKY

Height: 5'07" (1.7 m)
Weight: 308.6 lbs. (140.0 kg)

| NORMAL |

LOPUNNY

Height: 3'11" (1.2 m)
Weight: 73.4 lbs. (33.3 kg)

| NORMAL |

LUCARIO

Height: 3'11" (1.2 m)
Weight: 119.0 lbs. (54.0 kg)

| FIGHTING | STEEL |

LUMINEON

Height: 3'11" (1.2 m)
Weight: 52.9 lbs. (24.0 kg)

| WATER |

LUXIO

Height: 2'11" (0.9 m)
Weight: 67.2 lbs. (30.5 kg)

| ELECTRIC |

LUXRAY

Height: 4'07" (1.4 m)
Weight: 92.6 lbs. (42.0 kg)

| ELECTRIC |

MAGMORTAR

Height: 5'03" (1.6 m)
Weight: 149.9 lbs. (68.0 kg)

| FIRE |

MAGNEZONE

Height: 3'11" (1.2 m)
Weight: 396.8 lbs. (180.0 kg)

| ELECTRIC | STEEL |

MAMOSWINE

Height: 8'02" (2.5 m)
Weight: 641.5 lbs. (291.0 kg)

| ICE | GROUND |

MANAPHY

Height: 1'00" (0.3 m)
Weight: 3.1 lbs. (1.4 kg)

| WATER |

MANTYKE

Height: 3'03" (1.0 m)
Weight: 143.3 lbs. (65.0 kg)

| WATER | FLYING |

MESPRIT

Height: 1'00" (0.3 m)
Weight: 0.7 lbs. (0.3 kg)

| PSYCHIC? |

MIME JR.

Height: 2'00" (0.6 m)
Weight: 28.7 lbs. (13.0 kg)

| PSYCHIC |

MISMAGIUS

Height: 2'11" (0.9 m)
Weight: 9.7 lbs. (4.4 kg)

GHOST

MONFERNO

Height: 2'11" (0.9 m)
Weight: 48.5 lbs. (22.0 kg)

FIRE | FIGHTING

MOTHIM

Height: 2'11" (0.9 m)
Weight: 51.4 lbs. (23.3 kg)

BUG | FLYING

MUNCHLAX

Height: 2'00" (0.6 m)
Weight: 231.5 lbs. (105.0 kg)

NORMAL

PACHIRISU

Height: 1'04" (0.4 m)
Weight: 8.6 lbs. (3.9 kg)

ELECTRIC

PALKIA

Height: 13'09" (4.2 m)
Weight: 740.8 lbs. (336.0 kg)

WATER | DRAGON

PHIONE

Height: 1'04" (0.4 m)
Weight: 6.8 lbs. (3.1 kg)

WATER

PIPLUP

Height: 1'04" (0.4 m)
Weight: 11.5 lbs. (5.2 kg)

WATER

PORYGON-Z

Height: 2'11" (0.9 m)
Weight: 75.0 lbs. (34.0 kg)

NORMAL

PRINPLUP

Height: 2'07" (0.8 m)
Weight: 50.7 lbs. (23.0 kg)

WATER

PROBOPASS

Height: 4'07" (1.4 m)
Weight: 749.6 lbs. (340.0 kg)

ROCK | STEEL

PURUGLY

Height: 3'03" (1.0 m)
Weight: 96.6 lbs. (43.8 kg)

NORMAL

RAMPARDOS

Height: 5'03" (1.6 m)
Weight: 226.0 lbs. (102.5 kg)

ROCK

REGIGIGAS

Height: 12'02" (3.7 m)
Weight: 925.9 lbs. (420.0 kg)

NORMAL

RHYPERIOR

Height: 7'10" (2.4 m)
Weight: 623.5 lbs. (282.8 kg)

GROUND | ROCK

RIOLU

Height: 2'04" (0.7 m)
Weight: 44.5 lbs. (20.2 kg)

FIGHTING

ROSERADE

Height: 2'11" (0.9 m)
Weight: 32.0 lbs. (14.5 kg)

GRASS | POISON

ROTOM

Height: 1'00" (0.3 m)
Weight: 0.7 lbs. (0.3 kg)

ELECTRIC | GHOST

SHELLOS (EAST SEA)

Height: 1'00" (0.3 m)
Weight: 13.9 lbs. (6.3 kg)

WATER

SHELLOS (WEST SEA)

Height: 1'00" (0.3 m)
Weight: 13.9 lbs. (6.3 kg)

WATER

SHIELDON

Height: 1'08" (0.5 m)
Weight: 125.7 lbs. (57.0 kg)

ROCK | STEEL

SHINX

Height: 1'08" (0.5 m)
Weight: 20.9 lbs. (9.5 kg)

ELECTRIC

SKORUPI

Height: 2'07" (0.8 m)
Weight: 26.5 lbs. (12.0 kg)

POISON | BUG

SKUNTANK

Height: 3'03" (1.0 m)
Weight: 83.8 lbs. (38.0 kg)

POISON | DARK

SNOVER

Height: 3'03" (1.0 m)
Weight: 111.3 lbs. (50.5 kg)

GRASS | ICE

SPIRITOMB

Height: 3'03" (1.0 m)
Weight: 238.1 lbs. (108.0 kg)

GHOST | DARK

STARAPTOR

Height: 3'11" (1.2 m)
Weight: 54.9 lbs. (24.9 kg)

NORMAL | FLYING

STARAVIA

Height: 2'00" (0.6 m)
Weight: 34.2 lbs. (15.5 kg)

NORMAL | FLYING

STARLY

Height: 1'00" (0.3 m)
Weight: 4.4 lbs. (2.0 kg)

NORMAL | FLYING

STUNKY

Height: 1'04" (0.4 m)
Weight: 42.3 lbs. (19.2 kg)

POISON | DARK

TANGROWTH

Height: 6'07" (2.0 m)
Weight: 283.5 lbs. (128.6 kg)

GRASS

TOGEKISS

Height: 4'11" (1.5 m)
Weight: 83.8 lbs. (38.0 kg)

NORMAL | FLYING

TORTERRA

Height: 7'03" (2.2 m)
Weight: 683.4 lbs. (310.0 kg)

GRASS | GROUND

TOXICROAK

Height: 4'03" (1.3 m)
Weight: 97.9 lbs. (44.4 kg)

POISON | FIGHTING

TURTWIG

Height: 1'04" (0.4 m)
Weight: 22.5 lbs. (10.2 kg)

GRASS

UXIE

Height: 1'00" (0.3 m)
Weight: 0.7 lbs. (0.3 kg)

PSYCHIC?

VESPIQUEN

Height: 3'11" (1.2 m)
Weight: 84.9 lbs. (38.5 kg)

BUG | FLYING

WEAVILE

Height: 3'07" (1.1 m)
Weight: 75.0 lbs. (34.0 kg)

DARK | ICE

WORMADAM (SANDY CLOAK)

Height: 1'08" (0.5 m)
Weight: 14.3 lbs. (6.5 kg)

BUG | GRASS

WORMADAM (GRASS CLOAK)
Height: 1'08" (0.5 m)
Weight: 14.3 lbs. (6.5 kg)

BUG | GRASS

WORMADAM (TRASH CLOAK)
Height: 1'08" (0.5 m)
Weight: 14.3 lbs. (6.5 kg)

BUG | GRASS

YANMEGA
Height: 6'03" (1.9 m)
Weight: 113.5 lbs. (51.5 kg)

BUG | FLYING

LIFE LESSONS

Pokémon is so full of diverse characters and amazing storylines, but one question remains: What is it all about? Is it simply a young boy's coming-of-age story? Is it a story of unending friendship? Is it about the responsibility of putting your faith in your friends? Or is it, as so many claim, all of the above?

FRIENDSHIP

Ash has an incredible bond with Pikachu, and that bond is based on mutual respect, the ability to know what your limitations are, and love for someone who depends on you and whom you depend on. It is a relationship based upon mutual sacrifice. From the beginning, Ash has proven his willingness to sacrifice his time, energy, and health for the protection and betterment of Pikachu. With a friendship like that, it is no wonder why Pikachu never gives up when battling another Pokémon.

KINDNESS

Treat your friends and your Pokémon the way you want to be treated, and you'll live a happy and fulfilling life. Ash constantly challenges those who are abusive, be it with their Pokémon, or other humans. He often finds himself sticking up for the underprivileged and weak. What Ash doesn't do is lord over those he considers beneath him, even if they are outmatched. He may trash-talk, but he never bullies.

NATURE

Time and time again, the after-effects of fooling with the natural order of life is very bad. Most memorable is Team Aqua and Team Magma's insistence that their land mass/water mass ideology is better, with disastrous results. Taking a Pokémon out of its natural *modus operandi* and forcing it to your will is also going to bring retribution. Nature will find its balance with you or without you.

SPORTSMANSHIP

Simply stated, Ash wants to catch 'em all and he wants to win them all, but winning isn't everything. His style of taking on any challengers or stepping up to seemingly insurmountable odds may impress the ladies, but it doesn't always work out in his favor. Ash did not win his first tournament, placing in the top sixteen. He has lost numerous battles…

NEVER GIVE UP

…but he has also never given up, even when faced with defeat. His plucky determination has slightly changed over the years, and now Ash battles with less bravado and more strategy—and he's been winning more, too!

BRADY GAMES

PUBLISHER
DAVID WAYBRIGHT

EDITOR-IN-CHIEF
H. LEIGH DAVIS

LICENSING MANAGER
MIKE DEGLER

DIRECTOR OF MARKETING
DEBBY NEUBAUER

INTERNATIONAL TRANSLATIONS
BRIAN SALIBA

PROJECT MANAGERS
BRIAN SHOTTON
TIM COX

DESIGNERS
AREVA
DAN CAPARO
COLIN KING
TRACY WEHMEYER

SCREENSHOT EDITOR
MICHAEL OWEN

POKÉMON GROUP

DIRECTOR, BRAND MANAGEMENT
MAYA NAKAMURA

EDITORIAL DIRECTOR
LAWRENCE NEVES

LICENSING DIRECTOR
KELLY C. HILL

ASSOCIATE BRAND MANAGER
DUSTIN RODRIGUEZ

ACKNOWLEDGEMENTS

I would like to thank Areva for putting up with my constant badgering, hovering, and infinite tweaking. Your patience is remarkable, and this book would not be what it is without your efforts.

Dan's ability to make visual my incoherent blathering, and, even more surprising, make it look good amazes me every time I look at a page.

The authors, Cris and Katherine, are two amazing women: their talent and work ethic helped this book be all it could be. Their knowledge of the Pokémon world is truly mesmerizing.

Lastly, but most importantly, the steady reminder of what this book should be and what it means to Pokémon fans was always as close as my home. My son and daughter adore Pokémon. This book is for Orion and Meris. I love you.—Brian

Looks like we're Blasting Off again!

First American Edition 2008

08 09 10 11 9 8 7 6 5 4 3 2 1

Published in the United States by
DK/BradyGAMES, a division of Penguin Group (USA) Inc.
800 East 96th Street, 3rd Floor
Indianapolis, Indiana 46240

ISBN 978-0-7566-4430-7

Printed and bound by Lake Book, Melrose Park, IL

DK

LONDON, NEW YORK,
MELNOURNE, AND DELHI

BG
BRADYGAMES®